Lazy Idle Schemers

27 Dec. 2010

Anne & Bob

Here it is, at long last — I hope you enjoy it!
Thanks for your influence and support throughout the years

love – G.

Lazy Idle Schemers

Irish Modernism and the Cultural Politics of Idleness

Gregory Dobbins

ISBN 978-0-946755-50-9

Published by Field Day Publications in association with the Keough-Naughton
Institute for Irish Studies at the University of Notre Dame.

Set in 10.5pt/13.5pt Quadraat
Designed and typeset by Red Dog Design Consultants
Printed on Trucard and Munken Lynx

Field Day Publications
Newman House
86 St.Stephen's Green
Dublin 2
Ireland

www.fielddaybooks.com

For Desireé

Contents

Acknowledgements

To begin with, I am indebted to Field Day Publications for their interest in this project. I am deeply grateful to Seamus Deane for his enthusiasm, support, and editorial advice. I owe David Lloyd and P. J. Mathews a lot, for all kinds of reasons, but most of all for bringing this book to Field Day's attention. Thanks to David for his support and advice and to P. J. for his absolute and unyielding friendship throughout the years.

I have been fortunate enough to work with magnificent teachers throughout the years. Their influence upon me is incalculable. At Duke: Thanks to Fredric Jameson, Jan Radway, Michael Valdez Moses, Frank Lentricchia, and Alberto Moreiras. At Berkeley: Carolyn Porter, John Bishop, and the late Robert Brentano. In Thousand Oaks: Jack Farrell, Don Pearson, and Jim O'Brien. I must single out Ian Baucom not only for his mentorship, but for the close friendship we have developed over time.

I am blessed to have brilliant and wise friends. John Waters, my unofficial older brother, has been a source of strength and encouragement from the very first day I entered graduate school. I also want to thank Nigel Alderman, Jed Esty, Mike Rubenstein, Seán Kennedy, Christian Thorne, Simon Hay, Raul Aronovich, Dan Blanton, Amy Carroll, Dillon Brown, Greg Tomso, Kristin Bergin, and Jason Gebhardt for all that they have helped me with.

The University of California, Davis, has provided me with peerless colleagues. I want to thank in particular Margie Ferguson, David Simpson, Parama Roy, Scott Shershow, Beth Freeman, Scott Simmon, Joshua Clover, Lucy Corin, Frances Dolan, Seeta Chaganti, Matthew Stratton, Tim Morton, David Robertson, and Karl Zender for their help regarding matters great and small. My former colleague Riché Richardson helped make the transition from Duke to Davis smooth. Liz Miller and John Marx read large chunks of the manuscript on short notice, and it is better for their advice. Finally, I would like to recognize three invaluable comrades who provided crucial support: my current colleague

Mike Ziser and my former colleagues Catherine Robson and Bishnu Ghosh. Those three will always figure on any acknowledgments list I will ever produce.

I have received helpful advice from a number of scholars; many thanks to Declan Kiberd, Luke Gibbons, Guinn Batten, Margot Backus, Joe Valente, Phil Weinstein, Bhaskar Sarkar, Catherine Morris, Skip Thompson, Nicholas Allen, Joe Nugent, and Enda Duffy.

I am deeply beholden to my students and others who made an impact upon this book. Alysia Garrison deserves special credit; aside from being the primary graduate student I have worked with at U.C. Davis, she is also responsible for the index of this book. I am also grateful to Denise Harahus, Audrey Janello, Ionela Tanasie, Steven Blevins, Erin Paszko, Masha Boston, James Addona, Chris Schaberg, Aaron Cotter, Alice Henton, Dan Hoffheins, Mat Walker, Katie Davalos, Andy Zembo, and Alexis Kenyon.

Most of all I am indebted to my family. My parents Terry and Maureen Dobbins worked very hard to create the conditions in which I could someday write a book about laziness. My brother Ryan will always be my best friend; Ryan and his wife Kari provided invaluable support. I must also acknowledge Frederick Martín, Eddie Martín, Sylvia Carranza, Mary O'Shea and Gerrard Hussey for all of the practical help they have provided over the years. I would also like to honor the memory of Joseph Bradshaw, Joan Bradshaw, Josephine Rice, Brian Dobbins, and María Elena Martín. Finally, nothing at all would have been possible without the support of my wife Desireé Martín. Our son Santiago arrived right before the completion of this book and put everything in perspective. While the next book will be dedicated to him, this one is written in honor of his mother in tribute to her love.

Abbreviations

A   W. B. Yeats, *Autobiographies* (New York: Scribner, 1999)

AC   Eimar O'Duffy, *Asses in Clover* (London: Putnam, 1933)

AP   Walter Benjamin, *The Arcades Project* (Cambridge, MA: Harvard University Press, 1999)

ASTB Flann O'Brien, *At Swim-Two-Birds* (New York: Plume, 1976)

CWW Oscar Wilde, *The Collected Works of Oscar Wilde: Stories, Plays, Poems and Essays* (London: Collins, 1966).

D   Samuel Beckett, *Disjecta: Miscellaneous Writings and a Dramatic Fragment* (New York: Grove Press, 1984)

I   Walter Benjamin, *Illuminations: Essays and Aphorisms* (New York: Shocken Books, 1968)

KGB Eimar O'Duffy, *King Goshawk and the Birds* (London: Macmillan, 1928)

LM   Eimar O'Duffy, *Life and Money*, 3rd edn. (London: Putnam, 1935)

M   Samuel Beckett, *Murphy* (London: John Calder, 1963)

P   James Joyce, *A Portrait of the Artist as a Young Man* (London: Penguin Books, 1992)

SMS Eimar O'Duffy, *The Spacious Adventures of the Man in the Street* (London: Macmillan, 1928)

U   James Joyce, *Ulysses* (New York: Random House, 1961)

1   Introduction

'At your work, all of you!' shouts the fearsome Father Dolan, prefect of studies at Clongowes Wood College early in James Joyce's *Portrait of the Artist as a Young Man*. Dolan appears in the narrative briefly and memorably, addressing Stephen Dedalus's Latin class with the exhortation, 'we want no lazy idle loafers here, lazy idle little schemers. At your work I tell you!' (P, 50). Upon discovering that Stephen's hapless fellow student Fleming has failed to prepare adequately for class, he beats the student with a pandybat for being 'a born idler' (P, 49). Noting that Stephen is not doing the same Latin exercises as the rest of the class — he has broken his glasses and has thus been excused from class work — Dolan accuses him of 'scheming', or of coming up with an underhand plan to avoid work. Stephen, who is an excellent student and not guilty of shirking his responsibilities, is beaten; this is a traumatic moment for him:

> Stephen closed his eyes and held out in the air his trembling hand with the palm upwards. He felt the prefect of studies touch it for a moment at the fingers to straighten it and then the swish of the sleeve of the soutane as the pandybat was lifted to strike. A hot burning stinging tingling blow like the loud crack of a broken stick made his trembling hand crumple together like a leaf in the fire: and at the sound and the pain scalding tears were driven into his eyes. His whole body was shaking with fright, his arm was shaking and his crumpled burning livid hand shook like a loose leaf in the air ... The scalding water burst forth from his eyes and, burning with shame and agony and fear, he drew back his shaking arm in terror and burst into a whine of pain. (P, 52)

So Stephen comes to understand the arbitrary and cruel nature of power. There are no exceptions to Father Dolan's discipline, however merited the grounds for it might be. Dolan demonstrates that work is the crucial element in the relationship between obligation and punishment. One must work or face the painful consequences.

Almost fifteen years later, the incident still reverberates in Stephen's memory. Throughout *Ulysses*, he frequently remembers the phrase 'lazy idle schemer', usually when offered the possibility of some form of employment. In 'Circe', an apparition of Father Dolan emerges from a jack-in-the-box in order to remind him that he is a 'lazy idle schemer' (U, 561). But Stephen the child and the Stephen of 16 June 1904 have very different notions of the obligation to work. The older Stephen spends much of that day wandering the streets of Dublin in a boozy idleness, pondering, without coming to any conclusion, how he might undertake some innovative form of intellectual labour in the future. Father Dolan's accusation that the younger Stephen was a lazy, idle schemer was unjust, but it certainly describes the Stephen of *Ulysses* correctly. It thereby draws attention to something that, in my view, helps to organize the periodization of Irish literary history. Unlike the active and productive intellectuals of the Irish Literary Revival (some of whom, in fictionalized or semi-fictionalized form, appear in *Ulysses* as well), Stephen never really manages to get any work of any consequence done. His lazy scheming provides a central motif to one of the strongest tendencies within Irish modernism. Stephen's role in this novel as a 'lazy idle schemer' — a term I will be using to designate those would-be literary intellectuals who refuse the widely accepted obligation to labour — is prototypical of a series of such figures in the works of Eimar O'Duffy, Samuel Beckett, and Flann O'Brien. His idleness also challenges the ideologies of capital and the state that gradually strengthened during the long process of decolonization in Ireland. The cultural politics of Irish modernism are illuminated by an overwhelming narrative emphasis upon the representation of idleness.

While it was once controversial, the 'post-colonial turn' in Irish Studies is perhaps the most visible aspect of what Claire Connolly calls a 'critical orthodoxy' in Irish Studies over the last three decades.[1] Yet the application of that theory to Irish modernist texts has varied a great deal. On the one hand, the post-colonial theoretical approach has led many critics to insist upon the exceptionalism of Irish modernism. This was in part a response to metropolitan literary criticism's long-standing claim that Irish history had little importance for an understanding of writers like Joyce or Beckett.[2] A critical inquiry

---

1   See Claire Connolly, 'Theorising Ireland', *Irish Studies Review*, 9, 3 (2001), 301.
2   A statement by Franco Moretti in an essay about *Ulysses* offers a particularly egregious example: 'I have dealt — and shall continue to deal — with Joyce and *Ulysses* as expressions of English society and culture. Of course, it is a well-known fact that Joyce is Irish and that *Ulysses* takes place in Dublin. But if Joyce were an Irish *writer*, comprehensible and containable without any loose threads within Irish culture, he would no longer be Joyce; if the city of *Ulysses* were the real Dublin of the turn of the century, it would be the literary image *par excellence* of the modern metropolis. Cultural phenomena cannot be explained in terms of their *genesis* (what ever has emerged from the studies that interpreted Joyce on the basis of Ireland?); what counts is their objective *function*.' See Moretti, *Signs Taken for Wonders*, rev. edn. (London, 1988), 189–90.

into the particularity of Irish modernism was launched, reinforced by what Declan Kiberd calls 'a discrimination of modernisms', that recognized the distinct qualities of different national literary traditions.[3] On the other hand, the post-colonial theoretical approach to literary history has also had the opposite effect. One of the most significant attributes of the 'new modernist studies' has been its focus on the relation modernism had to a more recent understanding of transnationalism.[4] Thus, familiar figures from the modernist canon (including, at times, Irish writers like W. B. Yeats, Joyce, and Beckett) are reconsidered as part of a global movement that had both material connections and thematic links to non-European writers not previously considered in a modernist context.[5] The history of national specificity often recedes in this scholarship in comparison to the emphasis placed upon a global and — frequently — imperial history that enables the possibility of similarity between a broadly conceived group of international writers.

The concept of transnationalism has enabled a renewed understanding of the relationship modernism had to both imperialism and global capitalism. However, in its treatment of Irish writers, it occasionally runs the risk of reiterating older metropolitan assumptions about their relation to national history, which recent work in Irish Studies has so effectively challenged. Sometimes, the significance of either nationalism or national particularity is dismissed or reduced in favour of a cosmopolitanism 'in the service of antiracism, democratic individualism, and transnational community' that is somehow incompatible with cultural nationalism.[6] While no one would deny that such values have a place in Joyce's writing, they are by no means necessarily antithetical to nationalism or national specificity. Different strains of Irish nationalism have long valorized cosmopolitanism and insisted that there is a necessary, inextricable relationship between the two (as the writing of Joyce's contemporaries Thomas Kettle and Arthur Clery, to

---

For specific responses to Moretti's assessment of Joyce, see David Lloyd, *Anomalous States: Irish Writing and the Post-Colonial Moment* (Durham, NC, 1993), 11; Luke Gibbons, *Transformations in Irish Culture* (Cork, 1996), 165; and, in particular, Emer Nolan, *James Joyce and Nationalism* (London, 1995), 9. The rather considerable achievement of the reconceptualization of Irish modernism initially emerged in studies that interpret Joyce on 'the basis of Ireland'; see in addition, Enda Duffy, *The Subaltern Ulysses* (Minneapolis, 1994) and Andrew Gibson, *Joyce's Revenge: History, Politics and Aesthetics in Ulysses* (Oxford, 2002).

3   'All of which suggests that it is time for a discrimination of modernisms, a recognition that Irish modernism may not be at all the same thing as English modernism ... And French and American modernisms may be something else again.' Declan Kiberd, *The Irish Writer and the World* (Cambridge, 2005), 247.

4   See Douglas Mao and Rebecca Walkowitz, 'The New Modernist Studies', *PMLA*, 123 (2007), 737–48.

5   There are numerous examples of the recent 'transnational turn' in Modernist Studies, but for a representative selection, see Jahan Ramazani, *The Hybrid Muse: Postcolonial Poetry in English* (Chicago, 2001); Nicholas Brown, *Utopian Generations: The Political Horizon of Twentieth-Century Literature* (Princeton, 2005); John Marx, *The Modernist Novel and the Decline of Empire* (Cambridge, 2005), and Rebecca Walkowitz, *Cosmopolitan Style: Modernism beyond the Nation* (New York, 2006). All of these books deal with Irish modernist writers.

6   Walkowitz, *Cosmopolitan Style*, 56. For a prolonged critique of the way Irish nationalism has been profoundly misunderstood in previous generations of Joyce criticism, see Nolan, *James Joyce and Nationalism*.

cite just two examples, makes clear).[7] But more importantly, such contemporary notions of cosmopolitanism often treat nationalism in monolithic, unilinear, and frequently essentialist terms. Irish nationalism — or, as Partha Chatterjee suggests, any number of anti-imperialist nationalisms — is not one unified, coherent position that one can merely be in favour of or oppose, but rather embraces several different, even contradictory, positions.[8] The distinction between a form of nationalism committed to the capture of the state and a more general pervasive commitment to republicanism is important here. As Philip Pettit argues, the republican ideal has its origins in a conception of liberty as a form of non-domination.[9] In its most radical, utopian form, republicanism insists upon the universal extension of the principle of non-domination, rather than a narrower valorization of a particular form of identity identified with the interests of the state. In Irish cultural history, republicanism in this sense is opposed to the forms of domination identified with both colonial rule and the post-colonial state, but it nevertheless engaged with the terms of its own national specificity. While the specific political positions of each of the modernist writers I will be concerned with here were quite different, they share a general, typically republican, opposition to the exercise of domination.[10] Nationalism is, of itself, too broad and amorphous a concept to allow us usefully to say that writers such as Joyce or Beckett were simply for or against it. However, when particular aspects of Irish cultural nationalism coincided with a general opposition to forms of domination founded upon the exclusion of certain forms of identity — a position that ran through various strands of republican thought both before and after independence — they provided important co-ordinates for the emergence of Irish modernism.

But critical commentary is not alone in prioritizing a liberal conception of cosmopolitanism that sometimes fails to take into account the importance of national specificity. Occasionally literary criticism that is informed by a more radical understanding of cultural history makes a similar mistake, by an orthodox insistence upon retaining fidelity to theoretical concepts rather than entering into an account of the anomalies and particularities of Irish history.[11] As Joe Cleary has powerfully demonstrated, those

---

7   Thomas Kettle, 'The Economics of Nationalism', in *The Day's Burden* (London, 1918), 103–18; Arthur Clery, 'Cosmopolitanism and Nationality', in *The Idea of a Nation* (Dublin 2002), 74–76. See also Luke Gibbons, 'Constructing the Canon: Versions of National Identity', in Seamus Deane, ed., *The Field Day Anthology of Irish Writing*, 3 vols. (Derry, 1991), vol. 2, 950–1020.

8   See Partha Chatterjee, *Nationalist Thought and the Colonial World: A Derivative Discourse* (Minneapolis, 1993), 1–53.

9   See Pettit, *Republicanism: A Theory of Freedom and Government* (Oxford, 1997), 80–109.

10   Recent scholarship suggests that the term 'republicanism' is particularly useful for a more general consideration of Irish modernism at large. See, in particular, Nicholas Allen's *Modernism, Ireland and Civil War* (Cambridge, 2009), which argues quite persuasively that unrealized radical conceptions of republicanism provided a crucial determination for the emergence of Irish modernism. See also David Lloyd's article 'Republics of Difference: Yeats, MacGreevy, Beckett', *Field Day Review*, 1 (2005), 43–67.

11   For example, see Nicholas Brown, *Utopian Generations*, 213. Though Brown is more respectful of the colonial and anti-colonial co-ordinates of Joyce's writing than Moretti, he agrees that 'the ambitions of *Ulysses* plainly lie elsewhere', leading to the claim that 'it should be emphasized, however, that this

historical particularities must contribute to the formation of the theoretical concepts in the interpretation of Irish culture rather than the other way round.[12] The specificity of national history, and the persistence of nationalism in all of the different forms it took, proved to be both an inevitable determination and a significant realm of engagement for modernism in general, whether in the Irish or in other instances.[13] Idleness, as a concept, as a rhetorical stance and even as a vocation, I will argue, provides in Irish modernism a primary mode of critical engagement both with nationalism — towards which it was ambivalent — and, more importantly, with the particular nation-state that emerged in 1922, towards which it was much more antagonistic. If Irish modernism is indeed distinct from other national modernisms, then I want to suggest that the specific function idleness had within it is one of the primary indicators of that difference.

I begin with the supposition that Irish modernist writing has transnational dimensions while still retaining formal and thematic particularities that anchor it firmly to the cultural politics of Irish history. It follows that I insist on the necessary distinction between Irish modernism and the larger international culture movement it was connected to through literary institutions, circuits of readership and influence, and global trade and contact. In addition, I want to emphasize a necessary difference within Irish literary history, between the literature of the Revival and a later conception of Irish modernism. Idleness has a crucial part to play here as well. Whether as a narrative motif or as the basis for a more innovative method of formal representation, idleness helps to distinguish between the predominant aesthetic and social concerns of the Revival and the sporadic trajectory of a more experimental type of modernism that emerged with and after Irish independence in 1922. One long-standing periodization of Irish literary history insists that the Revival was clearly finished prior to 1922. The literature of the 1920s and 1930s could be understood as comprising, on the one hand, a more specifically Catholic and apparently ethnocentric commitment to certain aspects of the Revivalist project in the manner of intellectuals like Daniel Corkery or, on the other hand, as a loosely affiliated group of writers ranging from Sean O'Faolain to Flann O'Brien, grouped under the rubric of the 'Counter-Revival', because of their supposed shared dissatisfaction with the increasingly conservative

argument about the limitations of postcolonial criticism refers only to *Ulysses*, not to Irish literature in general'. Consequently, Brown's reading of *Ulysses* involves an understanding of Irish history derived from a standard Marxist theoretical standpoint, rather than from historical evidence that might suggest otherwise; see 38–39.

12 This position recurs throughout Cleary's criticism, but see the essay 'Toward a Materialist-Formalist History of Twentieth-Century Irish Literature', *boundary 2*, 31, 1 (2004), 207–42.

13 Jed Esty's *A Shrinking Island: Modernism and National Culture in England* (Princeton, 2004) offers a powerful example of how inextricably tied notions of national specificity could be with modernism. He demonstrates that modernism and changing conceptions of nationality were as interpolated with one another in the metropolitan centre of the British Empire as they were in the emerging post-colonial world.

climate of independent Ireland.[14] The plausibility of this account was tested by the prominent exiles, such as Joyce and Beckett, and ultimately relies upon the attribution of a shared political and social dissatisfaction, rather than on any sort of aesthetic similarities between the 'Counter-Revivalists'.

More recently, some critics have argued that the Revival itself was actually the first instance of a uniquely Irish modernism, and that the ethos of that moment continued to live on after independence in the form of works and events that appear to have a hitherto unrecognized affinity with a more international conception of modernism.[15] Though there are some very compelling versions of just such an understanding of literary history, it risks losing sight of the crucial political and aesthetic differences between the collective project of the Revival and the more disparate, disconnected writers committed to a more experimental version of modernist form such as the novelists I treat here or the group of Catholic modernist poets that includes Thomas MacGreevy, Brian Coffey, Denis Devlin, and Donagh MacDonagh.[16] The theorization of modernism must account for its significant formal differences from the cultural production of earlier periods. In a formal sense, each of the modernist writers I will be concerned with here wrote novels that clearly demonstrated what Fredric Jameson terms the 'autonomization' of the text, a process inherent to modernism characterized by

> the way in which the episodes of a narrative thus cut up into smaller segments tend to take on an independence and an autonomy of their own ... Joyce's *Ulysses* clearly offers the most striking exemplification of such narrative production, in which separate chapters end up going their own ways, developing separate styles and structures from each other, and finally looking as distinct from one another as the various organs in the body ... it tends to descend into the smallest units of the narrative, potentially making the individual sentences autonomous as well.[17]

If the texts of the Revival tended toward the construction of a national imaginary that could serve as a political and social ideal in actuality, then modernist writing produced

14   For the classic encapsulation of this perspective, see Terence Brown, *Ireland: A Social and Cultural History, 1922 to the Present* (Ithaca, 1985), 13–101. See also Brown's sections on 'The Counter Revival', in Deane, ed., *The Field Day Anthology of Irish Literature*, vol. 3, 89–232. For a powerful reconceptualization of this understanding of literary history, see Allen, *Modernism, Ireland and Civil War.*

15   Paige Reynolds, *Modernism, Drama, and the Audience for Irish Spectacle* (Cambridge, 2007), 8, argues: 'Irish revivalism and international modernism ... are two intersecting sets, and the term "Irish modernism" describes the sizable and significant site of common ground shared by these two movements. In this perspective, Irish modernism can be understood as a subset of practices employed by figures expressly associated by themselves, their peers, or subsequent critics with either revivalism or international modernism.'

16   A convincing exception to this tendency is Gregory Castle's *Modernism and the Celtic Revival* (Cambridge, 2001).

17   Fredric Jameson, *Brecht and Method* (London, 1998), 43.

something more akin to cancelled realist texts, which achieved a sense of formal autonomy from social actuality through the proliferation of a variety of different styles that demonstrated the artificiality of representation in general.[18] As a primary characteristic of modernism in general, the formal process of autonomization affiliates its Irish version with those other variations of modernist style found in other parts of the world. Yet, as Jameson allows elsewhere, autonomization does not occur in the same manner across the spectrum of modernist writing in general.[19] Cleary, for instance, notes the reversal of a key contradiction in the shift from the Revival to a more explicitly high modernist period. In his dialectical account of the relation between the Revival and modernism, he allows for the continuity between the two moments but also accounts for an important shift that signals the possibility of a break between periods:

> Ireland produced several great modernist writers — first Synge and Yeats, then Joyce, later O'Casey, Flann O'Brien, Ó Cadhain and Beckett — who managed between them to span three successive phases or generations of European literary modernism. In Synge and Yeats, the dialectic between the archaic (or the non-modern) and the modern tended to be weighted towards the archaic, which was associated with value, and to denigrate the modern, equated with degeneration and the loss of value … In Joyce's *Ulysses*, a tension between the archaic and the modern remains fundamental, but is no longer calibrated in terms of a tragic collision between pre-modern and modern cultural systems, as in Yeats and Synge … The wholly urban Irish milieu of Joyce's work shifts things decisively toward the 'modern' rather than the 'archaic' end of the spectrum, marking a decisive break with earlier literary modernisms.[20]

My argument here is consistent with Cleary's, though I will argue that the values of 'tradition' and 'modernity' (at least as they figured in a teleological conception of

---

18 Jameson writes in an earlier theorization of modernism that 'all modernistic works are essentially simply canceled realistic ones, that they are, in other words, not apprehended directly, in terms of their own symbolic meanings, in terms of their own mythic and sacred immediacy, the way an older primitive or overcoded work would be but rather indirectly only, by way of the relay of an imaginary realistic narrative of which the symbolic and modernistic one is then seen as a kind of stylization; and this is a type of reading, and a literary structure, utterly unlike anything hitherto known in the history of literature, and one to which we have been insufficiently attentive until now'. See Jameson, 'Beyond the Cave: Demystifying the Ideology of Modernism', in *The Ideologies of Theory: Essays 1971–1986. Volume 2: Syntax of History* (Minneapolis, 1988), 129.

19 Fredric Jameson, *The Modernist Papers* (London, 2007), xvii.

20 Joe Cleary, *Outrageous Fortune: Capital and Culture in Modern Ireland* (Dublin, 2006), 70. See also Emer Nolan, 'Modernism and the Irish Revival', in Joe Cleary and Claire Connolly, eds., *The Cambridge Companion to Modern Irish Culture* (Cambridge, 2005), 157–72. Nolan argues convincingly that one must look to the discourse of modernism to explain the tremendous innovation of the texts of the Revival compared to the literary works of previous generations.

modernization) will both be objects of contestation within the texts I will be concerned with. Yet at least two more important differences contribute to this sense of a break between the earlier writers of the Revival and the modernist writers that appear after *Ulysses*. One concerns the nature of historical representation, while the other has to do with the way work is conceptualized within the Revival and after.

Whether it was the opening of the Abbey Theatre or the founding of the Irish Socialist Republican Party, the beginning of the agricultural co-operative movements or the revival of the Irish language, all of the various forms of social and cultural activity identified with the Revival belong to a larger collective project. It had modernization as its goal; such an ambition required a belief in a teleological conception of progress, accompanied by an allied belief in the imminent realization of nationhood.[21] Despite this shared version of national history as driven by a modernizing impulse, the past was often represented as a timeless condition. This was especially true of the dramatic productions of the Revival, whether in the mythological works of writers like Yeats and George Russell (Æ) or in the scenes concerning daily life in rural Ireland that recur throughout the works of Lady Gregory and J. M. Synge (both of whom occasionally wrote in the mythological vein as well). In both cases, the exact historical designation of a given work is notoriously vague. Yeats's representation of Irish myth was explicitly committed to the evocation of a pre-modern time, while *The Well of the Saints*, the only play by Synge to even have a temporal designation in its description of the opening scene, takes place in the indefinite period of 'one or more centuries ago'.[22] Although many writers associated with the Revival responded to the immediate events of the present in their works (as any number of poems by Yeats suggest), their images of the past tend to lack historical specificity. By keeping the past vague, it was easier to represent values or positions that had an allegorical connection to the present. In this way, innovation could be introduced via the aura of the past through the representation of radically modern positions (such as, for example, James Connolly's commitment to the collective ownership of the land or Patrick Pearse's thoughts about pedagogy, which overlapped in certain respects with the Montessori method) as rooted in ancient Ireland.[23] The value of 'tradition', in this sense, could serve as a guarantor of an ongoing national — and crucially, in this case, non-sectarian — essence that persists through time.

---

21 My sense that the Revival extended beyond cultural production alone to include developments and movements committed to a collective notion of progress that extended to Irish culture, society, politics, and economics at large is influenced by P. J. Mathews's *Revival: The Abbey Theatre, Sinn Féin, the Gaelic League and the Co-Operative Movement* (Cork, 2003). On the underlying trope of modernization in twentieth-century Irish history, see Diarmaid Ferriter, *The Transformation of Ireland 1900–2000* (London, 2004), which shows that modernization was one of the primary ambitions for the nationalist movement right from the very beginning.

22 J. M. *Collected Works III: Plays: Book 1* (Gerrards Cross, 1982), 69.

23 I am indebted here to Declan Kiberd's position that tradition serves as a means to introduce innovation in Irish cultural history. This position is apparent in much of his criticism, but see in particular, *Inventing Ireland* (London, 1995), 207, and *The Irish Writer and the World*, 167.

However, in 1922, Yeats, Joyce, and Æ produced works that focused on the historical specificity of the recent past rather than the distant and vague time of the pre-modern. The 'Trembling of the Veil', the longest and most structurally complicated section of Yeats's *Autobiographies*, brought a new sense of historical precision to Yeats's narration of his life story. Unlike the earlier volume, *Reveries over Childhood and Youth* (1916), which presents a blurry account of his youth notably lacking in a precise chronology, 'The Trembling of the Veil' offers a more historically specific account of the period that began when Yeats arrived in London at the age of twenty-two in 1887 and ends with the beginning of his friendship with Lady Gregory a decade later. As well as providing a record of his development as an intellectual, Yeats includes a very detailed description of the early years of the Revival. His account emphasizes the complicity between recently founded cultural movements and new political organizations right from the beginning of the Revival (though in Yeats's telling of the story, cultural production is prior to and more significant than other forms of activism). The effect is strongly to suggest that recent contemporary political events, such as the formation of the Irish Free State, had their origins in the cultural work of the Revival. Yeats formulated the general project of his attempt at autobiography after reading Joyce's *Portrait of the Artist as a Young Man*. He provides a variation on that model in 'The Trembling of the Veil'.[24] He even asserts for himself a role in the authorship of the state. As he suggested in his Nobel Prize acceptance speech in 1923, 'indeed the young Ministers and party politicians of the Free State have had, I think, some of their education from our plays'.[25]

Joyce's *Ulysses*, with its detailed focus on the multiple details of one day in 1904, presents an account of the recent past that stands in stark juxtaposition to Yeats's. Though Joyce's novel is set in the heyday of the Revival, there is very little evidence of its vibrancy. Joyce represents it as a minor affair conducted by a coterie of privileged individuals removed from the daily life of the city. Stagnation prevails in his Dublin. His work suggests that the ambitions and practices of the Revival were woefully inadequate to overcome the general sense of colonial underdevelopment and impoverishment that characterized Irish life in the years leading up to independence. Finally, Æ's esoteric novel *The Interpreters* is set sometime in the future. It concerns a group of visionary rebels who have led an uprising against an unnamed empire on behalf of their nation; for the most part the narrative is made up of their conversations about their beliefs the night before they are due to be executed for their resistance. The novel is clearly presenting a mystical retelling of the events of Easter 1916; the main characters are thinly disguised caricatures of Yeats, Connolly, Standish O'Grady, Æ himself, and others. Æ's invocation of the recent past in this work is designed to raise questions about the interrelation between politics, spirituality, and culture for the newly independent state.

---

24 See R. F. Foster, *W. B. Yeats: A Life: 1: The Apprentice Mage* (Oxford, 1997), 526.
25 W. B. Yeats, *Autobiographies* (New York, 1999), 418.

According to Jameson, periodization begins when there is an awareness of the 'dialectic between the break and the period' in a given historical situation: 'What is at stake here is a twofold movement, in which the foregrounding of continuities ... slowly turns into a consciousness of a radical break ... the enforced attention to the break gradually turns the latter into a period in its own right.'[26] The passage between the high years of the Revival and the inception of the Irish Free State is anything but seamless. The violence that begins with the Easter Rising in 1916 and continues until the end of the Irish Civil War ruptures the then-prevailing sense of continuity, and, in turn, signals that Irish history had entered into the moment of the break, 'a period in its own right'. Writing in 1922, when it was possible to imagine that with the inauguration of the Irish Free State, Ireland had entered into a new condition, Yeats, Joyce, and Æ were in a position to represent the recent past as radically distinct from the contemporary moment. Such acts of historicization, according to Jameson, bring about the creation of the past as a distinct category in itself,

> by way of a powerful act of dissociation whereby the present seals off its past from itself and expels and ejects it; an act without which neither present nor past truly exist, the past not yet fully constituted, the present still a living on within the forcefield of a past not yet over and done with.[27]

It is in the quality of this sense of dissociation that one can distinguish the difference between *Ulysses* and these works by Yeats and Æ, even though they share affinities in their attempts to represent the specificity of the recent past. Though their understandings of the foundational values of the Revival differ from one another, both Yeats and Æ claim that Ireland, as it enters into a new historical period, must preserve its traditional myths. The cultural work of the literary intellectual, which helps to create and realize that aim, is at least as important, in their view, as the other forms of labour that build the nation. But, in contrast, *Ulysses* represents the values of the Revival as ineffective against the abject material conditions it depicts; more importantly, Stephen Dedalus, a lazy, would-be artist, is a brilliant and appealing version of the literary intellectual who is unwilling and unable to do the work of the nation that is so central to the ideology of the Revival. Joyce's idle intellectual makes the break between the Revival and a new strain of modernist writing. In addition to the new conjugation between 'tradition' and 'modernity' and the switch in temporal focus, there is no longer a celebration of labour; instead there is a valorization of idleness. This constitutes the third crucial difference between the affirmative project of the Revival and the more critical tendencies to be found within Irish modernism.

In part, idleness acquires such a significant meaning in Irish modernism because a strong work-ethic was so integral to the Revival. Tradition, for instance, was a central

26 Fredric Jameson, *A Singular Modernity: Essay on the Ontology of the Present* (London, 2002), 24.
27 Jameson, *A Singular Modernity*, 25.

category for the Revival because it proposed both the content of Irish cultural history as well as a structure in which that history could become legible. But the creation and retrieval of Tradition involved hard work; it was not simply a matter of style or aesthetics alone.[28] In respect to the present, the construction of tradition produced the 'national-popular' consent fundamental to any form of cultural nationalism.[29] In respect to the past, evidence of the persistence of tradition through history, however questionable or flimsy that might be, made it possible to assert and even measure historical progress through the centuries. During the Revival, what Michael Denning has referred to in the different context of the American 1930s as 'the laboring' of a national culture took place: national labour in the form of work was required to bring about the labour, or birth, of the new nation-state, anticipated by the persistence of tradition.[30] The necessity of the work of the nation became the basis for links between cultural expression and political and economic 'self-help' movements. Though these had very distinct social and political objectives, they shared something more than a frequent overlap of participants. Each of these formations was dedicated to the construction of some dimension of an Irish nation that had not yet come into political existence. The individual participants in these organizations saw themselves as engaged in a form of national work that encompassed the transformation of an imagined ideal into actuality in as many senses — political, social, cultural, or economic — as possible. The leaders of the Revival were therefore intellectuals committed to the production of abstract national values through their work. These values did not always coincide with those of the various nationalist political movements that emerged at the time — one thinks of some of the more arcane positions found in the writing of Yeats and Æ — but when they did, they served an important role in the elaboration of both national difference and in affirming the persistence of a distinct historical teleology. Because of the proximity of anti-imperialist revolution and decolonization, the position of the intellectual was inevitably a politicized one to begin with, whether or not an individual writer claimed that his or her work was apolitical.[31]

28 Bourdieu defines the literary field as the framework through which literature is produced in both a material and a symbolic way: 'The literary field (one may also speak of the artistic field, the philosophical field, etc.) is an independent social universe with its own laws of force, its dominants and dominated, and so forth. Put another way, to speak of the "field" is to recall that literary works are produced in a particular social universe endowed with particular institutions and obeying specific laws.' Pierre Bourdieu, *The Field of Cultural Production: Essays on Art and Literature* (New York, 1993), 163.
29 On the Gramscian conception of the 'national-popular', see David Forgacs, 'National-Popular: Genealogy of a Concept', in Simon During, ed., *The Cultural Studies Reader* (London, 1993), 177–90.
30 See Michael Denning, *The Cultural Front: The Laboring of American Culture in the Twentieth Century* (London, 1997), xvi–xvii, for his explanation of the concept.
31 As Jameson writes in the notorious essay 'Third-World Literature in the Era of Multinational Capitalism', the very conditions of possibility for any form of cultural production in a revolutionary, anti-imperialist context are defined in a political manner despite the agency of the literary intellectual: ... 'It being understood that in the third-world situation the intellectual is always in one way or another a political intellectual'. *Social Text*, 15 (1986), 74.

The participants in the Revival understood themselves as committed to one unified movement that brought together culture, politics and economics. As Yeats wrote in the postscript to *Ideals in Ireland*, a collection of essays published in 1901:

> Part of the power of this movement is that, unlike the purely political movement, it can use every talent and leave every talent in freedom ... it has the need of every delicate talent, for it would discover, as I understand all such movements, the form of the nation made perfect, the fiery seed as upon the divine hand, in the ideas and passions of the nation.[32]

All work identified with the movement had a part to play in the Revival; the Revival itself represented one multifaceted act of labour necessary for the birth of the nation. Writing from a more specifically economic perspective in 1905, Sir Horace Plunkett not only praised the overlap between the cultural wing of the Revival and the co-operative movement, but also regarded the Revival as the basis for the development of individual character:

> In the Gaelic Revival there is a programme of work for the individual; his mind is engaged, thought begets energy, and this energy vitalizes every part of his nature. This makes for the strengthening of character, and so far from any harm being done to the practical movement, to which I have so often referred, the testimony of my fellow workers, as well as my own observation, is unanimous in affirming that the influence of the branches of the Gaelic League is distinctly useful whenever it is sought to move the people to industrial or commercial activity.[33]

Plunkett emphasizes a conception of individual responsibility necessary for what Antonio Gramsci called 'the ethical State', a hallmark of bourgeois liberal democracy.[34] 'Individual character' in this case is not only contrary to a lingering stereotype of Irish idleness, which the productive work of the co-operative movement challenged; it was also the basis

---

32   W. B. Yeats, 'A Postscript', in Lady Gregory, ed., *Ideals in Ireland* (London, 1901), 106–07.
33   Sir Horace Plunkett, *Ireland in the New Century* (London, 1905), 155.
34   Gramsci explains his concept of 'the ethical State' in these terms: 'In my opinion, the most reasonable and concrete thing that can be said about the ethical State, the cultural State, is this: every State is ethical in as much as one of its most important functions is to raise the great mass of population to a particular cultural and moral level, a level (or type) which corresponds to the needs of the productive forces for development, and hence to the interests of the ruling classes. The school as a positive educative function, and the courts as a repressive and negative educative function, are the most important State activities in this sense: but, in reality, a multitude of other so-called private initiatives and activities tend to the same end — initiatives and activities which form the apparatus of the political and cultural hegemony of the ruling classes.' Antonio Gramsci, *Selections from the Prison Notebooks* (New York, 1971), 258. The self-help movements of the Revival are precisely the sorts of 'private initiatives' Gramsci refers to and which in this case help construct hegemony for the state that will come into being after independence. On the 'ethical State' and Ireland, see also Lloyd, *Anomalous States*, 9.

for a broader conception of national character that valorized the various attributes needed for proper forms of citizenship in the future.

Even the more radical voices of the Revival focused upon work as the basis of their respective projects. Both Connolly and Synge regarded the nature of modern labour as perhaps the largest problem facing Ireland at the turn of the century. Connolly, who considered his most famous work *Labour in Ireland* (1910) to 'justly be looked upon as part of the literature of the Gaelic Revival', regarded the liberation of the means of production through the general strike and ultimately through revolution as the best response to the alienation of labour.[35] Synge contrarily found an almost utopian integration of labour and art in what he regarded as the completely unalienated organic way of life he found on the Aran Islands.[36] By 1916, writing not long after the Easter Rising, Æ would consider that those workers who customarily performed 'servile labour' must be central to and at the forefront of the 'imaginative reconstruction of a civilization' as the new Irish state came into being.[37] In each case, Connolly, Synge, and Æ understand work as the fundamental basis for the alienation and material oppression inherent to modernity, and argue that the labouring of the national culture that occurred during the Revival provided the opportunity for a different conceptualization of a more liberated form of work in general. The sense that one must continue working on behalf of modernization and of the nation is pervasive throughout this period in the cultural debates about the nature and institutions of Irish literature.

After 1922, as the arrival of independence refashioned the labouring of the nation into the work of decolonization, the necessity of collective labour on behalf of the modernization of Ireland became a primary ideological value of both the state and civil society. A climactic passage in *The Victory of Sinn Féin* (1924) by the nationalist, pro-Treaty writer P. S. O'Hegarty captures the mood of the time. The greatest danger to an independent Ireland, in his view, was that the hard work that began during the period of the Revival might cease or be left unfinished; idleness, in this case, is as unfavourable a condition for him as it had been for Joyce's Father Dolan:

> If we are to have any future, it can only come to us through a development of character and through work … These will not be readjusted by substituting the Republic, or the Worker's Republic, or the Socialist Republic, or any other form of government, for the present one, but by hard work and honest dealing. There is no regeneration possible through sloth and license, but only through work and cleanliness … We must get back to simplicity and strenuousness. Jazz dancing, joy rides, fetes, and bazaars have never built a civilization, and never will build one. They only lead to fatty degeneration of the morals, of the character; to inefficiency and extinction.

---

35 James Connolly, *Collected Works*, 2 vols. (Dublin, 1987), vol. I, 22.
36 See J. M. Synge, 'The Aran Islands', *Collected Works: Volume II: Prose* (Gerrards Cross, 1982), 132–33.
37 Æ, *The National Being: Some Thoughts on an Irish Polity* (Dublin, 1916), 19.

We may go out in a blaze of light, and music, and garishness, as Babylon went out, but unless we produce something other than a craze for idleness and amusement, we certainly shall go out. There is more in life than amusement, and as a people we must find that out. We must rediscover work and rediscover honesty.[38]

O'Hegarty captures here the fundamental contradiction that serves as a condition of possibility for anti-colonial nationalism and anticipates the conservative tone of state-directed processes of decolonization in the decades to follow. On the one hand, the structure of the nation-state itself, as well as the ideology of modernization that justifies it, are themselves derived from colonial models; on the other hand, for nationalism to succeed, it must appeal to the masses for support through some kind of articulation of tradition and pre-colonial difference.[39] To O'Hegarty, the condition of independence guaranteed by the form of the Irish Free State (which, despite its implementation of a Gaelicized terminology, was closely modelled after its British predecessor) designates Ireland's arrival into a form of modernity in which the ongoing construction of the future can continue. Yet the singular quality of that modernity depends upon a conception of Irish difference heavily derived from a conservative understanding of Catholic morality and hostility to foreign influences like jazz, dancing, or socialism. Once more, the progress of the national character is seen to depend crucially on hard work. While there were major differences between the policies and positions of Cumann na nGaedheal during the period of the Irish Free State and those of Fianna Fáil after the election of Eamon de Valera in 1932, the specific formulation of the contradictory nature of anti-colonial nationalism evident in O'Hegarty's restatement of the national work-ethic would be a consistent, official position in Ireland.

It is evident, for example, in the formation in 1926 of a movement committed to the canonization of Matt Talbot, a recently deceased Dubliner dedicated to a variety of ascetic practices as penance for his dissolute life as a young man.[40] Talbot provides a useful example of exactly the sort of character O'Hegarty praises — he certainly would have been regarded in conservative circles as a more appropriate role model for the working class than Connolly — for not only was he holy, he was a dedicated labourer, best known for working long hours without a break and without receiving, or seeking, overtime pay. And a later example from the early 1930s demonstrates the persistence of the value of the national work-ethic. On the tenth anniversary of national independence in 1932, the Irish Free State

---

38 P. S. O'Hegarty, *The Victory of Sinn Féin* (Dublin, 1998), 130–31.

39 Partha Chatterjee in *Nationalist Thought and the Colonial World*, 43, calls the part of anti-colonial nationalism derived from local specificity 'the problematic', while that facet that draws upon the model provided by colonial nation-states he identifies as 'the thematic'. While the thematic tends to ensure that post-colonial political structures will reproduce colonial conditions, the problematic brings the possibility of instability.

40 For a representative early hagiographical account of Blessed Matt Talbot, see Sir Joseph Glynn's Catholic Truth Society pamphlet *Matt Talbot — A Dublin Labourer: 1856–1925* (Dublin, 1926).

took stock of its accomplishments by publishing the *Saorstát Éireann Official Handbook*, an overview of national life that serves as a guide to the new post-colonial nation and stands as a record of what the work of the nation had achieved. In addition to the formation of a liberal democratic nation-state, these achievements include the reorganization of both agriculture and industry, the introduction of new systems of social services devoted to the areas of education, local government, public health and transportation, the rural electrification project of the Shannon hydro-electric scheme, and the formation of a new system of taxation and public expenditure. Such acts of modernization, in the view of Bulmer Hobson, the handbook's editor, are part and parcel of nationalism itself, since 'constructive work and development in every direction which, under the old regime, could never have been attempted are now possible, and the energies which for generations were absorbed in the struggle for political autonomy set free for the work of social and economic reconstruction'.[41] Yet Hobson concludes his assessment with the brief warning: 'This work so recently begun will require many years of effort before the effects of past repression and neglect are eradicated'.[42] The work of the nation must continue as the former colony becomes a modern nation-state. Idleness, just as O'Hegarty had warned, was not only contrary to national character, but also inconsistent with modernization. From a contemporary historical perspective, and in the light of the more radical economic policies implemented during the 1960s by the Fianna Fáil government of Sean Lemass, it is easy to write off this period between independence and the onset of 'the Emergency' of World War II as backwards and hostile to modernization, insular and devoted (perforce) to an ideal of 'frugality'.[43] Yet, as the example of the handbook indicates, a commitment to some form of modernization through hard work had been a significant feature of state policy right from the very beginning — even if, as in the example of the veneration of Matt Talbot, work as a value or as a virtue can be seen in quite different lights.

But what of those who had no desire to do the work of the nation? Hobson shows no awareness of the ideological ambience such a national work-ethic produced. Although he suggests that none of that work would have been possible 'under the old regime' of the British Empire, the Irish Free State was far more dependent upon that empire than he cares to admit, as the new state-form and its social institutions differed only

41 *Saorstát Éireann Official Handbook* (Dublin, 1932), 16.
42 *Saorstát Éireann Official Handbook*, 16.
43 Cleary, *Outrageous Fortune*, 6, argues that the dismissal of de Valera's Ireland has itself now become a critical orthodoxy that signifies an investment in the ideology of modernization. In my view, the supposed backwardness of both the Irish Free State and de Valera's Ireland are only possible after a more intensified period of modernization that has as much to do with the intensification of global capitalism between the end of World War II and the 1970s as it has to do with the progressive tendencies of Sean Lemass (who, it should be remembered, was a key figure in the development of de Valera's protectionist economic policy himself). In subtle and contradictory ways, both the state and the Church served as agents of modernization. See John Kurt Jacobsen, *Chasing Progress in the Irish Republic: Ideology, Democracy and Dependent Development* (Cambridge, 1994), 50–59. On the history of the trope of modernization in Irish criticism, see Conor McCarthy, *Modernisation: Crisis and Culture in Ireland 1969–1992* (Dublin, 2000), 11–44.

in their Gaelicized names from their colonial predecessors.[44] Moreover, the multiple, revolutionary possibilities of the initial work that went into the decolonization of Ireland diminished considerably as the new state consolidated itself. Many works produced during the first two decades of Irish independence are marked by the conviction that the radical potential of decolonization was not completely actualized. Providing evidence of the bleakness of freedom within post-colonial Ireland, naturalism was the dominant genre during this period.[45] It proved to be effective in the critical exposure of the various shortcomings of decolonization and the ongoing forms of oppression that continued to characterize Irish life, yet it was ultimately self-defeating. For it was weakened by an inherent representational contradiction. The aesthetics of naturalism required the exposure of the repressive facets of Irish life as so monolithic and powerful that reform and change seemed impossible.[46]

In contrast, modernist writing in this period arguably offered a more radical response to the representation of Irish life and history, even if it too was ultimately flawed. The version of high modernism that began with the publication of Ulysses and acquired international renown had initially only an underground reputation in Ireland. An emphasis upon the radical and innovative nature of modernist formal representation is not a new position, since it is one of the primary components of its aesthetic ideology. The valorization of experimentation and complexity contributes to an insistence upon a condition of aesthetic autonomy that attempts to separate modernist art from any number of aspects of modernity — popular culture, daily life, and even the entire realms of politics and the social.[47] Yet, as Jameson's theorization of modernism suggests, the 'autonomization' of art does not assign it to the realm of the absolute and timeless, but is itself a historical process with political and social causes and consequences. In the Irish case, the more experimental formal qualities of modernist writing mark a deep engagement with the trauma of Irish history; but they also signal an important break from the stylistic patterns of the Revival.[48] The intellectual labour of formal representation itself changed as the Revival gave way to post-colonial independence. It is for that reason that the representation of what exactly the intellectual does — or rather, what exactly the intellectual *does not* do — became such a preoccupation within the line of Irish modernist novels initiated by the publication of Ulysses. Most of all, he does not work. An emphasis upon the representation of idleness, even the suggestion that idleness might stand in for innovative forms of creative work, prevails in the Irish modernist texts I am concerned

---

44 Lloyd, Anomalous States, 7.
45 See Cleary, Outrageous Fortune, 85–137.
46 Cleary, Outrageous Fortune, 134.
47 On the consolidation of the ideology of modernism during the transitional moment he calls 'late modernism', see Jameson, A Singular Modernity, 141–210; on the production and function of the concept of the autonomy of the aesthetic, see, in particular, 161–79.
48 See Luke Gibbons, 'Montage, Modernism and the City', in Transformations in Irish Culture, 165–69.

with here. First and foremost, such idleness signifies dissent from the ongoing project of the work of the nation, a project promoted by the state after independence; the cultural politics of Irish modernism lie precisely in its engagement with the concept of idleness.

2

From a Marxist perspective, work should be one of the most valuable experiences possible, since it is the fundamental form of human praxis. Michael Hardt and Antonio Negri suggest that 'the living labour of the expansive social subject is its joy, the affirmation of its own power ... the affirmation of labour in this sense is the affirmation of joy itself'.[49] But such affirmation is lost once one loses control of that labour. During an earlier phase of capitalism, Karl Marx argued that 'the activity of the worker is not his own spontaneous activity. It belongs to another, it is a loss of his self'; this in turn creates a condition of alienation so pervasive that it can be considered as one of the foremost consequences of modernity.[50] While contemporary life is characterized more strongly by forms of immaterial labour, rather than by the industrial work Marx writes of, the deadening sense of both alienation and estrangement persist.[51] Whatever one's class or global location, labour-time within the contemporary moment of globalized post-modernity is likely to be of a longer duration and greater intensity than earlier in the history of capitalism. Idleness has become something like an unattainable ideal. J. M. Coetzee, in an essay devoted to the examination of laziness in South African cultural history, suggests that 'the challenge of idleness to work, its power to scandalize, is as radical today as it ever was'.[52] Because it is so far outside of the conventional work-logic of our particular moment, an insistence upon the necessity of idleness might be considered humorous; yet the humour masks a utopian desire. Over the last decade, there have been many celebrations of idleness as a structure of feeling provoked by the deadening consequences of contemporary forms of work. A number of books aimed at a popular audience have appeared: *The Importance of Being Idle*, *Bonjour Laziness: Why Hard Work Doesn't Pay*, *How to Be Idle*, *Sloth*, and *Doing Nothing*; the humour of these works is effective only because the desire for idleness itself seems so eccentric and beyond reach in contemporary work-logic.[53]

---

49 Michael Hardt and Antonio Negri, *Labor of Dionysius: A Critique of the State-Form* (Minneapolis, 1994), xiii.
50 Karl Marx, *Early Writings* (New York, 1975), 326.
51 Hardt and Negri, *Labor of Dionysius*, xii.
52 J. M. Coetzee, 'Idleness in South Africa', in *White Writing: On the Culture of Letters in South Africa* (New Haven, 1988), 34.
53 See Stephen Robins, ed., *The Importance of Being Idle: A Little Lazy Book of Inspiration* (London, 2000); Tom Hodgkinson, *How to Be Idle* (New York, 2005); Corinne Maier, *Bonjour Laziness: Why Hard Work Doesn't Pay* (London, 2005); Wendy Wasserstein, *Sloth* (Oxford, 2005); and Tom Lutz, *Doing Nothing: A History of Loafers, Loungers, Slackers, and Bums in America* (New York, 2006). Hodgkinson has also revived the title *The Idler* for a journal he edits committed to celebrating the ethos of idleness in as many forms as possible. At a more theoretical level, see Scott Cutler Shershow, *The Work and the Gift* (Chicago, 2005).

Lazy Idle Schemers is inspired by a similar structure of feeling. Both the celebration and the stigmatization of idleness are nothing new. They are part of a longer historical narrative in which the imperative to work hard always became a dominant social value. Coetzee notes that this was not always the case. Idleness was once considered a necessary element of the contemplative life in medieval times, despite the long genealogy of the belief that 'idleness is a sin, that idleness is a betrayal of one's humanity'.[54] In the Middle Ages and beyond, the vice of sloth (*acedia*) was understood to be something akin to a sense of distance from the divine brought about by isolation, a form of depression.[55] Conversely, *otium*, the time set aside for self-cultivation through the contemplation of the mind and soul, provided a highly valued alternative to work. But sloth's association with melancholy and the lack of productivity associated with *otium* steadily reduced the benign reputation idleness once enjoyed. After the Protestant Reformation and the critique of *otium*, the assertion of the need for the discipline of regular, continual work became primary to what Max Weber called the Protestant work-ethic. Yet during the Counter-Reformation, the Catholic Church also became increasingly opposed to idleness. This was especially true of the Jesuit Order, with its insistence on diligence and rigour.

Adam Smith conceded that a certain measure of idleness was an inevitable consequence of labour, as workers switched to different tasks; but the division of labour within capitalism would fortunately banish this idleness through the specialization of work, thus saving time in the interests of productivity.[56] The reorganization of society that began by the end of the seventeenth century, with the appearance of such institutions as the workhouse and the insane asylum, was characterized by a regard for the ethical value of work as something that would improve one's self and society in general. In the nineteenth century, idleness was disapproved of for retarding the march of progress. The idleness of the 'native' and the battle to overcome it became standard features of colonial narratives. Especially in British imperial discourse, idleness, a lack of self-mastery, and a disinclination towards both industriousness and industry were salient characteristics of colonized peoples, including the Irish.[57] As in Matthew Arnold's 'On the Study of Celtic Literature', the indolence of the Celt required the countering discipline of the Anglo-Saxon. The idleness of the Irish was typically presented (along with Catholicism, superstition, an inclination towards violence, and intemperance) as a justification for opposition to Home Rule. As anti-colonial forms of nationalism came to reproduce certain elements of imperialist logic by becoming modernizing movements in their own right, they too tended to represent idleness as a register of backwardness. The rejection of colonial stereotypes

---

54 Coetzee, 21. Coetzee's essay provides a useful, compressed history of the values identified with idleness and work; for a more thorough cultural history of the relationship between work and idleness since classical times, see Sebastien De Grazia, *Of Time, Work, and Leisure* (New York, 1994).

55 See Siegfried Wenzel, *The Sin of Sloth: Acedia in Medieval Thought and Literature* (Chapel Hill, 1960).

56 Adam Smith, *The Wealth of Nations* (New York, 2000), 9.

57 See Syed Hussein Alatas, *The Myth of the Lazy Native* (London, 1977).

of native idleness is obviously central to the Revival's promotion of the work of the nation, and presents a defensive response to the sorts of positions espoused by Arnold and others. Yet idleness did not have strictly negative conditions after the end of the medieval period. Significantly, it came to be regarded as having an important connection to literature and art; the phrase 'majestic indolence' was crucial in some of the formulations of British romanticism,[58] and was only one item in an ever-expanding lexicon that linked the virtues of not endlessly striving with the attainment of wisdom — William Wordsworth and John Keats come readily to mind in this connection. To Immanuel Kant, the freedom provided within an idle moment enables the possibility of the contemplation of the beautiful, which in turn leads to a condition of disinterest in which one leaves behind the limitations of the self in order to achieve universal subjectivity. Both a Kantian conception of disinterest (in the writing of Oscar Wilde) and a romanticist celebration of the possibilities of idleness (through Yeats's debt to the romantics) are preludes to an Irish modernist formulation of idleness that ultimately operates as a materialist negation of that very concept of disinterest. In *Ulysses*, Joyce provided a critical response to both Wildean and Yeatsian understandings of the relationship between intellectual labour and indolence.

A number of writers and philosophers celebrate the subversive potential of idleness but, because of its insistence upon historical specificity (which I will understand, in the Irish case, as national specificity), my argument will draw heavily upon the theoretical work of Walter Benjamin, who sought to understand idleness in dialectical and materialist terms. In the notebooks concerning the Paris arcades known as the *Passagen-werk*, Benjamin devoted all of Convolute M to 'Idleness', and the topic reappears in a number of his late writings related to that project. Although the Convolute on idleness is brief, his scattered speculations provide crucial insight into understanding its theoretical consequences.[59] Idleness (or *mussigang*, which has also been translated as 'loitering' and to Benjamin is something distinct from *musse*, or 'leisure'), proves to be a crucial determination for the manner in which such paradigmatic figures of the arcades as the *flâneur* and the gambler perceive the world. More specifically, while 'experience is the outcome of work', according to Benjamin, 'immediate experience is the phantasmagoria of the idler' (AP, 801). By 'phantasmagoria', Benjamin means the almost mystical state produced by the perpetual display within the arcades of fetishized commodities, similar to that created by the optical illusions of late nineteenth-century magic lantern shows.[60] The spell of consumption in the arcades is such that the ongoing immediate experience of the moment becomes more prominent than a rhythmic sense of experience conditioned by the beginning and end of the labour process. The means by which a seemingly endless synchronic experience of the present takes priority over a diachronic sense ultimately turns out to be one of the

58 See Willard Speigelman, *Majestic Indolence: English Romantic Poetry and the Work of Art* (Oxford, 1995).
59 See AP, 800–06.
60 See Susan Buck-Morss, *The Dialectics of Seeing* (Cambridge, MA, 1989), 81–82.

primary sources of the pleasures of idleness, according to Benjamin: 'Idleness has in view an unlimited duration, which fundamentally distinguishes it from simple sensuous pleasure, of whatever variety' (AP, 806). Thus, in one sense idleness appears to Benjamin to be something like a surrender to fate — 'Whoever enjoys leisure escapes Fortuna; whoever embraces idleness falls under her power' (AP, 800) — and the bewitchment of commodities. Yet, in Benjamin's view, idleness, like so much else associated with the arcades, bears within it a contradictory dimension. Ultimately, idleness offers up one potentially subversive semi-practice that might contribute to the critique of the teleology of progress so central to Benjamin's project in texts like 'Theses on the Philosophy of History'.

The temporality of idleness — and moreover, the distance from the labour process that inflects that temporality — provide one source of its more subversive qualities for the various types of idlers Benjamin addresses. For the *flâneur*, idleness serves not only as a refusal of a labour process that stands as the very basis for the exploitation and social divisions inherent to the version of modernity crystallized within the arcades of nineteenth-century Paris. It also signals a rejection of an increasingly dominant conception of temporality conditioned by the pace and rhythm of what E. P. Thompson called the 'work-discipline' of industrial capitalism.[61]

In a well-known passage of his primary essay on Baudelaire, Benjamin refers to the brief moment in which it was fashionable for dandies to walk turtles through the arcades.[62] Through his adoption of the slowness of the turtle, the *flâneur* enacts a symbolic form of resistance to the intensification of the speed of daily life (which, Benjamin notes, was a consequence of the rationalization of the labour process) with the desire to live within a prolonged sense of the moment, ostensibly outside the flow of history. While such manifestations of idleness appear to stand outside the passage of time, in Benjamin's view the *flâneur* embodies the contradiction of past and present, and the analysis of the dialectical relation between archaic and modern in the inactivity of the idler gestures towards an alternative history of development critical of the commonplace assumptions that characterize the phantasmagoria of modernity.[63] Baudelaire manages to represent figures or motifs that evoke a suppressed history of values or practices contrary to the common sense of the present. While the *flâneur* has become so accustomed to the phantasmagoria of commodities in the arcades that its jarring effects no longer have an impact upon consciousness or perception, the idleness of the *flâneur* recalls the 'heroic indolence' that, according to Marx, prevailed before the triumph of industry that accompanied the rise of

---

61 Thompson suggested in his classic essay, 'Time, Work-Discipline and Industrial Capitalism', that the transition to a more industrialized form of capitalism entailed a dramatic restructuring of work habits, which also entailed a profound shift in the importance and experience of time. See E. P. Thompson, *Customs in Common: Studies in Traditional Popular Culture* (New York, 1993), 352–403.

62 See Walter Benjamin, 'The Paris of the Second Empire in Baudelaire', *Selected Writings: Volume 4, 1938–1940* (Cambridge, MA, 2003), 30–31.

63 AP, 806.

the bourgeoisie ('In bourgeois society, indolence — to take up Marx's word — has ceased to be "heroic"; Marx speaks of the "victory ... of industry over heroic indolence"', AP, 800).[64] As an 'archaic' remainder of the past, the heroic indolence of the *flâneur* contributes two crucial dimensions to an understanding of Baudelaire's poetry. On the one hand, idleness presents one of the many 'wish-images' Benjamin discovers in the arcades, which serve to enable the conceptualization of a future beyond capitalism.[65] On the other hand, the fact that the *flâneur*'s practice of heroic laziness lingers as something of an exception, despite its apparent social extinction, calls attention to the often brutal process of modernization by which it *became* the exception rather than the norm.

In Benjamin's view, leisure was profoundly different from idleness. While leisure remained essentially tethered to its reliance upon the regularity of work, idleness strives to escape any connection to work whatsoever: 'Idleness seeks to avoid any sort of tie to the idler's line of work, and ultimately to the labor process itself. That distinguishes it from leisure' (AP, 803). The temporality of leisure depends upon the priority of work. It is that which takes place between the end of one act of labour and the beginning of another. Rather than serving as some sort of older precedent for idleness, leisure anticipates much more closely the modern phenomenon of what Theodor Adorno called 'free time': that brief period of sanctioned rest between periods of work that presents itself as relief from labour but actually in its rational and compartmentalized form stands as 'the unmediated continuation of labor as its shadow'.[66] In Benjamin's view, idleness did not necessarily present an absolute alternative to modern forms of 'free time'. Historically, the appeal of idleness stemmed from its status as 'an early form of distraction or amusement' in which one could 'savour, on one's own, an arbitrary succession of sensations'. Yet 'it was to this need that the entertainment industry answered' (AP, 804). What Adorno later termed 'the culture industry' emerged and the commodification of the pleasure of idleness began in earnest, so that the structures of 'free time' might have content. Nor was idleness safe from being converted into a form of work in its own right; Benjamin suspected that the spontaneity that the apparent aimlessness of idleness masked might serve as 'a specific form of work-preparedness' (AP, 802) for such emerging professions as journalism, detective work, and even the ambulatory type of advertising practised by the sandwich-man, the 'last incarnation' of the flâneur (AP, 448). Yet the particular forms of idleness characteristic of the arcades and represented within the writing of both Baudelaire and the more middlebrow feuilletonists of nineteenth-century Paris had not yet been completely converted into socially acceptable forms of either entertainment or work, according to Benjamin; in its distance from the labour process, idleness still retained a subversive potential.

64 Benjamin refers to in one of Marx's articles in the *Neue Rheinische Zeitung*, to 'the victory of the bourgeoisie', which 'was at that time the victory of a new social order ... of industry over heroic laziness ...'. See Karl Marx, *The Revolutions of 1848: Political Writings: Volume I* (London, 1973), 192.
65 On the utopian capacity of the wish-image, see AP, 4–5.
66 Theodor Adorno, *Critical Models* (New York, 1998), 173.

Benjamin's formulation of exactly how such implications might be actualized within some sort of aesthetic practice is somewhat paradoxical. Since any given instance of idleness is radically particular to the specific conditions of a given time and place, a general account of the disruptive potential of idleness is not possible. However, within the particular conditions of modernity, the socially sanctioned forms of leisure that once provided the basis for the production of art have disappeared. Instead, leisure has been replaced by the more desultory condition of idleness, 'a precondition of artistic production. And often, idleness is the very thing which stamps that production with the traits that make its relation to the economic production process so drastic' (AP, 805–06). Just as the labour process ineluctably 'stamps' the commodity through its conversion of work into value, the semi-practice of idleness — or, as we might best define it after Benjamin's theorization of it here, the apparent inactivity that actually masks those 'unofficial' labours necessary for the production of art — leaves its inevitable mark upon the work of art. Since idleness — unlike labour — is not for sale within the context of modern bourgeois society, the values it produces as crystallized in the work of art itself will lie well outside the framework of evaluation that determines what is valuable according to the logic of the market. It is precisely in this manner that idleness subverts the values of cultural production — and in the context of Irish modernism it will enable a critical interrogation into the manner in which value was produced within the Revival. Potentially, the different values — in this case, aesthetic rather than economic — of modern art might allow for the possibility of positions and conditions external to those that are in accord with the common sense of bourgeois society. As Adorno would argue in a similar vein in *Aesthetic Theory*, through a process of negation the critical engagement of such alternative values enables the imaginative possibility of a social world different from the seemingly unchangeable conditions of capitalist modernity.

To Benjamin, the articulation of alternative values is closely connected to the apprehension of an alternate understanding of history recalcitrant to the progressive historicism that underwrites capitalism and its consequent conceptualization of modernity. The difference lies within the temporality of idleness. To return to the quote with which I began, according to Benjamin, history first becomes knowable through different types of 'experience', forms of knowledge closely tied to work and idleness: 'Experience (*Ehrfahrung*) is the outcome of work; immediate experience (*Erlebnis*) is the phantasmagoria of the idler' (AP, 801). The words *Ehrfahrung* and *Erlebnis* have various connotations for Benjamin, and the distinction between them is crucial for understanding the critique of modernization evident in *The Arcades Project*. *Ehrfahrung* is also translated as 'long experience' or 'connected experience' throughout various editions of Benjamin's writing, and it evokes notions of tradition and continuity. *Erlebnis*, by contrast, refers to particular or individual experiences of a given moment, and it entails a sense of the discontinuity of the present from the past. By implication, *Ehrfahrung* presupposes productivity and activity, while *Erlebnis* corresponds to consumption and passivity.[67] It is in the distinction between *Ehrfahrung* and *Erlebnis* that the differences between the Revival and the high modernist period that follows appear most stark: the work-ethic apparent in the Revival amounts to one ongoing attempt to construct a teleological understanding of *Ehrfahrung* that would explain and justify the persistence of Irish nationality, while the modernist novels I will be concerned with here are committed to the delineation of *Erlebnis* in the temporal context of colonial (and, eventually, post-colonial) modernity.

Ehrfahrung is defined by its sequential nature: 'What distinguishes long experience (*Ehrfahrung*) from immediate experience (*Erlebnis*) is that the former is inseparable from the representation of a continuity, a sequence' (AP, 802). *Ehrfahrungen* organize a series of related events into a type of narrative in which one can apprehend the passage of time. For this reason, *Ehrfahrungen* are important for literary purposes because of the sense of continuity and progression they provide.[68] Though they do not always take a specifically literary narrative form, *Ehrfahrungen* transmit the sorts of traditions, stories, and tropes that provide a sense of stability, as well as a guarantee of one's connection to a shared past; they provide a rationale for one's place in the world.[69] However, within the phantasmagoria of the modern city, in which the appearance of places, commodities, and things take priority over the reality of the history that produced them, the narratives of tradition and continuity produced by *Ehrfahrungen* are shattered by the shocks of modernity. Yet the disruption of *Ehrfahrung* provides certain critical opportunities as well. Another way to conceive of the interruption of that particular brand of *Ehrfahrung* would be to regard it as the moment of revolution — a cataclysmic event that would create the opening for the inception of a completely new historical process — or, to put it in terms consistent with Benajmin's 'Theses on the Philosophy of History', the moment of cessation in which a profound shock blasts a specific era out of the course of history.[70] In order to produce a critique of progression through time itself, it is first necessary to account for how that progression is represented — in other words, one must bring a critical eye to bear upon the particular form of *Ehrfahrung* that constitutes the dominant, authorized narrative that justifies progress through time.

The temporality of *Erlebnis* provides the possibility of a critique of progress — especially when progress takes the form of the narrative of modernization. Given Benjamin's discussion of *Erlebnis*, on first glimpse it would seem that such a possibility would appear unlikely. *Erlebnis* refers to the phenomenon of living within the phantasmagoria of false

---

67 See Buck-Morss, *The Dialectics of Seeing*, 104–05, 108, 188–89.

68 In notes connected to his essay 'On Some Motifs on Baudelaire', Benjamin suggests that the immediate experience of *Erlebnis* is 'by nature unsuitable for literary composition' in itself and that the intellectual labour of literary work 'is distinguished by the fact that it begets *Ehrfahrungen* out of *Erlebnissen*' (AP, 1007, n. 4).

69 In the essay on Baudelaire, Benjamin identifies them with the archaic festivals and rites of 'organic' communities. See I, 159.

70 Such a goal lies at the heart of Benjamin's critique of historical progress in that essay. See I, 261.

consciousness that seems to eradicate any accurate or objective perception of history and reality.[71] As a temporal condition that elucidates the immediate experience of the present, Erlebnis is synchronic rather than diachronic, and it fosters a sense of a perpetual present. It is for these reasons that Erlebnis is so difficult to represent in literary genres like the realist novel — as an ongoing sense of the unending duration of the current moment, Erlenbis lacks the means of differentiation necessary to the advancement of a narrative. Yet it is a precisely modern condition, and as the sense of Erlebnis becomes predominant it demands new methods capable of mapping it. Benjamin's concept of the 'trace' (Spur) offers a key to an alternative hermeneutics that would enable the knowledge of a history once provided by Ehrfahrung but now repressed by the teleology of progress. The trace refers to the imprint of objects or concepts that persist as fossils of prior, outmoded commodities and therefore as vestiges of prior moments in history. If one can come to terms with the implicit history suggested by the trace, then one can begin to construct an alternative form of representation that can register the sort of knowledge implicit to, yet disguised by, Erlebnis:

> With the trace, a new dimension accrues to Erlebnis. It is no longer tied to the sense of adventure; the one who undergoes an experience (Erlebnis) can follow the trace that leads there. Whoever follows traces must not only pay attention; above all, he must have given heed to a great many things … In this way there comes into play the peculiar configuration by dint of which long experience (Ehrfahrung) appears translated into the language of immediate experience (Erlebnis). (AP, 801)

In this manner, the apprehension and analysis of the trace enables the translation of the language of tradition into the language of shock; not only do the otherwise unrepresentable qualities of Erlebnis become legible for narrative purposes, but the repressed knowledge of the historical process that shattered the possibility of Ehrfahrung becomes discernible as well. By including those seemingly archaic or outmoded elements of the past no longer useful for progressive historicism, this alternate form of historiography enables an archaeology of the present that accounts for the passage of time without becoming complicit with the teleology of progress. Ultimately, idleness is not a condition defined by the absence of any work or activity whatsoever, but rather the context that enables a new form of intellectual labour committed to different forms of representation and analysis not yet recognized as legitimate or productive.

   Benjamin provides a method that might be worked out according to the distinct dictates of a specific context. Ultimately, my argument will take as a point of departure the claim that the post-Joycean Irish modernist novel delineates Erlebnis in a manner that enables one to discover a repressed history of trauma and conquest omitted from

71 As Benjamin states explicitly in AP, 804: 'Phantasmagoria is the intentional correlate of Erlebnis.'

progressive narratives complicit with the national work-ethic. This is one of the main differences between Irish modernism and that of other national traditions. While the narrative techniques of Joyce and others might appear to have similarities with the work of writers elsewhere, whether in formal experimentation or in the representation of idleness in general, the political charge Irish modernism bears makes it different. The representation of idleness throughout modernism in general is not unique, as any reader familiar with Marcel Proust, Franz Kafka, or T. S. Eliot's concession of 'the necessary laziness' of the poet in 'Tradition and the Individual Talent' would confirm.[72] But the representation of idleness in Irish modernism engages with matters having to do with nationality and decolonization. What is unique is the manner in which idleness in Irish modernism serves as both a form of dissent from the values of the Revival — and later, the post-colonial state — and as a basis for a Benjaminian hermeneutics of the trace that provides evidence of the differential nature of modernity within Ireland.

Benjamin insists that while it is possible to find some evidence of idleness as far back as primitive times, any discussion of it must be structured by attention to the particularity of temporal and geographical context. 'We should', he writes, 'try to show how deeply idleness is marked by features of the capitalist economic order in which it flourishes.' That economic order in Ireland was very far from the European/French order Benjamin focused on in his research on the arcades. In Ireland, the arrival of capitalism was mediated dramatically and suddenly by colonial violence, rather than through the more gradual development of the capitalist means of production that occurred within more metropolitan societies. If 'the only satisfactory semantic meaning of modernity lies in its association with capitalism', as Jameson argues, then the form it takes in Ireland is crucially determined by the trauma of colonization.[73] The various outmoded traces, fragments, and practices that the lazy idle schemers encounter while wandering the streets of Dublin in novels like *Ulysses* and *At Swim-Two-Birds* are not only fossils of prior modes of production, but also records of a pre-colonial culture and the violence that shattered it. By recovering these traces within the colonial form of *Erlebnis* represented within their texts, the Irish modernists provide the basis for an understanding of history that avoids the teleology of national progress present within the works of the Revival.

The fact that idleness provides the context in which all of this might occur is significant, for idleness itself in the form of 'heroic indolence' gestures toward a time before colonialism as well as capitalism. But to place an interpretative emphasis upon the practice of idleness in the Irish modernist novel risks the reaffirmation of another characteristic of the particular era in question: the colonial stereotype of the Irish as lazy, indolent, sentimental, undisciplined, and incapable of self-rule. Though I will engage with the category of the stereotype more closely in Chapter 3, I want to stress at this point that I do

72   T. S. Eliot, *Selected Prose of T. S. Eliot* (New York, 1975), 40.
73   Jameson, *A Singular Modernity*, 13.

not see the stereotype of Irish laziness as true in actuality but as functionally important in a rhetorical and political sense. The labour it took to write a book like *Ulysses* belies any stereotype of Irish laziness, even if it does represent idleness extensively. Nor will I argue at any point that the writers discussed in this book were themselves invested in the supposed truth of the stereotype of Irish laziness. Whether in the form of a Wildean brand of what Homi Bhabha has termed 'sly civility', as a marker of material impoverishment, or as evidence of a new form of non-alienated intellectual labour — all of which will be the case at different times in the discussion that follows — idleness signals a particular form of temporality inflected by the aftermath of colonization, rather than the assertion of a supposedly atavistic ethnic trait.

However, an understanding of the historicity of this particular stereotype does help clarify some of the larger aims of this project. One of the main rhetorical techniques of Irish nationalism involved what Lloyd has termed the 'transvaluation' of stereotypes in which negative attributes of the Celt were reconsidered as positive characteristics of the native Irish.[74] For example, nationalist discourse often reframed stereotypical beliefs about the sentimentality of the Celt as the piety and conviction of the unadulterated Irish. Idleness, in all of its slothful and financially perilous aimlessness, presents something quite different. It is no wonder that there were really no attempts within Irish nationalism or the Revival to transvalue the stereotypical idleness of the Irish into something more positive: it simply did not fit the narrative of modernization necessary to bring about decolonization. Yet modernization is a problematic concept in the context of Irish history, as it began with colonization, was mediated by violence and catastrophe, and frequently eradicated alternative social formations, beliefs, and practices that were in some instances more egalitarian than those imposed by the colonizer.[75] Lloyd argues that Irish society is marked by what he terms 'recalcitrance', a

> mode of resistance to official nationalism ... which has less to do with the difficulties of material conditions in the colony or with alternative modes of organization, and far more to do with cultural practices that are at once embedded in the popular imaginary and incompatible with nationalist canons of tradition and moral citizenship.[76]

In this case, idleness (at least in the manner in which it is represented within Irish modernism) marks the difference of the colonized Irish from the colonizer, and bears the traces of an otherness that resists assimilation to conventional forms of bourgeois

---

74 See David Lloyd, 'Counterparts: *Dubliners*, Masculinity, and Temperance Nationalism', in Derek Attridge and Marjorie Howes, eds., *Semicolonial Joyce* (Cambridge, 2000), 131–32, for a discussion of the 'transvaluation' of Irish stereotypes and some selected examples.
75 See Gibbons *Transformations in Irish Culture*, 6 and also 82–93.
76 Lloyd, 'Counterparts', 137.

nationalism derived from colonial models. Idleness, which is both the practice of wasting time and an attempt to live outside of a dominant form of temporality conditioned by work discipline, helps clarify the disparate nature of modernity in Ireland. Whether one recognizes what Lloyd calls 'the *non-modern* … a set of spaces that emerge out of kilter with modernity but nevertheless in dynamic relation to it' in Ireland, or one resists the possibility of what post-colonial theory has termed 'alternative modernities', at the very least the prevalence and function of idleness within works like *Ulysses*, the Cuanduine trilogy, *Murphy* and *At Swim-Two-Birds* help demonstrate that the specific experience of modernity in Ireland is as distinct from other parts of the world as Irish modernism is from other national literary traditions.[77] The practices of the lazy idle schemer — and more importantly, the understanding of Irish history that result from them — suggest the persistence of what Lloyd calls 'Irish Times', a 'temporal dimension composed simultaneously of multiple and incommensurable temporalities for which the terms "tradition" and "modernity" are only partial and certainly inadequate designations'.[78]

As Benjamin suggests throughout his writing about idleness, it is a profoundly ambiguous condition. One risks neglecting that ambiguity if one fails to propose certain crucial qualifications regarding the representation of idleness in Irish modernism. First of all, Ireland in the first two decades of independence was an underdeveloped, economically deprived, former colony that required a great deal of transformative work. While the conservative version of nationalism that eventually came to dominate the Irish Free State was restrictive and at times puritanical, to recognize it as such is not to diminish the considerable achievement brought about by the Irish nationalist movement — initially, at least, a much broader, egalitarian, inclusive and at times more radical movement than it is given credit for — in conducting one of the earliest successful wars of liberation against the British Empire. To opt out of the work of the nation in the manner of the lazy idle schemers of Irish modernism meant a refusal of what the work of the nation had become; it was not a position nostalgic for colonial rule. For the most part, the motif of idleness in the hands of the lazy idle schemers stood for the first halting attempts to formulate an alternative form of work, rather than an absolute refusal to work altogether. Secondly, the role of the lazy idle schemer, as represented through the figures of the aspiring intellectuals at the centre of each of the novels discussed here, is a particularly difficult position to inhabit. Unlike the forms of idleness found in other literary periods, like romanticism, within Irish modernism it involves a strong sense of abjection. Though O'Duffy presents idleness as a pleasurable utopian condition far superior to the depravity of capitalism, Joyce and Beckett represent it as something inextricably tied to melancholy, frustration, and even as analogous to insanity. While the inactivity of the lazy idle schemers registers dissent from both consecrated forms of intellectual labour and the work of the nation in general, it also

77 David Lloyd, *Ireland after History* (Cork, 1999), 2. Emphasis in original.
78 David Lloyd, *Irish Times: Temporalities of Modernity* (Dublin, 2008), 6.

signifies the frustration that arises out of a dearth of possible positions available within the Irish field of literary production. Idleness, therefore, is not a celebratory practice — it is a sign of post-colonial intellectual and economic underdevelopment.

Finally, this book will not concern Irish idleness in general. Modern Irish writing is not lacking in the varieties of idleness it represents. There is in particular a dramatic tradition dating back at least as far as Dion Boucicault that includes such notable shirkers of responsibility as the 'Captain' Jack Boyle in Sean O'Casey's *Juno and the Paycock* and Pat the caretaker in Brendan Behan's *The Hostage* that I will not be concerned with here. While these latter-day descendants of Boucicault's Shaughraun are certainly characterized by their capacity for both laziness and scheming, they are part of a different interrogation of the relationship between Irish identity and stereotypes of recalcitrance. Instead, this study will focus upon the inactivity of that particular type — a would-be intellectual who belongs to an emergent middle class, and within Irish modernism, this lazy idle schemer is specifically gendered as male. While there are various examples of idle women within the Irish modernist novel — most prominently Molly Bloom — the relationship women have both to work and idleness in these texts is often problematic. In *Ulysses*, Joyce critically represents women's labour as one of the means by which the patriarchal forms of domination that contribute to the general *ennui* of late colonial Dublin maintains its power; less critically, as in Beckett's delineation of the character Celia in *Murphy* as a clichéd version of the prostitute with a heart of gold, the representation of women is at times misogynistic. As an archetype of the literary intellectual, the lazy idle schemer is crucial to the ideology of Irish modernism — and that ideology could be just as problematic and repressive as it could be thematically or formally innovative. In this sense, the model of the intellectual one finds in the Revival was clearly more egalitarian than it was in Irish modernism, as such prominent figures as Lady Gregory, Maude Gonne, Alice Milligan, Eva Gore-Booth, Constance Markievicz, and a host of others demonstrate. Yet in order to avoid reproducing these blind spots about gender, it is important to recognize that women writers had different aims in mind. Most notably, they formulated their dissent from the work of the nation by postulating a form of intellectual labour different from that of the figures I will be concerned with here. Unlike the male modernist writers who privileged the motif of laziness, women writers like Mary Lavin and Kate O'Brien focused on specifically feminine forms of work. In the works of Kate O'Brien especially, sites of female labour, such as the convent in *The Land of Spices* or the classroom in *Mary Lavelle*, become alternative female public spheres in which women enjoy a degree of agency and satisfaction in their work prohibited to them at large in an increasingly conservative Irish society.[79]

---

79   See Kate O'Brien, *Mary Lavelle* (London, 1984) and *The Land of Spices* (London, 1988); notably, both of these novels were banned by the Censorship Board of the Irish government upon their publication in the years 1936 and 1941, respectively.

The difference between women's writing and the works of the writers I will be concerned with here raises a related point. This work in no way proposes to produce a definitive or all-encompassing theory of all of Irish modernism as such. To produce such an act of totalization would inevitably exclude writers and texts as much as it would include others; moreover, such a conception of literary history would risk reinstating the sort of teleological thinking that I argue at least one strand of Irish modernism formally reacted against. In line with the Benjaminian co-ordinates of this project, it seems far more compelling to me to regard Irish modernism as comprising a specific constellation of a particular time and place. According to Benjamin, 'by the virtue of the elements' of a number of different thematic or formal threads of a given emerging concept it is possible to discern a distinct constellation in which 'phenomena are subdivided and redeemed; so that these elements which it is the function of the concept to elicit from phenomena are most clearly evident at the extremes'.[80] The series of texts I will be concerned with here comprise just such an element within the broader constellation of Irish modernism, and in its distance from the Revival it marks a sense of the 'extreme' that establishes a break between the two periods; the investment in idleness evident in these texts is precisely what defines this subfield of Irish modernism. Yet the lazy idle schemer has a prehistory, and, in Chapter 2, I will examine some precedents for the modernist formulation of idleness. The roots of the modernist exploration of the connection between idleness and intellectual labour are found in the works of Wilde and Yeats. Wilde's representation of idleness presents a radicalization of that stereotype as something that opens up the possibilities of the valorization of scandal, a fundamental commitment to pleasure, and a flexible, performative notion of identity. Yeats, in turn, reformulated a Wildean concept of disinterested abstraction into a particular instance of what Gramsci would have called the national-popular. In *Autobiographies* and related writing, Yeats theorizes the dualistic nature of intellectual labour.

My chapters on Joyce comprise the largest section of *Lazy Idle Schemers*, and they present some of the central premises of my argument. In Chapter 3, I argue that a crucial strain of Joyce's representation of Stephen Dedalus in *Ulysses* involves confronting the positions regarding the relationship between idleness and intellectual labour found in the works of Wilde and Yeats and turning them on their heads in a materialist fashion that departs from the category of disinterest. By remaking the model of the intellectual found in the works of those two writers, Joyce conducts a critique of the manner in which the literature of the Revival produces symbolic values useful to the state-driven goals of an increasingly conservative nationalist movement, proposes a non-teleological understanding of history that raises important questions about the nature of modernity in Ireland, and inaugurates a dissident strand of Irish modernism critical of both colonial and post-colonial sociopolitical conventions. The materialist dimension to Joyce's representation

80 Walter Benjamin, *The Origin of German Tragic Drama* (London, 1977), 34–35.

of idleness, I suggest, stems from his encounter during his early years in Trieste with Italian socialism — a form of political commitment that took the theoretical position of the refusal to work as a central principle. Although Joyce eventually lost interest in socialism as a specific ideological doctrine, I argue that it nevertheless provided a means for him to reconsider the role of the literary intellectual. It is through the figure of the lazy idle schemer that Joyce redeems the usefulness of idleness, despite its apparent unproductive qualities. In Chapter 4, I focus on those early sections of *Ulysses* in which the narrative focuses on Stephen Dedalus. In these episodes of the novel, Joyce represents a negation of the conventional form of intellectual labour prevalent in the Revival in order to propose a critique of the process in which socially meaningful symbolic values come into being through the work of the nation.

My remaining chapters present three variations of a post-Joycean modernism that addresses the consequences of idleness in relation to the respective fields of economics, philosophy, and politics. In Chapter 5, I discuss Eimar O'Duffy, a neglected novelist whose Cuanduine trilogy (written between 1926 and 1933) provides an important missing link in the trajectory of Irish modernism between the publication of *Ulysses* and the later writers more frequently identified with Joyce. *King Goshawk and the Birds*, *The Spacious Adventures of the Man in the Street*, and *Asses in Clover* contain the most thoroughgoing critical refutations of the ideology and the imagery of the Revival of any of the works I am concerned with and propose that idleness should be considered the primary political value of Irish modernism. O'Duffy was closely involved with the Social Credit movement and outlined his economic beliefs in a lengthy and unusual work titled *Life and Money*, which I read as a theoretical supplement to his novels. While O'Duffy's immediate goal was the abolition of money, his novels celebrate what he termed 'the Leisure State', a utopian, decentralized form of social organization committed to a world in which people worked as little as possible.

My discussion of Beckett's *Murphy*, subject of Chapter 6, concerns the fate of the increasingly residual social and academic Anglo-Irish Protestant elite. Murphy is a quintessential lazy idle schemer, and his tortuous experience on the 'Job-path' presents some of the more humorous representations of the desire for indolence found within the novels discussed in my book. Yet the implications of Murphy's idleness go beyond his hatred of labour. Murphy's commitment to as absolute a form of inactivity as possible enables an inquiry into the social position of previously empowered institutional processes of cultural reproduction. On the one hand, Murphy's commitment to laziness enables the critique of philosophy. On the other hand, Murphy's belief in the necessary separation of the mind and body allows Beckett to satirize what I term (after a phrase used by the historian Joe Lee) 'Trinity sloth', a form of academic laziness that was self-reflexive and seemingly separate from the material reality of Irish social life surrounding it.

Finally, in a reading of Flann O'Brien's 1939 novel *At Swim-Two-Birds*, in Chapter 7, I argue that by the late 1930s idleness had become such a deeply ingrained characteristic of the ideology of Irish modernism that it no longer retained the recalcitrant possibilities it had in the works of earlier writers. The unnamed narrator of *At Swim-Two-Birds*, a paradigmatic example of the lazy idle schemer, idealizes laziness due to his desire to model his life after the characters in Joyce's novels. Nevertheless, I argue that in O'Brien's novel idleness retains a critical potential despite the apparent limitations of his version of the lazy idle schemer. Through a sustained comparison of *At Swim-Two-Birds* and the Constitution of 1937, I argue that the former is a text in which elements drawn from a number of different historical moments intersect with each other in a manner that contradicts the logic of modernization. While this formally and thematically radical dimension to *At Swim-Two-Birds* finally proves unsustainable within the novel's own terms, it nevertheless suggests the possibility of a temporality premised upon the pleasures of idleness, rather than the alienation of labour. Despite its ambiguities and limitations, there is an undeniably utopian dimension to the emphasis put upon the representation of idleness in Irish modernism; *Lazy Idle Schemers* is committed to a recovery of that utopian dimension. Idleness draws attention to work as a fundamental problem that national independence in itself would not solve, and registers attempts to resist the alienation and dissatisfaction produced by modern labour. As I will suggest in my Afterword, that position continues to have merit today even if our own historical moment is well past the end of the modernist period that produced these texts.

2   'Creation without Toil': Wilde, Yeats, and the Origins of the Lazy Idle Schemer

I

The lazy idle schemer does not lack precursors in Irish cultural history. Though Stephen Dedalus is the first fully fledged version of that would-be intellectual — and then, only within the pages of *Ulysses* — he nevertheless had his antecedents. The primary antagonist of the lazy idle schemer is the Yeatsian model of the engaged writer who is not only committed to the cultivation of his own self-development as an ongoing aesthetic project, but also to the delineation of a national imaginary. That presiding model of the intellectual in the era of the Revival was exemplified in a number of other figures ranging from Patrick Pearse to Lady Gregory, but Yeats's exploration of its possibilities was the most thorough and subtle of all. Social and political engagement was indeed central to his conception of his own role as an intellectual; yet idleness was an important element too. His autobiographical writing contains his most considered reflections on how the dichotomy between work and idleness conditions his public and private labour as an intellectual. Because the lazy idle schemer in Irish modernism is most usually represented in fictionalized autobiography, it is difficult to show how he is ultimately committed to negation rather than affirmation. For instance, many commentators seek to identify Stephen Dedalus, Murphy, or the unnamed narrator of *At Swim-Two-Birds* with their literary creators. Yet it is precisely the inactivity of all three of those fictional characters that Joyce, Beckett, and O'Brien overcame in and through their novels. The autobiographical tendency in Irish modernist writing is at least partly explained by Yeats's reputation as the most significant intellectual of the Revival, that 'restricted field of literary production', which sought to produce works that were deemed the more worthy for their distance from the mass market.[1]

But Yeats's view of the link between idleness and intellectual labour is as important for the enhanced prestige of the figure of the lazy idle schemer as for that of the committed artist, to which the modernist writers were so antagonistic. Yet Yeats's understanding of idleness, as he freely admits in *Autobiographies*, also owed a tremendous debt to Oscar Wilde. Wilde's writing in general provides a wide range of imaginative resources for the formulation of the lazy idle schemer. His critical writing, in particular, offers a number of positions on the relationship between work and idleness that will serve as a basis for Irish modernism. Yeats, in turn, revised some of Wilde's positions for his own anti-colonial cultural politics. This produced a version of the literary intellectual to which the lazy idle schemer would be both indebted and opposed. Irish modernism — most of all the status idleness had within it — would not have been possible without either Wilde or Yeats. Their notions of the utility of idleness for cultural production contributed to the representation of the lazy idle schemer in *Ulysses*.

2

In a collection of epigrams entitled *Phrases and Philosophies for the Use of the Young*, published in December 1894, Wilde asserted that 'the condition of perfection is idleness: the aim of perfection is youth' (*CWW*, 1206). The lazy idle schemer is young. Since he has not yet actually determined a course of action for a future that has yet to arrive — indeed, even to do so would be vulgar — he is identified as a member of a new generation that does not yet have a collective identity. This in part explains Wilde's appeal to subsequent writers. Despite their generational differences, both Yeats and Joyce early in their careers found in Wilde a useful model of the intellectual for the articulation of their own emerging aesthetic ambitions.[2] In his 1891 review of Wilde's short-story collection *Lord Arthur Saville's Crime and Other Stories* for the newspaper *United Ireland*, Yeats praised Wilde for his recalcitrant Irishness:

> 'Beer, bible, and the seven deadly virtues have made England what she is', wrote Mr. Wilde once; and a part of the Nemesis that has fallen upon her is a complete inability to understand anything he says. We should not find him so unintelligible

---

1   On the 'restricted field of production' as a characteristic of the broader terrain of cultural production in general, see Bourdieu, *The Field of Cultural Production*, 115–21.

2   While Wilde's influence upon Yeats and Joyce has long been acknowledged, it is only recently that his importance for the emergence of modernism in general has been recognized. See Ann L. Ardis, *Modernism and Cultural Conflict 1880–1922* (Cambridge, 2002), 45–77.

— for much about him is Irish of the Irish. I see in his life and works an extravagant Celtic crusade against Anglo-Saxon stupidity.[3]

Although Yeats's assessment of Wilde should be qualified by the nationalist orientation of *United Ireland*, he finds here two positions that will inflect his own early writing and the development of his aesthetic philosophy. On the one hand, Wilde seems to bear out an Arnoldian sense of racial difference, in which (in Seamus Deane's words) 'every virtue of the Celt was matched by a vice of the British bourgeois; everything the philistine middle classes of England needed, the Celt could supply'.[4] On the other hand, the quality of intelligence exemplified by Wilde's 'life and works' belied the lack of intellectual clarity of Arnold's imaginative, irrational Celt, who lacked the precision of the Anglo-Saxon. But Yeats believed in Arnold's Celt because he was an opponent of the deadening rationality of modernity, although he was troubled by Arnold's insistence on the racial destiny implied by such a figure. Wilde epitomized both the imaginative capacity of the Irish and their cultural distinctness.[5] Two decades later Yeats's autobiographical writings made clear that his own initial literary ambitions were very much the same as Wilde's.

Joyce too found in Wilde an anticipation of his own artistic ambition. In a piece for the Italian newspaper *Il Piccolo della Sera*, written to introduce a production of Wilde's *Salomé* in Trieste in 1909, Joyce suggested that the source of Wilde's inspiration made particular sense to a young dissident Catholic writer such as himself:

> Here we touch upon the vital centre of Wilde's art: sin. ... All his characteristic qualities, the qualities (perhaps) of his race: wit, the generous impulse, the asexual intellect were put to the service of a theory of beauty which should, he thought, have brought back the Golden Age and the joy of youth to the world. But deep down, if any truth is to be educed from his subjective interpretation of Aristotle, his restless thought which proceeds by sophisms rather than syllogisms, his assimilation of other natures alien to his own, such as the delinquent and the humble, it is the truth inherent in Catholicism: that man cannot reach the divine heart except across that sense of separation and loss that is called sin.[6]

Joyce's focus on sin inevitably reminds his readers of Wilde's scandalous reputation. Yet for Joyce, Wilde's relation to sin is rooted as much in his nationality as it is in his homosexuality, even if the national characteristics he exemplifies are rather distant from

---

3   W. B. Yeats, 'Oscar Wilde's Last Book', in *Uncollected Prose by W. B. Yeats, Volume 1: First Reviews and Articles 1886–1896*, ed. John P. Frayne (New York, 1970), 203–04.
4   Seamus Deane, *Celtic Revivals* (London, 1985), 25.
5   Yeats, 'The Celtic Element in Literature', 175
6   James, Joyce, 'Oscar Wilde: The Poet of "Salomé"', in *Occasional, Critical, and Political Writing* (Oxford, 2000), 151.

the attributes of Arnold's Celt. The possibility that the apprehension of beauty might bring about an eternal 'joy of youth', in which the passage of time would seem to have stopped, is one feature of the aesthetic theory Stephen Dedalus expounds in the final chapter of *A Portrait of the Artist as a Young Man*. More important for Joyce, however, are the ramifications of Wilde's aesthetic philosophy. Whether or not it succeeded on its own terms, Wilde's life and writing define or are defined by 'sin', that is by a position beyond the dictates of morality and propriety that must be the aspiration of any intellectual who strives to articulate new and different conceptions of value, even at the cost of isolation. Joyce suggests, via Stephen's ruminations concerning the relationship between aesthetics and convention in the opening episodes of *Ulysses*, that innovation often comes very close to heresy and carries with it similar punishments; yet, like ideas once thought blasphemous, it sometimes can come to be accepted as the foundation for a new conception of order. Like Yeats, Joyce uses Wilde as a persona through which he can project intimations of his own positions concerning the nature of aesthetics and intellectual labour.

At first glance, there is some distance between Yeats's primarily Celtic Wilde and Joyce's essentially Catholic Wilde; in each case, the writer produced a version that endorsed his own literary aspirations. Yet there is a link between these respective versions. It is to be found in Wilde's celebration of idleness, the 'condition of perfection' associated with youth. Idleness was precisely one of the characteristics of the Celt that, in Arnold's view, demonstrated the need for a controlling Anglo-Saxon impetus that would guide Celtic creativity towards a progressive future. Idleness became one of Wilde's scandalizing performances, aimed in part at satirizing Arnold's act of stereotyping. Yet idleness was already scandalous; it had sinful, decadent connotations. Wilde wrote in 'The Critic as Artist' that 'while, in the opinion of society, Contemplation is the gravest sin of which any citizen can be guilty, in the opinion of the highest culture it is the proper occupation of man … to do nothing at all is the most difficult thing in the world, the most difficult and the most intellectual' (*CWW*, 1039). All of Wilde's writing depicts idleness; people attending formal parties and the theatre, visiting places of resort, and engaging in witty conversations filled with paradoxes and epigrams. Yet as Jeff Nunokawa argues, there is a fine line between the form of inactivity that serves as a necessary condition for the processes of contemplation central to the creation and interpretation of art and the sorts of activities favoured by Wilde's well-to-do characters in which 'leisure is a duty that, while preferable to its counterpart, remains, nonetheless, another job to do'.[7] The 'great aristocratic art of doing absolutely nothing' (*CWW*, 38), as Wilde refers to it in *The Picture of Dorian Gray*, actually involves a lot of work. Rather than bearing many similarities to the form of inactivity that will later characterize the lazy idle schemer, the leisurely activities

---

7   Jeff Nunokawa, *Tame Passions of Wilde: The Styles of Manageable Desire* (Princeton, 2003), 105. For an excellent overview of the resistance towards the compulsion to work that runs intermittently through Wilde's writing, see Nunokawa 96.

practised by so many of Wilde's characters actually appear more similar to Adorno's notion of 'free time', a brief period carved out within a greater collective form of temporality determined by a rhythm derived from labour-time, which ultimately provides a mirror image of work in its organization, rigour, and duration. However, a more profound form of idleness emerges as a central value in essays like 'The Decay of Lying', 'The Critic as Artist' and 'The Soul of Man under Socialism'; this had a deep impact on Yeats and Joyce. The idleness of the literary intellectual in Irish modernism originates in Wildean idleness, and it is at one level closely identified with Wilde's own very public performance of the role of prototypical lazy idle schemer.

During his life, Wilde was famous for his pose of refined and languid idleness. Katherine Bradley recorded in her diary in 1890 that

> he is writing two articles at present in the Nineteenth Century on the Art of Doing Nothing. He is at his best when he is lying on a sofa thinking. He does not want to do anything; overcome by the 'maladie du style' — the effort to bring in deliberate cadences to express exactly what he wants to express — he is prostrate. But to think, to contemplate ...[8]

Yet Wilde was productive. Within a year of Bradley's observation, he published two volumes of stories, one novel, a collection of critical essays written over the previous year, the better part of two plays and numerous poems — all of this in addition to his occasional writing and speaking engagements. As Richard Ellmann suggests, 'languor was the mask of industry'.[9]

In 'The Decay of Lying', an essay written as a Platonic dialogue between two aesthetes on an idle day in a country house, Wilde sets out some of his central ideas about the nature of art. 'Life imitates art far more than Art imitates life' (CWW, 982). Ideally, doing nothing meant conceding the superiority of art to life. Contemplation took priority over action. In one sense Wilde's position suggests in Neoplatonic fashion that art possesses the attributes of an ideal prior and superior to any manifestation in the material world. Or, in Ernst Bloch's terms in The Utopian Function of Art and Literature, Wilde's account of art implies that it can be a model for something that will succeed it in the material world.[10] Art would transmit those various semi-utopian possibilities into the 'life' of the aesthetically educated. They, in turn, are transformed by them so much so that they become living works of art in their own right. Wilde's position might initially indicate that art avoids the material world by refusing to engage with life, but it actually provides an account of the particular ramifications art has within the material world. Since 'art never expresses

8   Quoted in Richard Ellmann, Oscar Wilde (New York, 1987), 306.
9   Ellmann, Oscar Wilde, 307.
10 See Ernst Bloch, 'The Conscious and Known Activity within the Not-Yet-Conscious, the Utopian Function', in The Utopian Function of Art and Literature (Cambridge, MA, 1988), 103–41.

anything but itself' (*CWW*, 987), in the view of Wilde's mouthpiece Vivian there is no worthy political or social inspiration in the creation of art. To Wilde, artists who set out to make a particular impact upon the world are nothing more than propagandists. However, the contemplation of art does indeed make an impact upon its audience, and art does have consequences through its reception, as it paradoxically seems to be both autonomous from, and directly engaged with, the world. Most importantly, by asserting that the reception of art conditions those who contemplate it to the extent that they ultimately approximate forms of art, Wilde suggests that it does not only involve the apprehension of beauty, but also promotes a condition of performativity that has profound consequences for the recipient's identity. In this sense, the 'idle' contemplation of art has consequences for the identity of the person who appreciates it. In the consequent transformation, qualities that are inherent to art, but that surpass the conventional forms of identity, are absorbed. Through the contemplation of art, an identity imposed by history can be transcended or exchanged for another; a performative alternative can be realized.

This clearly has a bearing on Wilde's articulation of his sexuality. Greek art, idealized by Wilde in 'The Decay of Lying' and elsewhere, evoked a form of sexuality alternative to socially sanctioned conceptions of 'the natural' and could provide the basis for a performative conception of an identity that is moulded by desire. Wilde's sexuality was complicated, and it is somewhat anachronistic to classify him in our terms as homosexual. That category of identity did not yet really exist as a social construction in the late nineteenth century in the way it does now; indeed, as Alan Sinfield argues, Wilde's personality and trial for indecent offences were crucial prerequisites for the formation of that identity.[11] Yet Wilde's preference for supposedly 'non-natural' sexual pleasure is connected to his valorization of idleness. And, further, idleness arguably forges the link between his sexuality and his Irishness. If idleness serves as a refusal of a labour process committed to the reproduction of commodities, Wilde's sexual preferences stand as a refusal of natural reproduction and ultimately are closely intertwined with his theorization of art.[12] Perhaps the cruellest irony of the outcome of the trial of 1895 was a sentence to two years of hard labour in Reading Gaol. Wilde spent most of his career arguing against the necessity to work; forced labour was an especially inhumane punishment for having chosen to explore a supposedly 'non-natural' identity. It is no wonder that so many of Wilde's major literary works — *The Picture of Dorian Gray*, *A Woman of No Importance*, and *The Importance of Being Earnest* among them — take as a central theme the performance of an identity different to that inherited at birth. But for Wilde, the preference for a performative rather than an imposed conception of identity had both a sexual and a national dimension. The transformation of his inherited national identity into a performative Englishness can be traced back to his arrival in Oxford as a university student in the mid-1870s.

---

11   See Alan Sinfield, *The Wilde Century: Effeminacy, Oscar Wilde and the Queer Moment* (New York, 1994).
12   See Regenia Gagnier, *Idylls of the Marketplace: Oscar Wilde and the Victorian Public* (Stanford, 1986).

Wilde remarked later, 'My Irish accent was one of the many things I forgot at Oxford.' This re-creation of his identity eventually became a performance of Englishness that, in the words of his biographer, placed him 'beyond rather than behind the English'.[13] Kiberd argues that Wilde's approximation of Englishness was strategic, in that it both enabled the acquisition of a position within British society but also offered the possibility of forging an alliance with a radical tradition that might provide connections in the future to an emergent Irish nationalism. Even if the youthful Wilde sought immediately to 'lose' his Irishness, like his nationalist mother he consistently supported Irish autonomy and specific nationalist causes — Charles Stewart Parnell and Home Rule — and publicly opposed British hysteria over the Phoenix Park murders.[14] But his performance of Englishness went to such an extreme that it came very close to parody. The evolution of his understanding of identity from a natural fact of birth, a given, towards a more performative concept of it, a creation, anticipates the work of much later theorists like Judith Butler in some respects; in others, this performance of a colonial archetype of Englishness anticipates the forms of mimicry and 'sly civility' eventually elaborated by Homi Bhabha. 'Sly civility', according to Bhabha, amounts to a possibly ironic or dishonest performance of a colonial identity or practice on the part of the colonized.[15] Rather than presenting an act of subservient obedience, the colonized subject's mimicry of a colonial model does not necessarily reiterate or reaffirm the priority of that role or behaviour, but instead repeats it with just enough suggestion of difference to provoke a sense of anxiety that threatens the legitimacy of the whole framework that established the difference between colonizer and colonized in the first place.

Wilde's notorious celebration of idleness — both in his writing and in his public life — is a critical element in the unique brand of sly civility he fashioned as a key part of his image. At one level, Wilde's affectation of the indolence of the British leisure class ironically exploits the alliance between the privilege and the preciousness of behaviour of the wealthy. But his performance of this identity parodies its assumption of entitlement precisely by failing to reproduce it exactly, by making it excessive, a spectacle, something not 'natural' but artificial. Yet at an even deeper level, Wilde's performance of British aristocratic laziness more alarmingly reveals its affinities with the stereotype of Irish idleness that Arnold and others argued was an inherent Celtic trait. Thus, in Wilde's public presentation of himself, in his representation of the members of the leisure class in his drama and prose, and, most of all, in the aesthete-personae of his critical dialogues, the imperfect performance of an Englishness defined by laziness melts into the ironic enactment of an Irish stereotype. The blur between the two national categories

---

13   Ellmann, *Oscar Wilde*, 38.
14   Kiberd, *Inventing Ireland*, 44. On the background to Wilde's family's investment in cultural nationalism and the impact it made upon him, see Richard Pine, *The Thief of Reason: Oscar Wilde and Modern Ireland* (New York, 1995), 117–23.
15   See the essay 'Sly Civility' in Homi Bhabha, *The Location of Culture* (London, 1994), 93–101.

was precisely Wilde's point.[16] If identity is performative to begin with, there is nothing natural about Englishness or Irishness in any sort of biological sense, whatever Arnoldian criticism claimed. Still, Wilde's radical conception of idleness bore within it a vision of proper duties of the intellectual and a refusal of conventional positions regarding the division of labour.

Wilde's most detailed discussion of idleness occurs in the two-part essay 'The Critic as Artist', published in 1890. Here, his focus shifts from the production of art to its consumption. Via the personae of the essay, Wilde takes the iconoclastic position that the critic inhabits a more important position than the artist, since 'the highest criticism deals with art … and is consequently both creative and independent, is in fact an art by itself, occupying the same relation to creative work that creative work does to the visible world of form and colour, or the unseen world of passion and of thought' (*CWW*, 1032). Central here is the standard separation between action and contemplation. This distinction follows from Wilde's famous statement that 'all art is immoral' (*CWW*, 1039) in 'The Critic as Artist'. In using the word 'immoral', Wilde goes out of his way to provoke the sense of scandal and sin that was to be one source of his appeal to Joyce. 'Immorality' initially means the refusal of 'energy' in favour of a commitment to a form of 'contemplation', which does not contribute to social reproduction. 'Morality' means the conventional and respectable forms of productivity necessary for the maintenance of society's needs. As Wilde's persona Gilbert explains,

> society, which is the beginning and basis of morals, exists simply for the concentration of human energy, and in order to ensure its own continuance and healthy stability it demands, and no doubt rightly demands, of each of its citizens that he should contribute some form of productive labour to the common weal, and toil and travail that the day's work may be done. (*CWW*, 1039)

'Energy' is a response to necessity, and therefore produces values, concepts, and acts that are useful; but the action provoked by such energy 'is limited and relative', since it does not contribute to the growth of individuality, even if it is required for the preservation of self and society. Ultimately, action stifles one's potentiality by limiting the capacity for individual development, because 'we are never less free than when we try to act' (*CWW*, 1040); the demands of external necessity do not allow for internal growth.

Art, in contrast, presents a response to necessity that refuses to recognize its centrality to human existence. While the result of action is the satisfaction of need, art functions through its complete evasion of the category of use-value. Wilde later famously declared

16   See Jerusha McCormack, 'The Wilde Irishman: Oscar as Aesthete and Anarchist', in Jerusha McCormack, ed., *Wilde the Irishman* (New Haven, 1998), 85.

in the 'Preface' to *The Picture of Dorian Gray* that 'all art is quite useless' (*CWW*, 17). The uselessness of art lies in its inability to produce anything that is socially necessary or meaningful, and it is in its fundamental unproductivity that one discovers its inherently 'immoral' quality. Gilbert states in 'The Critic as Artist':

> Society often forgives the criminal; it never forgives the dreamer. The beautiful sterile emotions that art excites in us are hateful in its eyes, and so completely are people dominated by the tyranny of this dreadful social ideal that they are always coming shamelessly up to one at Private Views and other places that are open to the general public, and saying in a loud stentorian voice, 'What are you doing?' whereas 'What are you thinking?' is the only question that any single civilized being should ever be allowed to whisper to another ... while, in the opinion of society, Contemplation is the gravest sin of which any citizen can be guilty, in the opinion of the highest culture it is the proper occupation of man. (*CWW*, 1039)

This idealized form of idleness, which Wilde calls 'contemplation', does not refuse any sort of energy or activity. As Gilbert acknowledges, it presented 'the noblest form of energy' for both Plato and Aristotle and, in the medieval period, *otium* was regarded as a blessed, even sacred, condition. By the end of the nineteenth century, however, the aesthetically minded 'dreamer' who avoids the labour process altogether by focusing upon what, by definition, has no immediate use-value is so far outside the social conventions of Victorian propriety that only an ethical vocabulary predicated upon such terms as 'sin' or 'immorality' can make sense of his position. For the refusal of the labour process — at least in respect to a form of work committed to the production of socially useful ends — could also open the way to rejecting all that was most stifling about modernity. Furthermore, Wilde's argument stresses that idleness — at least when configured according to the notion of 'contemplation' idealized in 'The Critic as Artist', rather than in the privileged type of leisured indolence that appears elsewhere in his writing — is not exactly the complete absence of any sort of energy or activity; instead, it signals an alternative form of intellectual labour not recognized as legitimate within capitalist modernity but which actually provides the basis for creative innovation.

In 'The Critic as Artist', the contemplation of art allows the critic to assimilate knowledge and experience otherwise not available through history and heredity. According to Gilbert, 'by revealing to us the absolute mechanism of all action, and so freeing us from the self-imposed and trammelling burden of moral responsibility, the scientific principle of Heredity has become, as it were, the warrant for the contemplative life' (*CWW*, 1040). In other words, everything that we inherit from the past (and Wilde means here both the particular past of one's own biological make-up and the whole ongoing cultural tradition that produces one's understanding of the world and of art) condemns us to the repetition of those activities that allow existence to continue. But at the same time, the capacity for intellectual labour inherited from the past also creates the conditions for a form of potentiality in which that inherited identity can be left behind:

> And yet, while in the sphere of practical and external life it has robbed energy of its freedom and activity of its choice, in the subjective sphere, where the soul is at work, it comes to us, this terrible shadow, with many gifts in its hands, gifts of strange temperaments and subtle susceptibilities, gifts of wild ardours and chill moods of indifference, complex multiform gifts of thoughts that are at variance with each other, and passions that war against themselves. (*CWW*, 1040)

Because of its essential uselessness, art allows the possibility that the realm of necessity might be left behind altogether. The idle contemplation of art enables one to transcend to a position beyond one's own interest or inherited identity in order to engage with other desires, experiences, and possibilities, as Wilde's mouthpiece Gilbert tells his interlocutor:

> And so it is not our own life that we live, but the lives of the dead, and the soul that dwells within us is no single spiritual entity, making us personal and individual, created for our service, and entering into us for our joy. It is something that has dwelt in fearful places, and in ancient sepulchres has made its abode. It is sick with many maladies, and has memories of curious sins. It is wiser than we are, and its wisdom is bitter. It fills us with impossible desires, and makes us follow what we know what we cannot gain. One thing, however, Ernest, it can do for us. It can lead us away from surroundings whose beauty is dimmed to us by the mist of familiarity, or whose ignoble ugliness and sordid claims are marring the perfection of our development. It can help us to leave the age in which we were born, and to pass into other ages, and to find ourselves not exiled from their air. It can teach us how to escape from our experience, and to realize the experiences of those who are greater than we are. (*CWW*, 1041)

Wilde's position here presents a variation on a Kantian conception of disinterest, with certain crucial qualifications. In *The Critique of Judgment*, Kant argues that the perception of the beautiful leads one into a condition in which one escapes interest and necessity; in this transcendent condition of disinterest, one leaves behind the particularity of identity through the recognition of the universal.[17] As Terry Eagleton suggests in a discussion of the earlier philosophers Shaftesbury, David Hume, and Edmund Burke, which is just as applicable to Kant: 'disinterestedness here means indifference not to others' interests, but to one's own. The aesthetic is the enemy of bourgeois egoism: to judge aesthetically

---

17 See Immanuel Kant, *Critique of Judgment* (Indianapolis, 1987), 46. On Wilde's debt to Kant, see Julia Prewitt Brown, *Cosmopolitan Criticism: Oscar Wilde's Philosophy of Art* (Charlottesville, 1997), 32–35.

means to bracket as far as possible one's own petty prejudices in the name of a common general humanity.'[18]

While no less radical in its response to the norms of bourgeois society, Wilde's theory of contemplation presents an inversion of this position. Rather than signalling the denial of one's own interests in order to arrive at a condition of universality, Wilde's position regards aesthetic contemplation as a means for the intensification of one's particular and hitherto unrealized desires. As in more traditional conceptions of disinterest, Wilde holds that the contemplation of art allows one to escape a version of interest defined by an inevitable condition of necessity; one is no longer oneself, with all of the immediate needs and burdens one has inherited from the past. Yet once this moment of aesthetic contemplation is achieved, one momentarily becomes — or, in other words, performs — a completely different identity defined by different experiences, different longings, different desires; as Gilbert continues, 'Yes Ernest: the contemplative life, the life that has for its aim not doing but being, and not being merely, but becoming — that is what the critical spirit can give us' (CWW, 1041). Desire — especially unconventional forms of desire too scandalous to articulate in proper society, such as those having to do with Wilde's own sexuality — still has a place in Wilde's theory of contemplation — it does not in Kant's — and it can be experienced in displaced fashion through art.[19] It is at this point in the argument that Wilde's earlier assertion that 'all art is immoral' finally proves to be legitimately sinful. While Wilde initially meant that art is immoral because it forces one to reject the compulsion to work on behalf of the relief of necessity, it also ultimately allows one to become more sinful — sinful, at least, in respect to the prudish mores of late Victorian society — through a more complete contemplation, understanding, and finally enjoyment of those desires prohibited by custom and law. Wilde goes on to provide a variety of specific literary examples of the sorts of legendary experiences available through art, but it is not too much of a stretch to perceive in it a displaced discussion of the very homosexual desires and practices for which Wilde would be vilified five years later.

The iconoclasm of this presentation of sin and immorality ignited the young Joyce's attraction for Wilde, as his brief essay on *Salomé* indicates. But Wilde's theory of contemplation had a deeper impact upon subsequent Irish writing. Wilde's position that the contemplation of art enables one to go beyond the limitations of one's self, provided the basis for Yeats's apprehension that art allowed one to bypass the cold rationality of modernity in order to become aware of those mystical and supernatural forces located just beyond the bounds of material existence. Ultimately, the idle contemplation of art enabled contact with what Yeats eventually called 'Spiritus Mundi', that vast storehouse of collective memory made up of Platonic ideas. Conversely, the young Joyce eventually came

18   Terry Eagleton, *The Ideology of the Aesthetic* (Oxford, 1990), 39.
19   My argument here is consistent with Nunokawa's discussion of the similarities and differences between a Kantian concept of disinterest and Wilde's theorization of contemplation in 'The Critic as Artist'; see Nunokawa, *Tame Passions of Wilde*, 117–18.

to an Aristotelian understanding of Wilde's discussion of contemplative transcendence. To Joyce, the rational interpretation of the form of an aesthetic object enabled the condition of impersonal impartiality and even the transcendence of the material context that governs the framework through which social being develops — a position made clear in *A Portrait of the Artist as a Young Man* in the juxtaposition of Stephen Dedalus's artistic credo with the misery of his impoverished condition.[20] In each case, the refashioning of Wilde by Yeats and Joyce raises questions regarding the emerging Irish nation. For Yeats, the contemplation of the particularity of Irish culture enables a universal condition of disinterest — that ideal position for what he would later term the 'unity of being' — without having to assimilate the dominant version of modernity emanating from Britain. For Joyce — or, at the very least, for Stephen Dedalus, as Joyce's more mature writing specifically rejects a number of the positions he held when he was younger — the contemplation of art enables one to enjoy an intellectually fulfilling form of stasis superior to the collective economic, social, and political paralysis of late colonial Ireland. Just as important for both Yeats and the young Joyce is the role of the literary intellectual Wilde advocates in 'The Critic as Artist'.

Wilde's entire argument in 'The Critic as Artist' depends upon the conceit apparent in the title of the essay: that, as Gilbert asserts, 'surely, Criticism itself is an art. And just as artistic creation implies the working of the critical faculty, and indeed, without it cannot be said to exist at all, so Criticism is really creative in the highest sense of the word' (*CWW*, 1026). Here, Wilde foregrounds the critic, the literary intellectual who contributes to art's ultimate value by perceiving it, interpreting it, and articulating its meaning. At first glance, such a position seems to be countered by the figure of the artist in Yeats's early poetry and Joyce's *Portrait of the Artist as a Young Man*. Yet Wilde's explanation of what the critic actually does is a more effective account of the cultural production of that figure than the romantic one of the artistic genius who creatively brings beauty into existence out of nothing. Crucial to the aesthetic projects of both writers — and in the case of Joyce, even more so in the mature works of *Ulysses* and *Finnegans Wake* — was their startling reconceptualizations of older material and attitudes in their work. According to Wilde, this is exactly what the critic does: 'It is Criticism, again, that by concentration makes culture possible. It takes the cumbersome mass of creative work, and distils it into a finer essence' (*CWW*, 1056). As is evident in a section of dialogue between Gilbert and Ernest, such a transformation presents the highest form of criticism:

---

20 Joyce's ironic and parodic representation of Stephen Dedalus has been a commonplace in Joyce criticism at least as far back as Hugh Kenner's *Dublin's Joyce* (Bloomington, 1956). But the discussions of art in Joyce's notebooks concerning aesthetics, which he wrote in his early twenties, are virtually identical to Stephen's positions in the final chapter of *Portrait* and demonstrate the extension of Wilde's discussion of disinterested transcendence into more specifically Aristotelian territory. See 'Aesthetics', in *Occasional, Critical, and Political Writing*, 102–07.

Ernest: The highest Criticism, then, is more creative than creation, and the primary aim of the critic is to see the object as in itself it really is not; that is your theory, I believe? Gilbert: Yes, that is my theory. To the critic, the work of art is simply a suggestion for a new work of his own, that need not necessarily bear any obvious resemblance to the thing it criticizes. The one characteristic of a beautiful form is that one can put into it whatever one wishes, and see in it whatever one chooses to see; and the Beauty, that gives to creation its universal and aesthetic element, makes the critic creator in turn, and whispers of a thousand different things which were not present in the mind of him who carved the statue or painted the panel or graved the gem. (*CWW*, 1030)

The problem with producing art is that it still involves some degree of energy — and therefore action, that activity which prevents complete realization of the self, even if it is not directed towards the satisfaction of need through the creation of something immediately useful. The idle contemplation of art, however, is far superior, as the critic is in a position to understand the values expressed by a given text or artefact and then articulate them to society at large.

According to Wilde, the critic stands at the centre of a culture. He both preserves and transfigures the form in which a given culture exists. The critic has a unique sense of what Wilde calls 'concentrated race-experience', or the cumulative imaginative deposit of a group of people who share a common culture and heritage. Gilbert explains at length:

The culture that this transmission of racial experiences makes possible can be made perfect by the critical spirit alone, and indeed may be one with it. For who is the true critic but he who bears within himself the dreams, and ideas, and feelings of myriad generations, and to whom no form of thought is alien, no emotional impulse obscure? And who but the true man of culture, if not he who by fine scholarship and fastidious rejection has made instinct self-conscious and intelligent, and can separate the work that has distinction from the work that has it not, and so by contact and comparison makes himself master of the secrets of style and school and understands their meanings, and listens to their voices, and develop that spirit of disinterested curiosity which is the real root, as it is the real flower, of the intellectual life, and thus attains to intellectual clarity, and having learned 'the best that is known and thought in the world', lives — it is not fanciful to say so — with those who are the Immortals. (*CWW*, 1041)

Wilde's assessment of the role of the critic here reads almost like a rough draft of any number of works by Yeats concerning either the duty of the literary intellectual or his own personal ambitions. A number of positions stand out in Gilbert's discussion, such as the notion that the intellectual has an almost sacred role in the transmission of 'racial' (or 'national', considering that Victorians tended to conflate race and nation) cultural experience to a society that may have lost a connection to it, or that the intellectual has a refined emotional capacity that makes him more receptive to possibilities that lie outside conventional rationality. Additionally, the intellectual, in this formulation, is — and should be — the primary arbiter of the value of culture, and himself enters into a form of immortality through his ultimate transformation into an aspect of culture itself.

All of these positions are present within any number of Yeats's works concerning culture, whether it be in the idealistic early essays regarding the necessity of a national theatre or the bitter and disillusioned late texts included in *On the Boiler*, whether it be the personal trajectory that marks the narrative of *Autobiographies* or the mystical understanding of history that makes up *A Vision*. Wilde's formulation of the role of the critic provided for Yeats a powerful model for the work of the literary intellectual during the Revival. Yet there was one more qualification to be made. Gilbert tells Ernest:

> The influence of the critic will be the mere fact of his own existence. He will represent the flawless type. In him the culture of the century will see itself realized. You must not ask of him any other aim other than the perfecting of himself. The demand of the intellect, as has been well said, is simply to feel itself alive. The critic may, indeed, desire to exercise influence; but if so, he will concern himself not with the individual, but with the age, which he will seek to wake into consciousness, and make responsive, creating in it new desires and appetites, and lending it his larger vision and nobler moods … and for this or that person toiling away, what do the industrious matter? They do their best, no doubt, and consequently we get the worst from them. It is always with the best intentions that the worst work is done. (*CWW*, 1053)

Wilde foreshadows the Revival in his description of how the literary intellectual exercises influence by awakening the 'age' to a level of consciousness in which culture affects history. Several times Wilde argues that good art cannot have a didactic purpose or an immediate relation to material reality; art produced for a specific purpose necessarily has a use-value, and therefore cannot provide the contemplative experience of transcendence that superior forms of aesthetic production achieve. Art cannot be explicitly political; yet, it certainly can have political consequences because it has the capacity — at least as mediated by the critic — to contribute to the formation of a collective consciousness. This is a logical and literal consequence of Wilde's opening position that life imitates art. For if one encounters an ideal in a work of art that presents a re-interpretation of the world, it can then become an element in the actual world through the act of contemplation.

This position underlies Yeats's entire understanding of the relation between culture and politics at the outset of the Revival. It explains his paradoxical position on the place of politics in that cultural movement. It allowed him to disavow any direct political inspiration in the works of the Irish National Theatre and other associated groups, while participating in political organizations and public protests. Though Yeats claimed that his work was rooted in the 'casual impulses of dreams and daily thoughts', he nevertheless believed that his writing had serious political consequences after it appeared (to the extent that in later years he would consistently assert that plays like *Cathleen ni Houlihan* created the conditions of possibility for events like the Easter Rising and the formation of the Irish Free State).[21] The problem with Wilde's position for Yeats and the Revival had to do with Wilde's explicit disavowal of the labour process. In a general sense, the Revival needed the idea of a national work-ethic if it were to make a significant impact upon Irish society. In a more personal sense, 'toil' was something that Yeats identified with the rigorous, difficult labour of writing. Yeats went to great lengths to articulate a relationship between toil and idleness in relation to creative labour that would allow him to hang on to a Wildean position without having to retain completely the emphasis upon the vital importance of doing nothing evident in 'The Critic as Artist'.

Anxieties about the centrality of idleness in Wilde's critical writing did not prove to be as problematic for the modernist writers who came to prominence after the Revival. Joyce, in particular, discovered in Wilde the idea that idleness could bear a radical political dimension. 'The Critic as Artist' has an undeniably elitist undertone, as when Gilbert declares that 'it is to do nothing that the elect exist'. Wilde's essay suggests that the role of critic is available only to a rarefied few. Yet the enlightened intellectual, so conceived, belongs to the leisure class that Wilde elsewhere treats in so ambivalent and critical a manner. In 'The Soul of Man under Socialism', his last significant treatment of idleness, Wilde reveals hostility towards the leisure class. But, within the corpus of Wilde's critical writing, it is unusual in its explicitly political approach. In it he forsakes the dramatized format of the Platonic dialogues and of his earlier essays on aesthetics and writes straightforwardly in his own voice. The essay demonstrates his support for the relatively new doctrine of socialism and suggests that it is the sociopolitical framework best suited to the implementation of the broader philosophical beliefs about art that he discusses elsewhere. Socialism for Wilde, like art, is predicated upon idleness. Just as in 'The Critic as Artist', Wilde acknowledges that those members of society who are committed to intellectual life

> are either under no necessity to work for their living, or are enabled to choose the sphere of activity that is really congenial to them and gives them pleasure. These are the poets, the philosophers, the men of science, the men of culture — in a word, the

---

21   See Yeats's essay 'An Irish National Theatre' published in *Samhain* in 1903, *Explorations* (New York, 1962), 115–16. This essay is prompted by criticism of the dramatic movement originating in the nationalist movement and responds to the accusation that the National Theatre was not national enough; yet it must be conceded that one reason for Yeats's refusal to commit to a more aggressive form of cultural nationalism might be the desire not to offend more conservative potential patrons.

real men, the men who have realized themselves, and in whom all Humanity gains a partial realization. (*CWW*, 1080)

The great unjust quality of modern life, however, is that only a privileged few are able to actualize themselves through their intellectual labour.

> Upon the other hand, there are a great many people who, having no property of their own, and being always on the brink of sheer starvation, are compelled to do the work of beasts of burden, to do work that is uncongenial to them, and to which they are forced by the peremptory, unreasonable, degrading Tyranny of want. (*CWW*, 1080)

The masses who work do not have access to idleness. In his conception of socialism the redistribution of idleness is an even more pressing need than the redistribution of wealth. Wilde's conception of socialism, which connects it to a specific political philosophy, had a pronounced impact upon the emergence of Irish modernism. Wilde's general view of aesthetics held that idleness was necessary for the act of contemplation, the highest creative act of all. Contemplation, in turn, led to a superior condition, which ultimately reproduced idleness. Wilde's essay has the value of suggesting that idleness is not just an abstract ideal, but also a material practice that can inspire a specific form of politics.

Since Wilde's central premise about the value of socialism — 'Socialism itself will be of value simply because it will lead to Individualism' (*CWW*, 1080) — emphasizes the importance of individuality without raising the matter of collectivity, the essay has frequently been interpreted as not committed to socialism at all.[22] The minimal role he assigns to the state in his conception of a socialist future has led to the suggestion that he actually favours something more akin to anarchism. This is misleading, as Wilde does not argue that individualism is an end in itself. The growth of individualism, which in its cultural manifestation means the production of art, should not be restricted to a privileged few: 'Under the new conditions Individualism will be far freer, far finer, and far more intensified than it is now. I am not talking of the great imaginatively realized Individualism of such poets as I have mentioned, but of the great actual Individualism latent and potential in mankind generally' (*CWW*, 1083). Although actually-existing individualism within Victorian society can only develop as a consequence of the accumulation of private property, in Wilde's view this actually limits the degree to which the individual can ultimately develop: 'Property not merely has its duties, but has so many

---

22 See, for example, Josephine Guy's essay '"The Soul of Man under Socialism": A (Con)Textual History', in Joseph Bristow, ed., *Wilde Writings: Contextual Conditions* (Toronto, 2003), 59–85, which argues that Wilde's essay actually lampoons and opposes socialism. For an effective refutation of Guy's argument, see Elizabeth Carolyn Miller, *Framed: The New Woman Criminal in British Culture at the Fin De Siècle* (Ann Arbor, 2008), 195–96.

duties that its possession to any large extent is a bore. It involves endless claims upon one, endless attention to business, endless bother. If property had simply pleasures, we could stand it; but its duties make it unbearable' (*CWW*, 1081). Ultimately, the division of labour prevents the growth of individualism. Those who benefit from the work of others may develop their individual potentiality to some limited extent, but for the most part they are distracted by the demands inherent in the accumulation of property; conversely, those who work for the benefit of others have no opportunity whatsoever to develop themselves. For modern work stands as the absolute enemy of individualism:

> And as I have mentioned the word labour, I cannot help saying that a great deal of nonsense is being written and talked nowadays about the dignity of manual labour. There is nothing necessarily dignified about manual labour at all, and most of it is absolutely degrading. It is mentally and morally injurious to man to do anything in which he does not find pleasure, and many forms of labour are quite pleasureless activities and should be regarded as such. (*CWW*, 1088)

Wilde's conception of socialism depends first and foremost upon the redistribution of idleness, not of property. While this would ultimately involve the abolition of property, and thus prevent the ensuing distractions that possessions entail ('nobody will waste his life in accumulating things, and the symbols for things') (*CWW*, 1084), it cannot proceed without the abolition of work.

Yet Wilde's argument does not predict a world without *any* work at all. There has to be manual labour to provide those basic necessities that would enable the condition of idleness. Very much in line with late nineteenth-century utopian thinkers, Wilde proposes that 'all unintellectual labour, all monotonous, dull labour, all labour that deals with dreadful things, and involves unpleasant conditions must be done by machinery' (*CWW*, 1089). Wilde's distinction between manual and intellectual labour is important, for it shifts the understanding of the manner in which work produces value from a strictly economic to a more abstract sense. In Wilde's view, no one who prefers to perform manual labour should be prevented from doing so, as long as the value it produces actualizes one's potentiality to the greatest extent possible. Those with no interest in manual labour — the greater part of humanity — should focus on those forms of work best developed through a commitment to contemplative idleness.[23]

> Every man must be left quite free to choose his own work. No form of compulsion must be exercised over him. If there is, his work will not be good for him, will not

---

23 'He may be a great poet, or a great man of science or a young student at a University, or one who watches sheep upon a moor; or a maker of dramas, like Shakespeare, or a thinker about God, like Spinoza; or a child who plays in a garden, or a fisherman who throws his net into the sea. It does not matter what he is, as long as he realizes the perfection of the soul that is within him.' (*CWW*, 1087)

be good in itself, and will not be good for others. And by work I mean simply activity of any kind. (*CWW*, 1082)

The socialist state should act as the primary protection against the compulsion to work. To Wilde, the state should exist primarily 'to be a voluntary manufacturer and distributor of necessary commodities ... to make what is useful' (*CWW*, 1088). The state should not govern beyond providing the assurance that no one will be compelled to work in the interests of another.

Wilde never betrays any sense that he is anything less than serious about his argument throughout 'The Soul of Man under Socialism'. Yet the apparent lack of ambiguity here does not dispel profound doubts about the feasibility of his argument. In 'The Critic as Artist', in one of Gilbert's asides, Wilde states:

What we want are unpractical people who see beyond the moment, and think beyond the day. Those who try to lead the people can only do so by following the mob. It is through the voice of one crying in the wilderness that the ways of the gods must be prepared. (*CWW*, 1043)

'The Soul of Man under Socialism' extends this argument further by reconsidering idleness in material terms and making it a political goal. Whether Wilde's conception of socialism would have been feasible is beside the point. His arguments about idleness are fundamentally utopian:

A map of the world that does not include Utopia is not worth even glancing at, for it leaves out the one country at which Humanity is always landing. And when Humanity lands there, it looks out, and, seeing a better country, sets sail. Progress is the realization of Utopias. (*CWW*, 1089)

Progress, in this sense, is something that comes to an end; it ceases once idleness becomes a social possibility for all of humanity. Wilde's conception of socialism signals the end of history and the refusal of temporal progression.

One other factor in 'The Soul of Man under Socialism' brought the argument closer to home: the relationship between idleness and Irishness. Nunokawa argues that Wilde's argument challenges the centrality of the compulsion to work in the ideology of late Victorian Britain, but ultimately does not effectively supplant it.[24] At worst, Wilde's valorization of idleness becomes a form of quiescence, in which the enjoyment of idleness serves as a compensation for the inability to pose an alternative to the inevitability of labour; at best it only reinstates the primacy of the labour process it attempts to oppose

---

24 See Nunokawa, *Tame Passions of Wilde*, 113–14.

by assuming that it is a social given, which one must inevitably endlessly react against until the unlikely arrival of utopia. But as Jerusha McCormack has noted, when it was first published in the *Fortnightly Review* in 1891, Wilde's essay on socialism was placed alongside an essay by the critic Grant Allen entitled 'The Celt in English Art'.[25] Allen's essay takes Arnold's distinction between the Celt and the Anglo-Saxon as a point of departure. It goes on not only to identify contemporary aestheticism with the Celtic temperament, but also to identify the Celt with the progressive values of liberty, equality, and brotherhood. Notably, Allen's essay singles Wilde out as a paradigmatic example of the rarefied Celt. McCormack asks, given the context of publication, 'how could Wilde's essay be read as anything other than as performative, a part of Wilde's own definition of himself to an English public, as an Irish artist — and provocateur?'[26] It is true that Wilde embarks upon a rhetorical attack on the way British society resorts to the banality of racial ideology when forced to examine itself, as McCormack argues. But it is equally true that Wilde's essay presents a radical inversion of the colonial positions that inform Allen's essay. While Allen is in general complimentary to 'the Celt', he nevertheless draws upon a long-standing prejudice about the essential backwardness of the Irish. 'The Soul of Man under Socialism' suggests that idleness, a glaring example of Irish delinquency, is actually the basis for an advanced form of progressive politics. Here, the 'sly civility' of Wilde's performative approach to identity, evident in his public life and writing, does not merely rehearse the paranoid distinction between colonizer and colonized, but inverts it so that the stereotyped behaviour of the Celt is recast as the harbinger of a future superior to the colonial present. Ultimately, idleness for Wilde was actually an interesting and satisfying form of work in its own right. It created the opportunity for a disengagement from the reified conditions of identity, a form of impersonal distance — a position the lazy idle schemer of Irish modernism later occupied. Before that occurred, however, this new regime of identity made a profound impact upon Yeats, who saw in Wilde a model for the literary intellectual.

3

Yeats associated idleness with the sense of desperation a writer feels upon not being able to write. Perhaps more than any other Irish writer before Beckett, Yeats wrote eloquently about not being able to write. He noted in a diary from 1909, later reworked for the autobiographical text *Estrangement* (which, in turn, later became part of the complete text of Yeats's *Autobiographies*):

25 See McCormack, 'The Wilde Irishman', 86–87.
26 McCormack, 'The Wilde Irishman', 87.

Two hours' idleness — because I have no excuse but to begin creative work, an intolerable toil. Little D—— F—— of Hyderabad told me that in her father's garden one met an opium eater who made poems in his dreams and wrote the title-pages when he awoke but forgot the rest. He was the only happy poet. (A, 358)

The ambiguity of the diary entry is telling. On the one hand, idleness brings about something comparable to the pleasure of intoxication here, as the imagination of having performed some act of intellectual labour is infinitely more satisfying than the hard work of actually having done it. Yet even when viewed benignly as a form of contemplation, idleness does not provide Yeats with much consolation for the painful feeling of indolence. Nevertheless, throughout his writing he persisted in pursuing the connections between idleness and the contemplation of art. The act of artistic creation, as a form of intellectual labour, brought the pleasures of idleness and the effort of art together. It was one of the crucial qualities of literary work that distinguished it from other forms of intellectual labour; Yeats suggested as much in another, more obscure autobiographical extract entitled If I were Four-and-Twenty, which demonstrates his debt to Wilde:

Now all these writers of economics overrate the importance of work. Every man has a profound instinct that idleness is the true reward of work, even if it only come at the end of life, or if generations have to die before it comes at all, and literature and art are often little but its preparation that it may be an intensity. I have no doubt that the idleness, let us say, of a man devoted to his collection of Chinese paintings affects the mind even of men who do physical labour without spoken or written word, and all the more because physical labour increases mental pursuits.[27]

To Yeats, here, all work — whether of a physical or intellectual nature — is a preparation for the reward of idleness, a condition anticipated in art; yet idleness itself can become menacing when it prevents work, particularly the sort of intellectual work that produces art.

If I were Four-and-Twenty was originally published in 1919 in a limited edition series by the Cuala Press, operated by Yeats's sisters Elizabeth Corbet Yeats and Susan Mary Yeats. Unlike the similar autobiographical limited editions Estrangement, The Death of Synge, and The Bounty of Sweden, If I were Four-and-Twenty was never incorporated into Autobiographies and was not reprinted until several years after Yeats's death. Yet there is a deeper reason why it remains a neglected text: it is a remarkably lazy piece of writing, meandering here and there in seemingly random directions, taking in brief observations about French Catholicism, socialism, Balzac, and the nature of family life along the way. It finally ends with Yeats's suggestion that if he were not so lazy, he would begin a new epoch in Irish history by producing a text that articulated the heterogeneous elements of the national

27 Yeats, Explorations, 278–79.

culture by describing the new doctrine of 'unity of being'.[28] Yet such a declaration of unrealized intellectual labour only proved to be the narrative moment of laziness that preceded the difficult work to come. Three years later, Yeats published *The Trembling of the Veil*, another, much better-known autobiographical piece, as the core of the longer text that would eventually become *Autobiographies*. Its publication in 1922 coincided with the epochal moment of the arrival of Irish independence, and it set about explaining the 'unity of being' and the literary intellectual's role of delineating it in precisely the manner Yeats had not bothered to do in the earlier *If I were Four-and-Twenty*.

The relationship between work and idleness in the performance of intellectual labour is of an intricate, dialectical nature for Yeats, and much of his writing concerns the complicated manner in which idleness, the opposite of work, might be channelled productively into the intellectual labour of writing. On the one hand, idleness signifies the inability to work; it identifies the crushing feeling of writer's block, which Yeats struggled against throughout his life. On the other hand, idleness provides the necessary moment of laziness at the root of poetic labour that allows for the possibility to enter into reverie, one of Yeats's favoured conditions. Idleness does not inevitably produce reverie, but under the right conditions of receptivity it allows one to come to an awareness of the images and symbols that make up the proper content of poetry.[29] To Yeats, good poetry is not possible without reverie. He wrote that Percy Bysshe Shelley's capacity for reverie served him well as a writer:

> I imagine that when he wrote his earlier poems he allowed the subconscious life to lay its hands so firmly upon the rudder of his imagination that he was little conscious of the abstract meaning of the images that rose in what seemed the idleness of his mind. Anyone who has any experience of any mystical state of the soul knows how there float up in the mind profound symbols, whose meaning, if indeed they do not delude one into the dream that they are meaningless, one does not perhaps understand for years.[30]

It is in reverie that one comes to an awareness of the symbols and images that mark the distance between private experience and the articulation of a national culture. Yeats even quotes Shelley's essay 'On Life', regarding 'those who are subject to the state called reverie', in order to drive the point home. The poetic value of the images that emerge from

---

28 'When Dr. Hyde delivered in 1894 his lecture on the necessity of "the de-anglicisation of Ireland", to a society that was a youthful indiscretion of my own I heard an enthusiastic hearer say: "That lecture begins a new epoch in Ireland." It did that, and if I were not four-and-fifty, with no settled habit but the writing of verse, rheumatic, indolent, discouraged, and about to move to the Far East, I would begin another epoch by recommending to the Nation a new doctrine, that of unity of being.' Yeats, *Explorations*, 280.

29 On Yeats's conflation of symbols and images, and the manner in which he regarded them as separate from allegories, see Denis Donoghue, *William Butler Yeats* (New York, 1971), 70–85.

30 'The Philosophy of Shelley's Poetry', in W. B. Yeats, *Essays and Introductions* (Dublin, 1961), 78–79.

reverie is rooted in what Yeats would later call 'Spiritus Mundi', that unconscious collective storehouse of understanding that he identified with a Platonic conception of the Ideal:

> Nor I think, has anyone, who has known that experience with any constancy, failed to find some day, in some old book or on some monument, a strange or intricate image that has floated up before him, and to grow perhaps dizzy with the sudden conviction that our little memories are but part of some great Memory that renews the world and men's thoughts after age, and that our thoughts are not, as we suppose, the deep, but a little foam upon the deep.[31]

Such images are thus not only of private importance to the poet; they also contain the collective values of a culture that (at least in the Irish case) is struggling to come into being. They inspire the sort of contemplation for their audience that will in turn provide the possibility of yet another condition of idleness, which will reproduce the condition of reverie. In this complicated description of the act of intellectual labour, Yeats redefines the artist, typically seen by society as an idler devoted to the production of useless objects, as an intellectual committed to the elaboration of a national culture. Just as in Wilde's assertion that life imitates art, in Yeats's view any concrete change in the real world only occurs if it has been prefigured in the work of the artist.

Yeats grappled with these problems as early as 1904 in the poem 'Adam's Curse'. As well as being a poem about his unrequited love for Maud Gonne, which asserts that women must labour to be beautiful while men labour to create beauty, it is an early attempt to theorize intellectual labour. The curse referred to in the title is that work will necessarily entail some degree of alienation:

> I said, 'It's certain there is no fine thing
> Since Adam's fall but needs much labouring.'

What troubles Yeats about modernity is the fact that the genuinely difficult intellectual labour of writers is no longer respected as useful:

> I said, 'A line will take us hours maybe;
> Yet if it does not seem a moment's thought,
> Our stitching and unstitching has been naught.
> Better to go down upon your marrow-bones
> And scrub a kitchen pavement, or break stones
> Like an old pauper, in all kinds of weather;
> For to articulate sweet sounds together

31   Yeats, 'The Philosophy of Shelley's Poetry', 79–80.

> Is to work harder than all these, and yet
> Be thought an idler by the noisy set
> Of bankers, schoolmasters, and clergymen
> The martyrs call the world.'[32]

Yeats's mentor Wilde had no problems with such a state of affairs; as he suggests in the 'Preface' to *The Picture of Dorian Gray*: 'We can forgive a man for making a useful thing as long as he does not admire it. The only excuse for making a useless thing is that one admires it intensely' (*CWW*, 17). To Wilde, the notion of a useful form of labour is itself a conventional bourgeois value, and is therefore not to be celebrated; art is to be valued precisely because of its apparent uselessness. Contrarily, Yeats demands in 'Adam's Curse' that the intellectual labour of the writer be afforded the same — if not greater — respect for its difficulty as any other form of labour. This is important to him, not because he hopes that people he clearly despises will recognize the dignity of the difficult nature of the work he performs, but because his ambition as a writer involved nothing less than the articulation of a national culture. Artistic labour should ultimately be regarded as the most useful form of intellectual work, because it directly brings about historical change. He self-consciously worked to elaborate that model of a national culture most clearly in his dramatic writing, through which the Irish audience could be unified into a national community by the contemplation of a performative national ideal.[33] In turn, his autobiographical prose offered Yeats the opportunity to theorize and reflect upon his work as an intellectual. Taken as a whole, the various texts that make up *Autobiographies* can be read as a prolonged analysis of the process through which one becomes a literary intellectual. The selected moments of his life represented in *Autobiographies* serve as minute allegories that provide him with the opportunity to theorize the relationship between work and idleness in the practice of intellectual labour.

In strictly chronological terms, *Autobiographies* begins in the late 1860s and ends in 1923, covering the period between Yeats's earliest memories of his childhood in Sligo to his acceptance of the Nobel Prize for literature. Yet *Autobiographies* was compiled from a number of texts written at vastly different periods in Yeats's career. It first appears as a complete text in 1938, comprising three sustained, previously published autobiographical narratives, as well as three shorter, previously published autobiographical fragments. Because the chronology of composition does not match the chronology of the narrative,

---

32 'Adam's Curse' in *The Collected Poems of W. B. Yeats: A New Edition*, ed. Richard J. Finneran (New York, 1989), 81.

33 As Yeats reflects in *The Bounty of Sweden* about the chosen theme of his Nobel acceptance speech: 'I have chosen "The Irish Theatre" for my subject, that I may commend all those workers obscure or well-known, to whom I owe much of whatever fame in the world I may possess. If I had been a lyric poet only, if I had not become through this Theatre the representative of a public movement, I doubt if the English committees would have placed my name upon that list from which the Swedish Academy selects its prize-winner.' (*A*, 405)

one faces certain difficulties in assessing *Autobiographies*.[34] In addition, Yeats took dramatically different and contradictory positions on many topics over his long career.[35] *Autobiographies* provides a particularly acute case of such contradictions. He is at his grumpiest and most authoritarian in discussing the years 1896 to 1902 in 'Dramatis Personae', the section of the narrative composed last and nearest the end of his life in 1935. Yeats's representation there of various events and controversies of the early years of the Irish Literary Theatre allows him to demonstrate how he learned from Lady Gregory the values of nobility, refinement, and aristocratic grace. Yet his account of his relations with George Moore and Edward Martyn during the same controversies becomes an opportunity to espouse his support for some form of social eugenics. This is a position he began to advocate increasingly after his authoritarian turn in the 1930s (when he adjusted Wilde's defence of non-reproductive sexuality into an authoritarian conception of sexual reproduction). Meanwhile, there is then an abrupt shift in the next section, 'Estrangement', devoted to the year 1909 — which, written in that year, provides a more idealistic, youthful and less self-assured perspective on himself and his life. Despite these narrative inconsistencies, it is possible to isolate specific sections of *Autobiographies* that clarify Yeats's most perplexing anxieties.

'The Trembling of the Veil' is the longest, most sustained, and arguably richest section of *Autobiographies*. It is here that Yeats most clearly explains his understanding of how he works creatively, both privately as a writer and publicly as an engaged intellectual; consequently, it can be read as a handbook about how he became (or how a writer should become) a literary intellectual and contributed to the national work of decolonization. This in turn mutates into what was to become a canonical account of the role of the writer in Ireland for the next several decades. There is a specific historical reason why the model of the Yeatsian intellectual stands out most clearly in this section of *Autobiographies*. Up until 1922, most literary works of the Revival depicted an ancient mythological moment or a seemingly unchanging conception of rural life as versions of Irish tradition. This provided 'proof' of a distinct cultural conception of Irishness, which, in turn, legitimated the progressive historicist drive of a nationalist movement to retain that cultural distinctiveness in the creation of an independent nation-state consistent with the conventions of Western European modernity.

Crucial texts published in the year of Irish independence centre on the immediate past of the early years of the Revival. It is of course possible to find slightly earlier texts concerned with the representation of their recent past. Yeats published *Reveries over Childhood and Youth*, the first volume of the work that would become *Autobiographies* six years earlier, and around the same time George Moore began publishing *Hail and Farewell*, the three-volume

34 On the generally uneven qualities of *Autobiographies*, as well as an assessment of its relation to other notable Irish autobiographical works of the period, see Eamonn Hughes, '"You Need not Fear that I am not Amiable": Reading Yeats (Reading) Autobiographies', *Yeats Annual*, 12 (1996), 84–116.

35 See Marjorie Howes, *Yeats's Nations: Gender, Class, and Irishness* (Cambridge, 1996), 14.

memoir of his experience of the Revival. 'The Trembling of the Veil', however, stands as Yeats's first attempt to lay claim to the Revival as specifically his creation, by providing an authoritative, general account of the importance of intellectuals for the work of the nation. Instead of suggesting that literary work was the preserve of a bohemian group of idlers, an image Yeats railed against in 'Adam's Curse', in 'The Trembling of the Veil' he asserts that the work of the writers of the Revival produces a crucial precondition for the realization of national independence.

The strangest quality of 'The Trembling of the Veil' is its refusal of most of the conventional features of autobiographical writing. The narrative specifically focuses on the years 1887 to 1897, but Yeats rarely provides dates. Although this period covers the years in which he produced his first volumes of poetry, he almost never refers to them. Moreover, he rarely represents himself as a participant in current historical events. His refusal to provide a more vivid sense of his inner life in his description of major events in Irish history exemplifies one of the attendant frustrations of reading 'The Trembling of the Veil'. In those moments in which he does actually provide a stronger sense of opinions he once held, those positions are often odd enough to make one question the narrative as no more than a kind of self-reflective, even self-defensive, personal history.

Nevertheless, despite the nebulousness of the account of his own acts and opinions during the period in question, Yeats provides a comprehensive history of his relationship to just about every important intellectual he came into contact with during this formative period of his life. It was a quality of 'The Trembling of the Veil' that especially frustrated Æ, who reviewed the book in his journal the *Irish Statesman*:

> What I regard as the chief defect of these autobiographies will, I think, be considered by others as their main virtue. The poet tells us but little about his internal life, but much about the people he has met, and he has met many famous people of his time … I hold that there is only one person that a man may know intimately, and that is himself. If he be a man of genius what he could tell us about his own inner life would be of much more value than anything he could tell us of the external life of others … I read this biography as I would look at some many-coloured shell, from which the creature inhabiting it, who might have told us about its manner of being, had slipped away leaving us only the miracle of form to wonder at.[36]

Æ's assessment of 'The Trembling of the Veil' is both accurate and mistaken at the same time. On the one hand, his description of Yeats's record of relationships with 'famous people' identifies the main focus of the work and his comparison of its structure to 'a many-coloured shell' is perceptive. On the other hand, it is not so much that Yeats's internal life is entirely missing from that structure, as that Æ's does not realize that this

---

36   Æ, 'The Memories of a Poet', *Irish Statesman*, 4 December 1926, 302.

very absence is itself part of Yeats's account of the formation of a national intellectual. Yeats implicitly suggests throughout the early sections of *Autobiographies* that there were no intellectuals in Ireland capable of articulating the 'unity of being'; in a negative sense, what the various intellectual mentors Yeats discusses throughout fail to provide for the nation ultimately emphasizes all that Yeats *does* provide.

'The Trembling of the Veil', comprising five 'books', does indeed have an elaborate structure that expresses 'a miracle of form to wonder at', in which the first and the last two chapters mirror each other. Book One and Book Four concern Yeats's residency in England, while Books Two and Five concern his life in Ireland. All of the famous people mentioned were role models for the young Yeats. He begins by ranting against the accomplishments of science, rationality, realism, and naturalism, symbolized for him by the artists Carolus-Duran (Charles–Auguste–Émile Durand) and Jules Bastien-Lepage, and the scientists Thomas Henry Huxley and John Tyndall.[37] Throughout the rest of the narrative Yeats repeatedly invokes that quartet of names to indicate what he feels to be the misdirected ambitions of Victorian intellectual work, and the rest of 'The Trembling of the Veil' tells of his quest to find alternative models. The intellectuals mentioned in the initial sections serve as models; those discussed in Book Four and Book Five provide an important element of the English and Irish contexts for his enterprise. Book Three, entitled 'Hodos Chameliontos' ('the way of the chameleon'), concerns Yeats's relationships with various figures from the subculture of Victorian occultism and reflects some of the preoccupations of *A Vision*, which Yeats began to write soon after. Book Three emphasizes the importance of the supernatural dimension for Yeats's writing. It also serves as a metaphor for Yeats's formulation of intellectual labour in general by its mode of bringing together the polarities of work and idleness.

In the earlier autobiographical volume 'Reveries Over Childhood and Youth', Yeats remembers at one point an anecdote from his youth in Sligo in which an Englishman, ignorant of the local folklore, complains to a local car-driver that the Irish are inherently lazy for failing to alter the course of a river in order to cultivate more fields.[38] In a roundabout way, the anecdote has a bearing on his account of a dinner meeting with Wilde and their mutual friend, the (hard-working) English editor W. E. Henley. Henley and Wilde knew each other through their work as editors for the same publishing firm; while Henley works five hours five days a week, Wilde works one hour three days a week.

37 See A, 114–15.
38 'I knew stories to the discredit of England, and I took them all seriously. My mother had met some English who did not like Dublin because the legs of men were too straight, and at Sligo, as everybody knew, an Englishman had once said to a car-driver, "If you people were not so lazy, you would pull down the mountain and spread it out over the sand and that would give you acres of good fields." At Sligo there is a wide river-mouth and at ebb tide most of it is dry sand, but all Sligo knew that in some way I cannot remember it was the spreading of the tide over the sand that left the narrow Channel fit for shipping. At any rate the car man had gone chuckling all over Sligo with the tale. People would tell it to prove that the English were always grumbling.' (A, 60)

While Henley admires the 'genius' of Wilde's wit and conversation, he also marvels at the 'indolence' he is permitted. Yet not long after, Yeats discovers that Wilde's idle repartee with Henley was actually a form of work in its own right:

> And when I dined with Wilde a few days afterwards he began at once 'I had to strain every nerve to equal that man at all'; and I was too loyal to speak my thought: 'You and not he said all the brilliant things'. He, like the rest of us, had felt the strain of an intensity that seemed to hold life at the point of drama. (A, 125)

What appears as indolence in Henley's eyes is actually a highly wrought form of performative idleness that represents an alternative form of intellectual labour. Wilde worked very hard affecting the pose of laziness. He ridicules Henley's industriousness in a manner comparable to the Sligo car-driver's ridicule of the 'grumbling Englishman'. It is an important moment for Yeats. The problem with Wilde, Yeats comes to realize, is that he does not go far enough. Contrary to what Wilde actually suggested in his own writing about the necessity of idleness, his laziness stops just short of the difficulty of creative work:

> I think, too, that because of all of that half-civilized blood in his veins he could not endure the sedentary toil of creative art and so remained a man of action, exaggerating, for the sake of immediate effect, every trick learned from his masters, turning their easel painting into painted scenes ... Such men get their sincerity, if at all, from the contact of events; the dinner-table was Wilde's event and made him the greatest talker of his time, and his plays and dialogues have what merit they possess from being now an imitation, now a record, of his talk. (A, 130)

For Yeats, Wilde's exaggerated performance of the Irish stereotype of laziness finally failed to break out of a conception of identity that is English in origin; it stopped short of falling into reverie. The result is an art that is imitative rather than inspirational. Wilde's writing for Yeats stands only as an imitation of the ideal. In order to produce art that is a model for historical change, idleness must be transformed into the 'sedentary toil of creative art'.

Yeats's understanding of 'toil' is clarified in his account of William Morris's approach to creative work, which he presents as a dialectical reversal of Wilde's approach. Whereas Wilde appeared to be idle but actually laboured arduously to create that impression, Morris, 'a never idle man of great physical strength', appears to work very hard in order to enact alternative, fulfilling forms of unalienated labour that enable him to call himself (as Yeats notes he did in *The Earthly Paradise*) 'the idle singer of an empty day' (A, 132). Although Yeats takes issue with a number of Morris's positions (particularly his socialism and egalitarianism), he admires the manner in which Morris is committed to the creative practice of discovering new forms of 'making and doing':

He did not project, like Henley or Wilde, an image of himself, because having all his imagination set upon making he had little self-knowledge. He instead imagined new conditions of making and doing; and in the teeth of those scientific generalizations that cowed my boyhood, I can see some like imagining in every great change, and believe that the first flying-fish first leaped not because it sought 'adaptation' to the air, but out of horror of the sea. (A, 133)

In Yeats's view, the value of Morris's approach to craftsmanship lay in its attempt to forge a completely new practice; it involved, in Morris's own terminology, a transformation of labour from 'useless toil' to 'useful work'.[39] Morris's distinction between 'toil' — difficult, unsatisfying forms of labour that required great effort — and 'work' — the joyful, creative practice by which value is produced — is at one with the distinction between the alienated industrial labour of nineteenth-century capitalism and the skilled forms of artisanship he sought to revive through socialism. But Yeats, in describing his work as a writer, redefines 'toil' and 'work'. Ultimately, in 'The Trembling of the Veil' he subsumes the examples of both Wilde and Morris in his account of the work of the literary intellectual. The creative act of intellectual labour involves a series of reversals: the Yeatsian intellectual begins in a condition of idleness, which, as with Wilde, eventually becomes a form of work. Yet rather than stopping (as Wilde did) once it becomes difficult and unsatisfying, the Yeatsian intellectual persists through this form of 'sedentary toil', which ultimately becomes a realization of 'work' that is at once pleasurable and productive of some abstract concept of value through the condition of reverie.

In the sections of 'The Trembling of the Veil' devoted to Ireland, Yeats explores the nature of the national cultural values the Irish writer should seek to establish. The earlier 'Reveries Over Childhood and Youth' ended with Yeats being introduced to the Fenian activist and writer John O'Leary, who impressed upon him the need to articulate some sense of a national culture. The meeting had a profound impact on him:

I began to plot and scheme how one might seal with the right image the soft wax before it began to harden. I had noticed that Irish Catholics among whom had been born so many political martyrs had not the good taste, the household courtesy and decency of the Protestant Ireland I had known, yet Protestant Ireland seemed to think of nothing but getting on in the world. I thought we might bring the two halves together if we had a national literature that made Ireland beautiful in the memory, and yet had been freed from provincialism by an exacting criticism, a European pose. (A, 104–05)

---

39 See Morris's essay 'Useful Work versus Useless Toil', in *News from Nowhere and Other Writings*, ed. Clive Wilmer (London, 1993), 287–306, for his distinction between toil and work.

'The Trembling of the Veil' is just as focused on the 'scheming' described here as it is with the delineation of how one works as an intellectual. Eventually, he did describe the 'unity of being', the object of his ambition as an intellectual, as the possibility of a common culture between Irish Catholics and Protestants. This formulation operates, he explains, through 'a comparison to a musical instrument so strung that if we touch a string all the strings murmur faintly' (A, 164). The unity of being embraces not only religious or ethnic, but social and class differences as well; in this state, different parts of the nation make up a beautiful, symbiotic whole — yet the identity of each part remains 'tuned' to a specific position in the manner of Yeats's metaphorical instrument. Ancient Irish tradition provides a resource for the creation of a national community:

> Might I not, with health and good luck to aid me, create some new Prometheus Unbound; Patrick or Columcille, Oisin or Finn, in Prometheus' stead; and instead of the Caucasus, Cro-Patrick or Ben Bulben? Have not all races had their first unity from a mythology that marries them to rock and hill? We had in Ireland imaginative stories, which the uneducated classes knew and even sang, and might we not make those stories current among the educated classes, rediscovering for the work's sake what I have called 'the applied arts of literature,' the association of literature, that is, with music, speech, and dance; and at last, it might be, so deepen the political passion of the nation that all, artist and poet, craftsman and day-labourer would accept a common design? (A, 166–67)

The problem with Yeats's decision to valorize a collective sense of Irish tradition as the writer's most decisive realization of communal 'value' is that it succeeded too well, and ultimately proved to be easily appropriated by what Eagleton calls the 'archaic avant-garde'.[40] Since at least the nineteenth century, values presented as 'archaic' or 'ancient' often served to disguise the most advanced and progressive forms of modernization. The value of tradition produced by the Yeatsian intellectual is no exception to this contradiction. Moreover, the distinct sense of national particularity proclaimed in the 'unity of being' provided an imaginative resource for a political movement committed to the actualization of the Irish nation through the formation of an independent state. This was at least part of Yeats's intention, and the publication of 'The Trembling of the Veil' confirmed that. While Yeats initially participated in that state as a member of the Irish Senate, he became one of its first notable dissidents as the Irish Free State set about introducing legislation that catered to a conservative, restrictive form of Catholicism that Yeats had initially hoped the cultural values of his unity of being would supersede. He helped create tradition as a sacred, canonical value that was then used for modernizing

---

40 See Terry Eagleton, *Heathcliff and the Great Hunger* (London, 1995), 273–319.

purposes. What is more, the international esteem afforded Yeats and other writers of the Revival contributed to post-colonial Ireland's prestige as a distinct, independent nation.

'Dramatis Personae', the next section of *Autobiographies* that technically picks up where the narrative of 'The Trembling of the Veil' leaves off (though it was not written until 1934), registers in its higher quotient of bitterness and cynicism Yeats's disillusion with the new state. Yet there remains one final crucial aspect to account for in Yeats's formulation of the work of the intellectual in 'The Trembling of the Veil'. While the representation of the work of the literary intellectual in this text centres upon the complicated interplay of toil and idleness in the production of cultural values, one of Yeats's persistent complaints as far back as 'Adam's Curse' had been that the arduous process of literary creation was not generally appreciated as real work. In 'The Trembling of the Veil', he addresses the more socially acceptable forms of public intellectual labour that contrast with the devalued, difficult work of the writer. He reflects upon remembering the applause he received at the end of one of his first public lectures:

> I did not examine this applause, nor the true thoughts of those I met, nor the general condition of the country, but I examined myself a great deal, and was puzzled at myself. I knew that I was shy and timid, that I would often leave some business undone, or purchase unmade, because I shrank from facing a strange office or a shop a little grander than usual, and here was I delightedly talking to strange people every day. It was many years before I understood that I had surrendered myself to the chief temptation of the artist, creation without toil. Metrical composition is always very difficult to me, nothing is done upon the first day, nor one rhyme is in its place; and when at last the rhymes begin to come, the first rough draft of a six-line stanza takes the whole day. At that time I had not formed a style, and sometimes a six-line stanza would take several days, and not seem finished even then; and I had not learnt, as I have now, to put it all out of my head before night, and so the last night was generally sleepless, and the last day a day of nervous strain. But now I had found the happiness that Shelley found when he tied a pamphlet to a fire balloon. (A, 170–71)

Much of 'The Trembling of the Veil' — and *Autobiographies* in general — reveals how Yeats became a socially respected celebrity through his activities as a public intellectual. Yet compared to the difficulty of writing, such work does not involve any degree of toil; it is much more similar to idleness in its simplicity (even if it falls short of the valued condition of reverie). Both public and private forms of labour are aspects of the work of the literary intellectual. Yet in characteristic fashion, Yeats reverses the qualities of each as they exist in the eyes of society at large: that which looks like disreputable idleness is actually difficult, arduous work, fundamental to the labour of the literary intellectual; what looks like socially respectable work is actually a relatively easy form of creation without toil, secondary to the labours of the literary intellectual and comparable to the pleasures of idleness.

In order to do both successfully, however, it is necessary to discover a means to regulate the idleness of the intellectual. Yeats finally arrives at such knowledge at the end of 'The Trembling of the Veil'. Importantly, it is a lesson he learns from Lady Gregory. Reflecting upon the first time he stayed at her estate at Coole Park while attempting to write an ultimately abandoned novel, Yeats remembers:

> When I was in good health again, I found myself indolent, partly perhaps because I was affrighted by that impossible novel, and asked her to send me to my work every day at eleven, and at some hour to my letters, ratting me with idleness if need be, and I doubt if I should have done much with my life but for her firmness and her care. After a time, though not very quickly, I recovered tolerable industry, though it has only been of recent years that I have found it possible to face an hour's verse without a preliminary struggle and much putting off. (A, 283)

Significantly, Lady Gregory stands as the emblematic figure throughout *Autobiographies* who provides the financial means that allows Yeats to avoid the conundrum regarding intellectual labour he addressed in 'Adam's Curse'. Yet such patronage involved the responsibility to labour as an intellectual nevertheless. Lady Gregory mediates between the positive and negative forms of idleness, as she provides the conditions of leisure in which the abject idleness of the inability to write is transformed into the national work of the literary intellectual that arises from reverie. Yet the conditions of patronage that enabled the productive transformation of idleness existed in Ireland only for that limited number of aspiring intellectuals who stood to gain from a personal investment in a form of social relations that originated in the violent colonization of Ireland. While there were other Revivalists who joined Yeats in their enthusiasm for an increasingly residual social order that provided the financial wherewithal to set about doing the work of the nation, after 1922 a much larger group of increasingly powerful nationalists felt that the work of the nation that would bring into being a normative conception of Western modernity would also finally eradicate the social order on which Yeats placed such importance. Between these two positions stood a heretical strain of schemers who refused to participate in either process. These schemers also deployed the motif of laziness in their alternative form of cultural politics — although the commitment to indolence evident in the modernist texts that focused upon the lazy idle schemer would be of a much more radical nature than Yeats's productive transformation of it in his canonical formulation of the work of the literary intellectual.

3 'Count Me Out': *Ulysses* and the Right to Laziness

I

James Joyce's youthful interest in socialism has long been acknowledged, but remains relatively neglected. The conventional understanding of it runs as follows: between 1904 and 1907 there is tangible evidence that Joyce considered himself a socialist, though one can infer that his conviction dated from a year or two earlier. In ten of his published letters dating from that period, all of them written to his brother Stanislaus, Joyce discusses different aspects of socialism, usually with specific reference to the Italian form of it he encountered in leftist newspapers like *L' Asino* and *Avanti!* A few of these fleeting references demonstrate real enthusiasm. But Joyce never developed any allegiances to a specific party or ideological doctrine; as he wrote to Stanislaus from Rome in 1906, 'of course you find my socialism thin. It is so and unsteady and ill-informed.'[1] In a very gloomy letter of 1907 he seemed to renounce socialism: 'The interest I took in socialism and the rest has left me ... I have no wish to codify myself as anarchist or socialist or reactionary.'[2] On the basis of this apparent renunciation, his biographer Richard Ellmann suggests, Joyce's political opinions never amounted to much beyond an under–theorized, mundane humanism apparently unconcerned with any of the larger political questions of his era.

---

1 Richard Ellmann, ed., *Letters of James Joyce: Volume II* (New York, 1966), 187. (Hereafter, *Letters II*). See also, John McCourt, *The Years of Bloom: James Joyce in Trieste 1904–1920* (Madison, 2000), 65. Though Trieste was part of the Austro-Hungarian Empire during this period, its socialists looked to the syndicalist-influenced socialism of Rome rather than to the 'Austro-Marxists' of Vienna. For Joyce's relation to nationalism during his time in Trieste, see Eric Bulson, 'An Italian Tongue in an Irish Mouth: Joyce, Politics and the Franca Lingua', *Journal of Modern Literature*, 24, 1 (2000), 63–79.
2 *Letters II*, 217.

This position served as a critical commonplace that persisted for a number of decades.[3] Though subsequent research (notably the later work of Ellmann himself, as well as of his student Dominic Manganiello) reassessed the relationship of Joyce's political interests to his writing, much of it focused on the explication of allusions or the clarification of biographical matters.[4] There was no inquiry into what influence socialist theoretical paradigms had upon the formal or thematic characteristics of the work in the first phase of Joyce commentary, which indicated instead an implicit anarchist element.[5] Though some have since then argued for the necessity of taking Joyce's socialism seriously, its impact on his writing remains largely unexplored.[6]

The available evidence does not suggest that he maintained his interest in socialism consistently into his mature years. I argue, however, that Joyce's flirtation with socialism is important, because it illuminates how the role of the literary intellectual in relation to anti-imperialist nationalism is interrogated in *Ulysses* and how he undoes the dominant Revival paradigms of cultural production in order to pose more specifically modernist alternatives. One of the earliest, ostensibly socialist, co-ordinates to Joyce's interest seems to have been Oscar Wilde's *The Soul of Man under Socialism*, a work that he proposed translating into Italian.[7] Wilde's argument that an understanding of 'work' should include all creative possibilities rather than only those activities that create socially sanctioned values — and that socialism could be the political transformation that recognizes this aspect of intellectual labour — is echoed in Joyce's letters. In an early statement of his interest in socialism, Joyce distinguishes his beliefs from those of moderates like his university friend Francis Skeffington. The influence of Wilde's pamphlet is apparent:

> It is a mistake for you to imagine that my political opinions are those of a universal lover: but they are those of a socialistic artist ... Some people would answer that while professing to be a socialist I am trying to make money: but this is not quite true at least as they mean it ... What I wish is to secure a competence on which I can rely, and why I expect to have this is because I cannot believe that any State requires my energy for the work that I am at present engaged in.[8]

3   Richard Ellmann, *James Joyce*, new and rev. edn. (Oxford, 1982). In reference to Ellmann's liberal humanism, see Kiberd, *The Irish Writer and the World*, 245.
4   See Richard Ellmann, *The Consciousness of Joyce* (London, 1977), 73–95, and Dominic Manganiello, *Joyce's Politics* (London, 1980). On Manganiello's book, see 'Introduction', in Derek Attridge and Marjorie Howes, eds., *Semicolonial Joyce* (Cambridge, 2000), 15.
5   Ellmann, *The Consciousness of Joyce*, 82–86; Manganiello, *Joyce's Politics*, 207–11, 220.
6   Margot Norris's excellent *Joyce's Web: The Social Unraveling of Modernism* (Austin, 1992), 8, calls for the recuperation of 'a socialist or leftist version of the artist'. See also, McCourt, *The Years of Bloom*, 65–73.
7   Manganiello, *Joyce's Politics*, 220.
8   *Letters II*, 89.

For Joyce, as for Wilde, the state maintains a social order in which only certain types of work are considered socially useful. Truly innovative artistic labours are anathema both to the state and to the common sense of a market economy. The sort of socialism that both Wilde and Joyce advocated would not only regard creative intellectual labour as socially valuable, but would also establish a form of patronage that allowed for the artist to focus on cultural production as a primary form of work rather than the sundry forms of employment (which in Joyce's case ranged from language teacher to bank clerk) otherwise necessary for subsistence. While such an understanding of socialism might have lacked theoretical depth, the possibility of refusing to perform conventional forms of work lay at the heart of Joyce's interest in radical politics.[9]

Such a position helps to explain Joyce's intellectual investment in the Italian form of socialism he encountered in Trieste in 1905. Joyce was most interested in the positions of Arturo Labriola, the leader of the radical wing of the Partito Socialista Italiano, known for its anticlericalism and its disavowal of parliamentary politics.[10] As a syndicalist Marxist, Labriola held that economics preceded politics in importance and that the labour-power of the working class was the basis for the revolutionary potential of the proletariat. To Labriola, revolutionary socialism would not ultimately come from the political success of a vanguard party but through complete abstention from both politics and work. For Joyce, this provided an important point of connection to contemporary Irish politics, as he saw a similarity between Labriola and Arthur Griffith, the leader of Sinn Féin.[11] Though Labriola was a radical socialist and Griffith was unabashedly in favour of the development of an Irish form of capitalism — a difference that has led some critics to dismiss Joyce's comparison and therefore his understanding of politics — there are indeed points of connection between the two figures. Both political leaders regarded participation in parliamentary politics as a form of complicity with the state; furthermore, both held that political and social transformation would occur primarily through economic activity.[12] According to Labriola and the syndicalists, the primary resource the proletariat possessed was its capacity to work. By refusing to work through the act of the general strike, the

9   See Letters II, 205–06, for the following 'epiphany' from a 1907 letter to Stanislaus: 'Anyhow I shall never be a model bank clerk ... No more at present: rushing off to WORK. [Scene: draughty little stone-flagged room, chest of drawers to left, on which are the remains of lunch, in the center, a small table on which are writing materials (He never forgot them) and a saltcellar: in the background, small-sized bed. A young man with a snivelling nose sits at the little table: on the bed is a Madonna and a plaintive infant. It is a January day.] Title of the above: The Anarchist.'

10   See McCourt, The Years of Bloom, 14.

11   Letters II, 174–75: 'Labriola spoke yesterday, the paper says, with extraordinarily rapid eloquence for two hours and a half. He reminds me somewhat of Griffith. He attacked the intellectuals and the parliamentary socialists.'

12   It is important to note, however, that Griffith's emphasis on the productive possibilities of capital presents a key divergence from Labriola's emphasis on the productive, creative capacities of the worker. Joyce noted this difference and found Labriola's position more attractive. See Letters II, 187.

proletariat could begin the revolution that would bring about the formation of a new, liberated society.

Whatever interest Joyce may have had in the possibility of economic and social revolution, the concept of the general strike certainly appealed to him as a model of a commitment to literary innovation. Writing to Stanislaus Joyce in 1906, he used syndicalist rhetoric to begin to formulate the break between the dominant literary conventions of the Revival and his own emerging modernism:

> If it is not too farfetched to say that my action, and that of men like Ibsen etc., is a virtual intellectual strike. I would call such people as Gogarty and Yeats and Colum the blacklegs of literature. Because they have tried to substitute us, to serve the old idols at a lower rate when we refused to do so for a higher.[13]

Joyce understands writing here as a value-creating process in which one works to produce literature for others who will benefit from it; the values in question are the canonical conventions of what Bourdieu terms the 'restricted field of literary production.'[14] Yeats, Oliver St John Gogarty and Padraic Colum were akin to strike-breakers because of their willingness to produce symbolic values complicit with the 'old idols' of the existing social order. In the Revival, these values depended upon the primacy of a reconstructed Irish tradition that was useful in helping to endorse the associated progressive dynamic of an emergent cultural nationalism. Radical writers like Henrik Ibsen — and, Joyce hopes, himself — signalled their opposition to those conventional literary values by refusing to work at all. Through the refusal to work, both the syndicalist Marxist and the Ibsenite/ Joycean literary intellectual commit to idleness instead. Not coincidentally, the notion that idleness served as a revolutionary alternative to work was also widespread within the polemics of turn-of-the-century Italian socialism. Antonio Labriola (who was unrelated to the syndicalist leader Arturo Labriola), the first Italian Marxist theorist of note, played a crucial role in the foundation of the form of socialism Joyce encountered in Trieste. Notably, Antonio Labriola opposed a conception of the socialist future that rested upon the amelioration of working conditions alone — such a position would only play into what he called 'the empty dream, the abracadabra, of the *Right to Work*' — and instead emphasized a utopian vision in which the right to idleness took priority.[15] His position stems from the earlier work of Paul Lafargue, who argued in 1880 in *Le Droit à la Paresse* (*The Right to be Lazy*) that idleness was a valuable revolutionary tactic.[16] To Lafargue, the contrast

---

13 *Letters II*, 187.
14 See Bourdieu, *The Field of Cultural Production*, 29–73, 161–75.
15 Antonio Labriola, 'In Memory of the Communist Manifesto', in *Essays on the Materialistic Conception of History* (Chicago, 1908), 39. See also his *Socialism and Philosophy* (St. Louis, 1980), 62.
16 For the relationship between Lafargue's writing and cultural production, see Kristin Ross, *The Emergence of Social Space: Rimbaud and the Paris Commune* (Minneapolis, 1988), 47–74.

between work and leisure revealed a basic contradiction of capitalism that can only be resolved by the introduction of the concept of idleness.[17] Idleness is not only a condition that enables withdrawal from the contradictions of capitalist society, it also anticipates the utopia that comes into being after the arrival of socialism. Idleness characterizes a society in which work provides the same satisfaction as leisure because both are now part of a transformed, unified creative process in which everyone has complete control of their own labour and works for the collective good by working for oneself.

Joyce's interest in socialism eventually recedes — at least in the sense that there are not many references to it in the letters written after his early years in Italy (though there are allusions to socialism in all of his fictional works). Since the attraction socialism had for Joyce stemmed from his desire for a means of subsistence that would allow him to focus on his writing rather than having to work as a teacher or bank clerk, it is reasonable to speculate that the eventual patronage of Harriet Shaw Weaver (who was a committed Marxist herself) provided a private form of the Wildean brand of socialism for which Joyce had earlier expressed enthusiasm.[18] Weaver's beneficence enabled the new forms of intellectual labour Joyce sought in his writing. I argue that socialism made a profound impact upon Joyce's writing and the emergence of an Irish modernist aesthetic, for Italian socialism's principles of the refusal to work and the right to idleness aided his prolonged interrogation of the formation of the literary intellectual in the Revival. The Revival provided the imagery and symbolic content for an anti-imperialist form of nationalism that had finally succeeded in its revolutionary aims only weeks before the publication of *Ulysses* in 1922. Joyce, in historicizing an earlier moment in that process by setting all of its action on one day in 1904, offers a deflected inquiry into the role played by writers in the construction of the imaginative preconditions of post-colonial independence. While the more conventional writers of the Revival who appear in, or are referred to in, *Ulysses* are committed to the work of the nation, Stephen Dedalus signals an alternative form of dissent from the state-directed nationalism that came to dominate Irish politics during the years of the novel's composition. Though Leopold Bloom figures more prominently than Stephen Dedalus in readings of the novel's politics, Stephen is just as important to a post-colonial understanding of it. Bloom's otherness troubles exclusionary conceptions of identity. Stephen's idleness raises a number of questions — about modernist formal innovation, about the representation of a non-teleological idea of temporality, and about the colonial forms of modernity.

17 Ross, *The Emergence of Social Space*, 61: 'Lafargue suggests a revolutionary practice whereby the true threat to existing order comes not from some untainted working class but from a challenge *between* labour and leisure, producer and consumer, worker and bourgeois, worker and intellectual.' Emphasis in original.
18 Margot Norris briefly discusses the relation between Harriet Shaw Weaver's communism and patronage in *Joyce's Web*, 36–37.

2

To begin with, idleness here has its origin in colonial stereotypes of the Irish as unruly, undisciplined, and indolent, despite the large Irish contribution to the industrial revolution in both Britain and the United States. Its stereotypical status enhances the political impact of its deployment within Irish modernism, however untrue it may have been in historical actuality. Homi Bhabha and a number of other post-colonial theorists have argued that it is not the supposed accuracy or falsity of a given stereotype that matters as much as its status in an ambivalent discursive representation that at once registers both the presumption of superiority and the inherent paranoia of colonial ideology.[19] Since anti-imperialist nationalism inevitably functions as a derivative discourse of colonialism, cultural nationalism must necessarily engage with the stereotype.[20] For the most part, Irish nationalism responded to colonial stereotypes in one of two ways: it either disavowed the stereotype altogether, or, through a process of transvaluation, it reclassified it in positive terms as an exemplification of Irish difference.[21] Whether or not a particular stereotype might be useful for the rhetorical clothing of nationalism — however distorted the characteristic in question may have been — it had to do with temporality, as the distinction Deane draws between 'the character of nations' and 'national character' makes clear.[22] Deane finds that this distinction dates from the emergence of nationalism in the nineteenth century and refers to the tension between the character of nations, that progressive 'explanatory element in the story of a progression from the narrow ambit of the new territory or space of the state', and national character, that static or regressive 'controlling voice in a recalcitrant community narrative that refuses, with decreasing success, to surrender its particularities, to yield itself either to the state or to any comparable transnational, or "universal" goal or condition'.[23] Cultural nationalism thus faced a contradictory dilemma that proves to be one of its own conditions of possibility. In order to accelerate the process that would allow the character of nations to unfold into a modernity typified by statehood, it must repress those aspects of the national character that prevent progress. Yet, in order to maintain an iteration of the character of nations that is not wholly derivative of the model imposed by colonial violence, cultural nationalism must retain as many facets of national character as possible, in order to signal the particularity of local difference.

There are three ramifications of this contradiction that cultural nationalism has to deal with. To begin with, those potentially stereotypical qualities of the national character

---

19   See Bhabha, *The Location of Culture*, 81–82.
20   See Chatterjee, *Nationalist Thought and the Colonial World*, 1–53.
21   On the Irish nationalist transvaluation of stereotypes, see Lloyd, 'Counterparts', 131–33.
22   See Seamus Deane, *Strange Country: Modernity and Nationhood in Irish Writing since 1790* (Oxford, 1997), 49–99.
23   Deane, *Strange Country*, 49.

that might be reclassified in positive terms must not prevent or hinder the overarching progressive drive inherent in the development of the character of nations. While something like the stereotype of the superstitious and dogmatic Irish Catholic might be recoded as signifying a commitment to morality that could have a place in the cultural nationalist project, a stereotype like drunkenness, with its connection to wastefulness, self-destructive indulgence, and even violence or irrationality, clearly would not.[24] It is crucial that the value in question, even if it is identified with the past, be useful for the imagination of the future. The fact that the concept of tradition can only be understood as a crucial dimension of the process of modernization is a further ramification of the contradiction between the character of nations and national character.[25] Deane argues that 'modernity defined itself as the new emerging from the old; it needed the presence of archaic elements in order to articulate its difference from them'.[26] The celebration of the traditional, the ancient, and other ostensibly native vestiges of the past, characteristic of cultural nationalism, should not be regarded as the fetishization of the pre-modern or the desire to retrieve some sort of edenic pre-colonial essence. Instead, the rediscovery and embrace of tradition on the part of cultural nationalism serves as the basis for a progressive historical narrative that promises a revolutionary future through the confirmation of a specifically national past. Tradition itself in these terms presents just another mode of modernization. Finally, for all of this to be possible, cultural nationalism must either develop or appropriate new narrative forms that can allow for the simultaneous presence of national character and the progressive logic that drives the character of nations.[27] Since the specificity of local national tradition must be accounted for at all costs, representational forms and genres must depart to at least some extent from the models provided by the culture of the colonizer.

   In the Revival all three of the ramifications of the temporal contradiction of cultural nationalism were confronted. The plays, poetry, and other assorted antiquarian writings may have varied, but they shared a common project of delineating those aspects of the national character that would help enable an imaginative construction of the nation, which could become a reality through enough hard work. This was as true of those concerned with ancient legendary material as it was of those more concerned with the representation of a more contemporary version of the west of Ireland. Both offered evidence of a persistent national character that could evolve into the character of the Irish nation. The intellectuals, activists, and writers of the Revival substituted an apparently timeless conception of the west for the actual traumatic history of the more recent past; they not only largely evaded the consideration of certain historical events (such as the Famine or the Land War), which might have provided evidence of fatally intransitive attributes of the national character, they

24 See Lloyd, 'Counterparts', 132.
25 Deane, *Strange Country*, 51.
26 Deane, *Strange Country*, 53.
27 Deane, *Strange Country*, 54.

also converted the past into the Past, a more general concept suitable for the teleological narrative required by nationalism.[28] Though Yeats might have had misgivings about both the concept of modernity and some of the more ethnocentric forms of Irish nationalism that emerged in this period, he cleared the imaginative space for the Irish version of modernization enacted by state-centred nationalism.

Idleness was remarkably difficult to transvalue into a more positive dimension of the national character. It signalled the very opposite of all of the energy and work needed to build the nation in both a literal and imaginative sense, and it supported other stereotypical conditions such as drunkenness, sexual promiscuity, and indebtedness. Joyce included all of these forms of behaviour in *Ulysses*, but not to celebrate their status as stereotypes or to reverse their perceived values. Instead, he utilized them for a representation of Ireland distinctly at odds with nationalist common sense. Idleness stood contrary to just about every concept of progress possible. It had no utility, neither in relation to the construction of the nation-state nor to the elaboration and development of a new aesthetic. It is true that idleness is celebrated in Yeats's work through figures such as the indigent tramps or leisurely aristocrats of many of his plays and poems, as well as in his general understanding of intellectual labour. He reversed the values associated with work and non-work and re-inscribed idleness as an essentially purer form of intellectual labour; but this was part of his general rejection of modern bourgeois conventions and of contemporary propriety. Yet Irish idleness at the turn of the century had more to do with the abysmal and impoverished condition of colonial underdevelopment rather than the actualization of some stereotypical racial trait. If many did not work in Dublin in 1904, it was often because there was little work available. Unemployment presented a virtually insurmountable social obstacle for the would-be professional middle class Joyce knew. His representation of their collective frustration dated back as far as the depiction of paralytic malaise in *Dubliners*. That collective sense of *ennui* emphasized the abject social conditions that the Revival and the nationalist movement would have to overcome to realize their aims. Joyce frequently and consistently argued, whether explicitly in his early critical statements concerning his enthusiasm for Ibsenian naturalism or more implicitly in mature writings such as *Ulysses* and its representation of poverty, that the chosen and preferred expressive forms of both the Revival and Irish nationalism were not suitable for such a realization.

Idleness suggests the possibility of an innovative form that represents the wretched material conditions of late colonial Ireland but nevertheless resists complicity with the teleological progressive narratives that lay at the heart of Irish nationalism. Benjamin argues that idleness is a condition that places an emphasis on a synchronic conception of temporality, because its sensation of an unending duration of the moment displaces an ordered awareness of the succession of temporal units in the progressive and regimented

28 Deane, *Strange Country*, 50–51.

manner characteristic of labour-time. As the idler lingers and moves through modernity, he or she encounters the full temporal heterogeneity of the present, in which the dominant motifs and characteristics of the contemporary moment stand in juxtaposition to the ghostly traces, relics, and fossils of the past. The possibility exists, Benjamin suggests, that one might read them against the grain and begin to come to an alternative historical understanding of the processes of historical change. Such alternative forms of historiography would demand new representational forms; it was the role of the literary intellectual, dedicated to the anatomization of idleness, to provide them. Translated into the late colonial context of the Revival, such an understanding of idleness would provide the opportunity of a more radical understanding of historical change. Rather than an embarrassing stereotype resistant to efforts to recode it as something more positive, idleness not only drew attention to the miserable social conditions any revolution worth its salt would have to overcome but also presented the possibility that recalcitrant elements drawn from the national character might provide the basis for a thoroughgoing critique of the derivative structures of the character of nations. Most importantly, idleness, so understood, provided an opportunity for the dissident intellectual who sought to devise new representational forms which overcame the dilemma that Deane argues is inherent to Irish discourse in the years leading up to independence.

Inactivity in *Ulysses* registers all of these issues and provides a context for Joyce's interrogation of the relationship between intellectual labour and symbolic value. By raising the issue of national character — albeit in a deflected manner — relatively early in the novel, Joyce emphasizes the tension between a stereotypical conception of idleness and the representation of it as a register of the material reality of colonial underdevelopment. Through images of, and allusions to, passivity and torpor in 'Lotus Eaters', Joyce draws a connection between idleness and colonial stereotypes. In one of Leopold Bloom's orientalist fantasies as he passes the window of the Belfast and Oriental Tea Company, he thinks about the effect of weather upon character:

> So warm ... The far east. Lovely spot it must be: the garden of the world, big lazy leaves to float about on, cactuses, flowery meads, snaky lianas they call them. Wonder is it like that. Those Cinghalese lobbing around in the sun, in *dolce far niente*. Not doing a hand's turn all day. Sleep six months out of twelve. Too hot to quarrel. Influence of the climate. Lethargy. Flowers of idleness. (U, 71)

To Bloom, idleness is intrinsic, but develops under the influence of climate. It is a marker both of an otherness essentially foreign to an Irish sensibility (particularly to his own perspective of the world, which is conditioned by his professional hard-working activities as an advertising salesman) and of an almost utopian, desirable sensuality he generally lacks (except for the odd time in which warm weather has the same effect upon him as on the inherently idle 'Cinghalese'). Such ruminations suggest that Bloom has internalized what Alatas has called 'the myth of the lazy native' — that feature of national character so often attributed to the colonized, in which an irrational commitment to enjoyment takes priority over the practical and industrious work-ethic necessary to bring about progress and modernization.[29] While Bloom does indeed wonder whether his thoughts about the exotic East are accurate — obviously it is only in fantasy that he encounters the eroticism and sumptuous details of the tropics — the imagery and assumptions of his pondering fall squarely within the terms of colonial stereotypes. Joyce's representation of Bloom's travels through Dublin routinely provides glimpses of the idleness of its other citizens as well. Not long after his brief fantasy of Ceylon, Bloom encounters such local idlers as C. P. M'Coy (a character in *Dubliners* and *Ulysses* who has difficulty maintaining a job and is best known for an elaborate scheme in which he steals luggage from other people) and Bantam Lyons (a gambler whose profession is identified in one guide to Joyce's works as primarily a 'punter and habitué of pubs').[30] Though Bloom apparently fails to recognize that the stereotypical qualities of indolence that govern his idea of the native had long been applied to the Irish as well, the novel does not; it depicts a version of Ireland in which the 'flowers of idleness' are already growing upon local soil. The difference between Bloom's stereotypical fantasies and Joyce's representation of the city and its citizens is crucial. While the stereotype of native idleness implies the *necessity* of colonial rule, Joyce's depiction of idleness ultimately suggests that it is a *consequence* of colonial rule. Throughout *Ulysses*, Joyce generally represents idleness and work as mutually problematic and symptomatic of everything that needs to change to allow for a potentially more promising future.

Remarkably little work — at least in the sense of wage-labour — ever gets done in *Ulysses*. In 'Nestor', Stephen does teach at a primary school but, after collecting his salary, he spends the rest of his day wandering around Dublin, drinking and getting into various kinds of discussions; by the end of the day he suggests that he will not return to his job in the morning. Bloom too does some work on 16 June 1904, but in both the episodes in which he can be said to be working — 'Aeolus' and 'Scylla and Charybdis' — the narrative focus is on Stephen. Bloom spends the bulk of his time more as a *flâneur* than as a salesman. Molly Bloom spends most of the day in bed, and apparently never leaves 7 Eccles Street; her profession at any rate is rather unusual. Meanwhile, numerous less important characters circulate who do not seem to be doing any work at all. *Ulysses* presents a taxonomy of idleness, ranging from the cut-rate inactivity of barflies like Nosey Flynn and Bantam Lyons to the more shabby-genteel form of idleness that characterizes the newspaper editor Myles Crawford and his educated companions at the newspaper office. Uniquely, Lenihan demonstrates a number of these different modes of inactivity

29 For an elaborate and prolonged interrogation of this stereotype in the context of East Asia, see Alatas, *The Myth of the Lazy Native*, esp. 70–82.

30 See Shari Benstock and Bernard Benstock, *Who's He When He's at Home: A James Joyce Directory* (Urbana, 1980), 117.

as he manages to move through just about every drink-related site of idleness in the novel. The primary reason for all of this indolence is the limited opportunities that exist in an underdeveloped colonial economy. Those jobs that are available in the middle-class world that is the focus of Joyce's writing provide little room for advancement or personal creativity (as Bloom's spotty history of employment attests) or involve working within the bureaucracy of the imperial administration (as in the case of Martin Cunningham, Jack Power, and others). Very few of Joyce's idlers possess the financial wherewithal to undertake a lifestyle committed to leisurely enjoyment. By contrast with Yeats's writing, where the two terms are more closely related, idleness and leisure are antithetical in *Ulysses*. Aside from an occasional wealthy tourist, like Haines in 'Telemachus' or cameo appearances by representatives of the British Crown in 'Wandering Rocks', the so-called 'idle rich' have a minimal presence in *Ulysses*. The Revival self-reflexively stressed its own work-ethic and the turn-of-the-century cultural nationalist movements similarly placed an emphasis upon the value of all of the hard work that needed to be done to hasten the arrival of independence. But Joyce's representation of widespread idleness in the Dublin of his novel stands contrary to both. In many respects the idleness of Dublin in *Ulysses* seems to be an extension of the collective paralysis of the city Joyce represented in *Dubliners*. The fact that so many of the idlers of *Ulysses* have already appeared in that earlier collection only adds to the sense of inertia.

Work does occur in *Ulysses*, but Joyce represents it as something that is just as problematic as idleness. Stephen's opinion of his job is especially grim; he compares his salary to a monthly hanging. He formulates a number of positions concerning time and history in this episode that will later be connected to idleness and alternative forms of intellectual labour. It is equally true that Bloom manages to get a little work done during the day, even if the focus of the novel is more squarely on Stephen's idleness. Yet Bloom has a history of difficult relationships with previous employers, and many of his reflections throughout the day demonstrate frustration with his job. Moreover, Bloom's profession briefly enables Joyce to demonstrate how the logic of work provides an ideological strategy of containment for modern desire, ambition, and even enjoyment.[31] Adorno argues that one of the most fundamental characteristics of modernity is the process by which the relatively limited social role of a 'profession' comes to dominate every other aspect of life. Work imposes its limitations even on the imagination of freedom.[32] In 'Ithaca' there is a comical demonstration of what Adorno later calls the 'free time' of modernity. As the objective third-person narrator of that episode notes, at night Bloom frequently meditates on his past experience and fantasizes about a better future, a practice that 'habitually before retiring for the night alleviated fatigue and produced as a result sound repose and renovated vitality' (U, 720). Notably, the style of this section evokes the sonorities of

31 On 'strategies of containment', see Fredric Jameson, *The Political Unconscious* (Ithaca, 1981), 52–54.
32 See Adorno, 'Free Time', in *Critical Models*, 167–68.

commercial language, suggesting that the rhetoric that characterizes Bloom's occupation not only pervades his consciousness, but even the supposedly 'objective' style of the episode. These fantasies take a number of forms, but invariably, as the catechismic style suggests, there is a final fantasy:

What were habitually his final meditations?

Of some one sole unique advertisement to cause passers to stop in wonder, a poster novelty, with all the extraneous accretions excluded, reduced to its simplest and most efficient terms not exceeding the span of casual vision and congruous with the velocity of modern life. (U, 720)

Even in his fantasies Bloom cannot escape his occupation. Even if he were able to produce his imagined 'one sole unique advertisement', it would not be a cause of wonder for very long. Advertising functions by attaching an aura of unique or 'magic' specificity to an otherwise standardized commodity or service. However, this specificity is immediately superseded by new advertisements that also boast 'magic' qualities.[33] The objects of Bloom's final meditations are frustratingly unattainable.

Yet Joyce's representation of work in *Ulysses* goes beyond such depictions of his two primary characters. In a more general sense, much of the work in the book happens liminally; it highlights both the social disparities of a colonial economy and the ideological blind spots of cultural nationalism. This is particularly true concerning the work performed by women. Women perform a great deal of the incidental work on 16 June 1904; some of them, such as the milk seller of 'Telemachus' or the barmaids of 'Sirens', briefly have a prominent place in the novel; others, like Blazes Boylan's secretary, Miss Dunne, or Stephen's younger sisters, Katey, Boody, and Maggy (all of whom appear in 'Wandering Rocks'), provide only glimpses of Dublin's working world.[34] But women's labour in *Ulysses* also takes a contradictory form. While women frequently provide for the survival of their families through their labour, they are consequently at greater risk than the men, as the early death of May Dedalus or the precarious financial state of the recently

---

33   See Raymond Williams, 'Advertising: The Magic System', in *Problems in Materialism and Culture* (London, 1980), 170–95.

34   The Dedalus sisters may present a special case. While it has generally been presumed that the laundry the sisters wash in 'Wandering Rocks' belonged to the Dedalus family, Bonnie Kime Scott has suggested that the sisters have taken in other people's laundry in order to provide for the family household, which is evidently maintained by Maggy. 'This very low-paid example of domestic labour is in stark distinction to the behavior of their father Simon Dedalus, who stands out as one of the characters of the novel least inclined to work.' See Bonnie Kime Scott, 'Diversions from Mastery in "Wandering Rocks"', in Kimberly Devlin and Marilyn Reizbaum, eds., Ulysses: *En-Gendered Perspectives: Eighteen New Essays on the Episodes* (Columbia, SC, 1999), 146.

widowed Mrs. Dignam indicate.[35] The poverty of characters like the Dedalus sisters indicates that low-paid and unskilled work like laundering or domestic service were often the only forms of employment readily available. The status of women's work further illustrates that the social conditions of Irish society are in need of a more thoroughgoing transformation than is offered by national independence alone. The numerous shadowy references to women's working conditions imply a gendered division between the public and private spheres,[36] whereby men were to work in occupations that would lead to the construction of the nation, and women were to work in a more strictly domestic sense as wives and mothers.[37]

Joyce isolates a crucial foundational moment in the consolidation of both the aesthetic ideologies of the Revival and the political ideology of Irish nationalism. Rather than confirming those ideologies, however, his representation of widespread idleness and dead-end work draws attention to those recalcitrant elements of what Deane terms national character. Ulysses emphasizes two glaring obstacles to the general process of modernization in Joyce's representation of work and idleness. Yet to consider it entirely negatively is to neglect one of the more important principles of the internal logic of his book: parallax. As has long been observed throughout several generations of Joyce criticism, it is virtually impossible to find evidence of the straightforward advocacy of any single position. Just as in the astronomical principle of parallax that Bloom thinks about during the 'Lestrygonians' episode, Joyce tends to construct his objects of representation according to different perspectives. If both work and idleness exist in Ulysses as negative terms, according to the principle of parallax it is quite likely that they might be understood in positive terms as well.

35 See Kimberly Devlin, 'Visible Shades and Shades of Visibility', in Devlin and Reizbaum, eds., Ulysses: En-Gendered Perspectives, 84.

36 Some of the most exploited women workers in Ulysses are the prostitutes of 'Circe'; Clair Wills suggests that their presence especially disrupts the process by which Irish nationalism approximated colonial positions by demonstrating the hypocrisy and oppressive qualities of both colonial and nationalist frameworks of value. See Clair Wills, 'Joyce, Prostitution, and the Colonial City', South Atlantic Quarterly, 95, 1 (1996), 79–95, 85.

37 There were numerous voices within the nationalist spectrum that objected to this separation of gender and work. Ireland had a very vibrant feminist movement in the years preceding national independence, which frequently overlapped with the nationalist movement, as the participation of such notable figures as Maude Gonne, Constance Markievicz, Eva Gore-Booth, and Hannah Sheehy-Skeffington in both movements demonstrates. The more leftist variations of groups dedicated to national liberation — such as Connolly's republican socialist movement — were also equally committed to the liberation of women. Nevertheless, more conservative forms of nationalism that became dominant after independence effectively silenced these positions. By the 1930s, any woman who held a job in which the state provided a salary was required to resign her position upon marriage in order to devote herself to wifehood and motherhood; married women were not eligible for these jobs in the first place. For an overview of the role of Irish women in the anti-colonial struggle, see Margaret Ward, Unmanageable Revolutionaries: Women and Irish Nationalism (London, 1983).

The concept of work is ultimately redeemed by the existence of *Ulysses* itself. Its variety of styles, its pretence to totality, the degree to which it seemingly compresses several different times and places into one very specific delineated time and place — all exemplify Maurice Blanchot's modernist notion of *désoeuvrement*, that characteristic of a literary text by which a work can never be said to be fully complete.[38] No matter how great the Herculean labour in the composition of *Ulysses*, something had to be left out. While it initially suggests an all-encompassing sense of totality, it ultimately celebrates its own fragmentation, 'unworking', its own *désoeuvrement*. Such an understanding of intellectual labour is important for a political understanding of the book. As Blanchot suggests, the mark of completion is also the mark of exclusion. Completion represents that moment in which something is excluded from the work in question; that which is excluded becomes the object of scorn, in that it signifies a repressed otherness and reaffirms the wholeness of the work that excludes it. A work that insists upon its own completion at the expense of that which is excluded has a certain totalitarian quality, while the work that is never complete holds forth the possibility that otherness might still have a place within it. Jean-Luc Nancy has argued that such a theoretical model has clear affinities with the possibility of an egalitarian community predicated upon difference rather than similarity. A community committed to its own *désoeuvrement* or 'unworking' is always in process and allows for the incorporation of new, as yet unrealized, identities, while a community committed to the centrality of one singular identity does not allow for the possibility of the inclusion of otherness.[39] Nancy's understanding of *désoeuvrement* also extends to *Ulysses*. Leopold Bloom, an Irish Jew who is not Jewish according to Jewish law, who has also been baptized as both a Protestant and a Catholic and at different points in the book inhabits the subject positions of male, female, transgendered, heterosexual, bisexual, and homosexual, disrupts any of the empowered forms of community predicated upon the singularities of nation, religion, and gender throughout the novel. He stands as an incarnation of the principle of 'unworking'. But an understanding of work predicated upon multiplicity and incompletion rather than the alienated types of employment Joyce represents throughout *Ulysses* already suggests some other, completely different, understanding of labour. It is thus not surprising to find that Blanchot's term *désoeuvrement* is often translated into English as 'idleness'. Since idleness is so closely connected to a redeemed concept of work reconfigured as Joycean modernist labour, it is necessary to understand how Joyce's representation of laziness might open up the possibility of something beyond colonial *ennui* alone.

Given that idleness is understood as a stereotypical element of colonial polemic to be countered by a nationalist inspired work-ethic, or as evidence of the uneven development

38 On *désoeuvrement* and the relationship between its aesthetic and political ramifications, see Shershow, *The Work and the Gift*, 163–205.
39 See Jean-Luc Nancy, *The Inoperative Community* (Minneapolis, 1991), 31.

that characterizes a dependent colonial economy, it remains difficult to consider it in unproblematic terms, no matter how strongly one wants to redeem it as a concept. Idleness in a general sense should in no way be construed as an entirely positive condition; at different moments in Ulysses it is identified with clichéd notions of Irishness, masculine privilege, and even with a casual complicity in an abject and impoverished status quo. For all of these reasons, idleness in Ulysses and in Irish modernism in general should not be romanticized. Idleness in Ulysses has presented problems for critics of Joyce since its publication; this has especially been the case for early Marxist or socialist critics of the novel.[40] In the 1930s, for example, the Marxist critic Alick West attacked it for its failure to represent work and evaluated it solely in terms of its representation of consumption.[41] Even in Benjamin's theorization of idleness — which attempts to regard it as a potentially subversive form of behaviour — it is linked to the spell cast by fetishized commodities encountered on display within the arcades, while Erlebnis, the form of temporality Benjamin identifies with idleness, is the time of passivity and apparent permanence that contributes to some of the more oppressive qualities of modernity (even if Benjamin ultimately reads Erlebnis against the grain as well).

Yet the late colonial setting of Ulysses adds another dimension to consumption and its relation to idleness. While commodities are not missing from the world of Ulysses, those depicted in the most fetishistic manner (such as the clothes and make-up desired by Gerty MacDowell or the books that represent escape from oppressive domestic conditions for Stephen's sister Dilly) are defined by a given character's inability to possess them. Just as the general representation of idleness registers the uneven development of late colonial Dublin, Joyce's representation of commodities focuses on forms of desire defined by poverty. Even those commodities that are most consumed — most notably, alcohol — are identified with practices that reveal the contradictions of Irish nationalist ideology, as does idleness.[42] Time is what is ultimately most consumed by the idlers of Ulysses; the novel persistently draws attention to the relation between politics and temporality. The relationship idleness has to consumption is ambiguous; this ambiguity extends to the meaning of idleness in general, not only in Ulysses, but also in all the other modernist works that appear after it. Benjamin reads the representation of idleness in Baudelaire and the assorted texts and practices of the arcades against the grain to open up the possibility of a new form of historiography not predicated upon a progressive and dominant conception of temporality. Similarly, Joyce's representation of idleness prefigures alternative forms of intellectual labour that could avoid the limitations of both the literature of the Revival and the discourse of Irish nationalism. This is especially true in respect to Joyce's representation of the emergent type of intellectual who would come to be seen as an archetypal character within Irish

40   For an overview of the early Marxist critical reaction to Ulysses, see Alan Roughly, James Joyce and Critical Theory (Ann Arbor, 1991), 217–26.
41   Alick West, Crisis and Criticism, and Selected Literary Essays (Norwood, 1975), 120–21.
42   See Lloyd, 'Counterparts', 133.

modernism. Stephen Dedalus's idleness is something more than the bad behaviour of an abject and dissatisfied would-be intellectual who has experienced the trauma of personal loss and the vicissitudes of poverty. His idleness is the primary characteristic of that paradigmatic figure of Irish modernism, the lazy idle schemer.

3

At one point in 'Wandering Rocks', Buck Mulligan discusses Stephen Dedalus with his former Oxford classmate, Haines. Noting that Haines has missed Stephen's long-promised interpretation of Shakespeare ('the happy hunting ground of all minds that have lost their balance', as Haines puts it) (U, 248), which had been delivered in the previous episode, 'Scylla and Charybdis', Mulligan expresses his doubts about Stephen's capacity to become the artist he so ardently desires to be. Stephen and his ideas do not correspond to Mulligan's notion of the late nineteenth-century philhellenic aesthete: 'He will never capture the Attic note. The note of Swinburne, of all poets, the white death and the ruddy birth. That is his tragedy. He can never be a poet' (U, 249). The Hibernophile Haines, on the other hand, whose assumptions about the nature of Stephen's interpretation of *Hamlet* are the exact opposite of what Stephen actually argued ('I am sure he has an *idée fixe* ... Such persons always have.'), has stereotypical ideas about the Celt's supposed lack of a sense of destiny or morality, derived from his reading of Celtic philology. While neither Mulligan's ideas about aesthetics nor Haines's interest in Gaelic antiquarianism refer to Wilde or Yeats directly, their remarks stem from a casual understanding of movements and positions associated with precisely those two emblematic models of the literary intellectual by whom Stephen has been preoccupied all day. Despite his earnest attempts to assert himself as an artist in his own right, it is a commonplace assumption among his Dublin acquaintance that he is not one; Lynch reminds Stephen in 'Oxen of the Sun', after hearing from him about the godlike powers of the artist, that self-identification as an artist will suit him better only 'when something more, and greatly more, than a capful of light odes can call your genius father' (U, 415).

Nevertheless, both the conversation between Haines and Mulligan, and Lynch's later attempt to bring the drunken Stephen down to earth, suggest that Stephen might amount to someone notable after all. In response to Haines asking whether Stephen wrote anything for any of the emerging organs of the Irish Literary Revival, Mulligan responds

> – Ten years, he said, chewing and laughing. He is going to write something in ten years.
> – Seems a long way off, Haines said, thoughtfully lifting his spoon. Still, I shouldn't wonder if he did after all. (U, 249)

Although this section of 'Wandering Rocks' does not seem especially consequential, beyond serving to reinforce the general sense of condescension both of these characters feel towards their room-mate in the Martello Tower, it stands as one of those occasional moments in *Ulysses* that becomes retrospectively ironic in the light of Joyce's ultimate achievement as a writer. Roughly ten years after 16 June 1904, the actual James Joyce (rather than the fictional Stephen Dedalus) would finally succeed in his efforts to publish the collection *Dubliners*, as well as begin to produce the first chapters of *A Portrait of the Artist as a Young Man*. There is a similar moment in 'Scylla and Charybdis' when one of the Revivalist intellectuals at the National Library declares, in a conversation that pointedly ignores Stephen's presence, 'our national epic is yet to be written ... [George] Moore is the man for it' (U, 192). The dismissive manner of certain characters in *Ulysses* towards Stephen's potential as a writer and the actual success of the historical figure who created him is certainly ironic now. But one of the greatest traps of Joyce criticism is to assume too direct a connection between Joyce and his characters. While he undeniably drew upon his own experiences in everything he wrote, as Beckett suggested of *Finnegans Wake*, 'the danger is in the neatness of identifications'.[43] It is important to have a basic sense of uncertainty about Stephen's future, since his role as a lazy idle schemer suggests he will never actually accomplish anything. The conversation between Mulligan and Haines focuses upon something else, a key characteristic of the lazy idle schemer: the philosophical problem of potentiality.

Stephen's potential cannot be disregarded. But the relationship between actuality and possibility is a much deeper philosophical issue than the question of whether or not one is a notable writer according to the dominant values of the Revival. Stephen, remembering his reading of Aristotle, thinks about potentiality at various points in the initial chapters of *Ulysses*. Giorgio Agamben finds in Aristotle's theorization of potentiality the possibility of a radical form of politics.[44] Agamben focuses on the distinction Aristotle makes between a generic form of potentiality (that is, for example, that any given child theoretically has the potential to become any number of things when she or he grows up), which is of little philosophical interest to him, and a more precise form that depends upon one having knowledge or a specific ability, such as that demonstrated by 'the architect ... that has the potential to build ... the poet that has the potential to write poems'. What is most important about this form of potentiality — which refers exactly to the type of intellectual labour that serves as the basis for Stephen's professional vocation as a writer — is that it might never be actualized:

> Whoever already possesses knowledge, by contrast, is not obliged to suffer an alteration: he is instead potential, Aristotle says, thanks to a *hexis*, a 'having' on the basis of which he can also *not* bring his knowledge into actuality by *not* making a

43 D, 19.
44 See Giorgio Agamben, 'On Potentiality', in *Potentialities: Collected Essays in Philosophy* (Stanford, 1999), 177–84.

work, for example. Thus the architect is potential insofar as he has the potential to
not-build, the poet the potential to not-write poems.

Agamben argues that the capacity for *not* acting is precisely what makes humans different
from other living beings and that every human potentiality depends upon one's relation to
one's own incapacity or privation. Ultimately, the possibility of liberation is to be found,
not within a concerted course of action, but rather in a principle of refusal, which involves
a chosen commitment to inactivity.

> To be free is not simply to have the power to do this or that thing, nor is it simply to
> have the power to refuse to do this or that thing. To be free is, in the sense that we have
> seen, *to be capable of one's own impotentiality,* to be in relation to one's own privation.[45]

In other words, to be capable of one's own impotentiality means to commit to idleness
rather than work, despite the fact that work might be a distinct possibility. Idleness, in
general, may have any number of negative connotations, ranging from colonial stereotypes
to political quietism, but when understood more precisely in relation to the conditions of
possibility for intellectual or creative labour, it encapsulates an aporetic commitment to
the critique of the production of value within a given symbolic economy. For the lazy idle
schemer who desires an as-yet-unrecognized form of modernist representational work, to
be capable of one's own impotentiality serves as a mandatory first step.

Leopold Bloom is one of the many characters in *Ulysses* who recognize Stephen's
potentiality as an intellectual; it is one of the reasons Bloom is attracted to him. Yet Bloom
misrecognizes Stephen as an organic intellectual of the Revival. A brief scene in the late
episode 'Eumaeus' underscores this, and also Stephen's own capacity for impotentiality.
Bloom attempts to begin a conversation with Stephen about the necessity of hard work.
In contemplative mood, he reflects upon the prejudiced and abusive varieties of Irish
nationalism he encountered during the day; he then proposes his own commitment to a
more properly social democratic form of patriotism:

> I'm, he resumed, with dramatic force, as good an Irishman as that rude person I
> told you about at the outset and I want to see everyone, concluded he, all creeds
> and classes *pro rata* having a comfortable tidysized income, in no niggard fashion
> either, something in the neighbourhood of £300 per annum. That's the vital issue
> at stake and it's feasible and would be provocative of friendlier intercourse between
> man and man. At least that's my idea, for what it's worth. I call that patriotism. *Ubi
> patria,* as we learned a small smattering of in our classical day in *Alma Mater, vita
> bene.* Where you can live well, the sense is, if you work. (U, 644)

---

45   Agamben, *Potentialities*, 183. Emphasis in original.

Stephen remains sceptical:

> Over his untasteable apology for a cup of coffee, listening to this synopsis of things
> in general, Stephen stared at nothing in particular ... Then he looked up and saw the
> eyes that said or didn't say the words the voice he heard said — if you work.
> – Count me out, he managed to remark, meaning to work.
> The eyes were surprised at this observation, because as he, the person who owned them
> pro tem. observed or rather, his voice speaking did: All must work, have to, together.
> – I mean of course, the other hastened to affirm, work in the widest possible
> sense. Also literary labour, not merely for the kudos of the thing. Writing for the
> newspapers which is the readiest channel nowadays. That's work too. Important
> work. After all, from the little I know of you, after all the money expended on your
> education, you are entitled to recoup yourself and command your price. You have
> every bit as much right to live by your pen in pursuit of your philosophy as the
> peasant has. What? You both belong to Ireland, the brain and the brawn. Each is
> equally important. (U, 644–45)

Bloom misreads Stephen as a young writer connected to the Revival. Yet Stephen has
distinct reservations about the Revival's underlying assertion that the writer is obliged to
do the work of the nation. He is much more committed to his capacity for impotentiality;
he tells Bloom, 'you suspect that I may be important because I belong to the *faubourg Saint
Patrice* called Ireland for short ... but I suspect ... that Ireland must be important because it
belongs to me'. He is stressing here his still-unrealized capacity to make Ireland an object
of representation, rather than to work on its behalf. Consequently, Bloom's attempt to
speak about work and the nation is doomed to fail; as Stephen finally puts it at the end of
the vignette, 'we can't change the country. Let us change the subject' (U, 645).

   While this discussion is fleeting, it nevertheless provides an important frame for a
discussion of the cultural politics of *Ulysses*. Most importantly, Bloom suggests that the
intellectual worker should be considered just as necessary to the work of the nation as the
peasant, the traditional labourer of Irish cultural nationalist rhetoric. Bloom takes for
granted that 'all must work, have to, together'. Bloom understands that the literary work
of the Revival — that form of cultural production that takes place in what Bourdieu would
call 'the restricted field of literary production' — involves the production of symbolic
value.[46] Just as his own position in the emerging field of advertising depends upon a
form of immaterial labour committed to the production of the affective dimension of
commodities rather than the commodities themselves, Bloom suggests in 'Eumaeus' that
the intellectuals associated with the Revival through their forms of immaterial labour
produce the symbolic values necessary for political and social transformation. Literary

46 See Bourdieu, *The Field of Cultural Production*, 115–20.

work is part of the work of the nation. The Revival, in this sense, supplies what Benjamin would call the *Ehrfahrung* of a national(ist) conception of history — those narratives that serve as a record of historical continuity and provide a rationale and justification for national belonging.

Stephen's response to Bloom suggests that he understands the Revival in precisely the same manner — it is just that he is not interested in working within this particular economy of symbolic value. While Bloom's understanding of literary labour presupposes that a complete withdrawal into a disinterested, purely aesthetic position is not possible for the writer, Stephen's rejection of the more familiar *Ehrfahrungen* of the Revival — with its emphasis on a traditional past that serves to fuel a forward-looking modernization — does not denote a rejection of national specificity or even of politics. If it stands as a refusal to do the work of the nation as demanded by the Revival and certain forms of cultural nationalism, it does not stand as the affirmation of a certain kind of cosmopolitanism that identifies with the empire (Buck Mulligan is the main representative of this). Instead, Stephen's recalcitrance signals the desire for an alternative form of intellectual labour that seeks to respond more effectively to the material reality of colonial Dublin. His desire for new aesthetic forms or interpretative methods responds specifically to his need to apprehend and represent the present. His sense of the present, in both personal and historical terms, is haunted by the past and has a seemingly uncertain future. Yet it is characterized most strongly by a sense of immediacy. In other words, Stephen's thoughts about the nature of intellectual labour throughout the day are more concerned with the present temporal heterogeneity of what Benjamin called *Erlebnis*, rather than the teleological sense of *Ehrfahrung* that characterizes so many narratives of the Revival. The sensation of living within *Erlebnis* is not unique to Stephen. Bloom's experiences and perceptions throughout the day clearly register *Erlebnis*, particularly in the manner that it conditions the form of Joyce's writing. It would be possible to understand Bloom's *flânerie* as a slightly different form of idleness, and to delineate the sensation of *Erlebnis* as a structural element of the novel. To focus on Stephen's response to *Erlebnis* provides a slightly different interpretative opportunity. Stephen possesses a greater awareness of the temporality of *Erlebnis* than Bloom, and it motivates his speculation about aesthetic innovation early in the novel. Moreover, as a lazy idle schemer, Stephen enables Joyce to interrogate the formation of literary intellectuals and respond to the production of symbolic value during the Revival.

An overwhelming sense of the impoverishment of a colonial form of *Erlebnis* predominates throughout the novel. There is very little suggestion of the vibrancy of the Revival in the version of Dublin represented in *Ulysses*; it is something that primarily takes place outside the focus of the narrative.[47] The Dublin of *Ulysses* does not seem to be far removed from that of *Dubliners*: frozen, static, repressed, underdeveloped, and bereft of a

---

47   See Mathews, *Revival*.

vitality that would challenge the ideological strictures of Jansenist Catholicism or British imperialism. Transformation or change — whether in the personal lives of the respective characters or in a social or political collective sense — does not seem to be impending or even possible. The temporal limits of the narrative of the novel — one random day in 1904 — intensify the sense of historical foreclosure. While Dublin, Ireland, and all those who live within it in *Ulysses* have pasts — and that history has left its traces everywhere within the internal and external lives represented within the city — Joyce, writing from a vantage point ten years or more into the future, provides very little clue as to what lies ahead. On the one hand, we are left with uncertainty about what the future will bring. On the other hand, Stephen's final thought — his memory of reading the prayer for the dead at his mother's death — is the same as one of his first thoughts of the day. The combination of uncertainty and repetition help to construct a general sense of a temporal impasse. Time does not pass in a continuous sequence, but rather seems to be fixed into an ongoing sense of the 'now'. One might argue that it is the role of the 'mythic method' and Homeric correspondences to provide a sense of temporal progression; however, the Homeric references do not ultimately 'work'. The most important thematic connections between *Ulysses* and *The Odyssey* (such as the meeting of Telemachus and Odysseus, the slaughter of the suitors, or the erotic reunion between Odysseus and Penelope) are those that fail to develop. This distinction between a sense of continuous history characterized by the progression of events and a seemingly endless sense of immediate history or experience in which nothing ever seems to change is Benjamin's distinction between *Ehrfahrung* and *Erlebnis*. If one of the primary representational goals of the Revival is a narrative form of *Ehrfahrung* that accounts for the possibility of historical progress and change, the version of Dublin represented in *Ulysses* registers a much more prominent form of *Erlebnis*, which suggests that Revivalist efforts will be doomed to failure. According to Benjamin, the distinction between *Ehrfahrung* and *Erlebnis* has to do with the relation between work and temporality. The teleological sense of progress and continuity one finds in *Ehrfahrung* is 'the outcome of work'; *Erlebnis*, on the other hand, 'is the phantasmagoria of the idler'.[48]

The Dublin represented in *Ulysses* is an instance of 'the phantasmagoria of the idler', and the term 'lazy idle schemer', a phrase associated with Stephen's childhood, which he remembers throughout the day, identifies him as a type of aspiring intellectual who refuses to work as do writers identified with the Revival. Bloom's attitude towards work in 'Eumaeus' is a gentler version of Stephen's first encounter as a child with the view that 'all must work' — the infamous 'pandybat' incident in *A Portrait of the Artist as a Young Man*. By 16 June 1904, however, Stephen's dissolute behaviour suggests that the phrase 'lazy idle schemer' more accurately identifies the young adult than it had the young child. It certainly presents a more accurate designation than the name of 'artist'. It has long been suggested that the title *A Portrait of the Artist as a Young Man* presents a gloss upon that

48 AP, 801.

book's ironic representation of Joyce's pseudo-autobiographical character. Joyce criticism often takes Stephen's role as an artist for granted — despite the fact that over the course of two novels Stephen only manages to write two very derivative poems of questionable quality.[49] While Stephen certainly performs the role of artist in conversation and manner in both novels, his failure to produce any work rather undermines his claim. Stephen's desire for alternative forms of representation and interpretation, his interrogation of the manner in which literary intellectuals produce symbolic values, his aimless wandering throughout the day, and — most of all — his inability to write, all contribute to his status as a lazy idle schemer.

Unlike the Yeatsian intellectual, who can more properly be said to have earnestly set forth to forge in the smithy of his soul the uncreated conscience of his race to a much greater degree than Stephen Dedalus ever did, the lazy idle schemer is a figure of negation, recalcitrant to both the conventions of social propriety and the canonical values of the Revival. The lazy idle schemer refuses the imperative to do the work of the nation and instead poses the question of whether or not alternative forms of intellectual labour resistant to the progressive drive of modernization might be possible. As a model of a particular kind of intellectual characterized by his inactivity rather than his productivity, Stephen serves as an archetypal character, emblematic of Irish modernism, for a number of works that came after *Ulysses*. He is certainly not the first idler of note in Irish literature. Stephen's social position, unlike that of the earlier idle aesthetes, is not maintained by the luxury of privilege. More importantly, Stephen's idleness in *Ulysses* signals his dissent from the values and commitments of the more familiar Yeatsian intellectual, and thus opens up the possibility of the kinds of formal innovation and thematic recalcitrance that would characterize Irish modernism after Joyce. The refusal of the politicized values associated with the cultural nationalism of the Revival initially suggests that the lazy idle schemer might be just another version of the writer that refuses any engagement with the social through a disinterested retreat into the realm of the purely aesthetic. There was nothing new about this type of literary intellectual. In fact a whole critical tradition has consistently read both Stephen and Joyce himself in such terms. However, Joyce represents Stephen's idleness as rooted in a form of materialism — both corporeal and historical — that is far removed from the versions of disinterest Wilde and Yeats identified with idleness. In *Ulysses*, Joyce's representation of the formation of the lazy idle schemer poses the possibility of a different form of intellectual labour grounded in a materialist awareness of the world and the body. For Joyce, idleness becomes a means to register an innovative type of modernist work not yet recognized as such. Rather than simply producing different values, the labour of lazy idle scheming involves the critique of the production of value rather than the production of value itself. This critique takes place through a performative critical analysis of the terms in which intellectual labour

---

49   On the essential irony of *A Portrait of the Artist as a Young Man*, see Kenner, *Dublin's Joyce*, 109–33.

is understood and it opens up the possibility of alternatives not yet recognized as legitimate. Lazy idle schemers like Stephen are therefore not actually literary artists, even if they presume themselves to be so or desperately desire it as a vocation. Instead, lazy idle schemers never really actualize their potentiality. They embody the negation of that more traditional, aesthetically minded intellectual who works to create acceptable and conventional symbolic values that have a social and political importance in their art.

Since what I am calling the lazy idle schemer does not actually work as an artist and resists other forms of employment, it is difficult to say what this would-be intellectual actually does. Yet Marx's theorization of 'unproductive' labour provides terms that help to clarify the distinctions between Stephen's idleness and the immaterial labour of other characters in the book. In 'Results of the Immediate Process of Production', the draft of what would have been the final section of the first volume of *Capital*, Marx briefly considers the question of what relation 'unproductive' labour has to his preferred model of productive labour, analysed so extensively throughout the rest of his writing.[50] Marx argues that there are two different forms of intellectual labour. One type of immaterial activity 'results in commodities which exist separately from the producer, i.e. they can circulate in the interval between production and consumption as commodities, e.g. books, paintings, and all products of art distinct from the artistic achievement of the practising artist'.[51] Since this form of intellectual labour contributes to the production of surplus value, in that it results in commodities, it is consistent with Marx's definition of 'productive labour' and could include not only the artistic endeavours but also other kinds of creative activities that contribute to the value of a commodity (like, say, advertising). The other type of immaterial labour Marx identifies is less important, since he regards it as a form of 'unproductive labour' that does not produce surplus value; it occurs when 'the product is not separable from the act of producing', which is to say, when activities find fulfilment in themselves and do not result in a separate, objectified commodity.[52] This performative type of immaterial labour includes certain forms of art (such as music, dance, or drama), but also includes the work of those who provide various types of service, ranging from domestic to educational work. Marx more or less neglects this category of labour, but it has become perhaps the most common mode of production in the post-modern world. Paolo Virno, who calls it work that 'involves a *virtuoso performance*', argues that it is the prototype for waged labour in general in the post-Fordist world.[53]

In the world of *Ulysses*, however, Marx's categories help distinguish Stephen from both the other two primary characters of the novel, as well as other members of the Dublin

---

50 Karl Marx, *Capital: Volume One* (London, 1976), 1038–49. My discussion here is indebted to Paolo Virno's interpretation of virtuosity in 'Virtuosity and Revolution: The Political Theory of Exodus', in Paolo Virno and Michael Hardt, eds., *Radical Thought in Italy: A Potential Politics* (Minneapolis, 1996), 189–212.

51 Marx, *Capital: Volume One*, 1048.

52 Marx, *Capital: Volume One*, 1048.

53 Virno, 'Virtuosity and Revolution', 191, 193. Emphasis in original.

intelligentsia he encounters throughout the day. In his employment as an advertising salesman, Bloom helps to generate the affective aura of a given commodity, a process that contributes to its market value. Such a form of work can be identified with the first category of immaterial labour discussed by Marx — as can the various labours of those characters, whether they are the journalists of 'Aeolus' or the literary intellectuals of 'Scylla and Charybdis', who produce distinct, published texts as a consequence of their work. As a singer and performing artist, Molly Bloom is quite literally a virtuoso and a perfect example of Marx's second category of intellectual labour. But Stephen Dedalus is much harder to place. He aspires to the sort of artistic success that would identify him with the first category of intellectual labour, and he certainly assumes the appropriate airs and rhetoric. Yet this is role-playing more than anything else. In those moments in which he is most noticeably working as an intellectual committed to new representational practices, he enacts interpretive performances; he does not produce a literary work. This performative dimension connects Stephen with the second type of intellectual labour Marx identifies. But ultimately Stephen falls into an intermediate position — which is precisely the category of the lazy idle schemer. Its virtuosity consists of the performance of possibilities that either ultimately amount to nothing or never get completed.

The labours of the lazy idle schemer, such as they are, thus depend upon the virtuosity of the performance of an intellectual role. Somewhat paradoxically, however, nothing more is produced through that work of virtuosity than the performance of a potentiality that will never be actualized. In turn, the form of impotentiality refuses the process by which symbolic value is customarily produced. If the work of the Revival centres upon the refashioning of selective elements of the national character in order to construct a progressive conception of the character of a nation that would become actualized through the state, lazy idle scheming consists of placing an emphasis upon idleness, an otherwise useless component of the national character, in order to launch a critique of the production of values that contribute to state-centred nationalism. Although Stephen is first called a 'lazy idle schemer' in A Portrait of the Artist as a Young Man, it is not until the 'Telemachiad' that one begins to see the unworking of conventional models of the literary intellectual, a concern for an alternative, non-teleological understanding of history, the desire for a new form of representation, and a growing dissatisfaction with those possibilities of work that did exist for a young Irish intellectual. Later, 'Aeolus' and 'Scylla and Charybdis' explore aspects of the temporal concepts of Erlebnis and Ehrfahrung, respectively. Although his 'work' in both episodes — spoken performances delivered in an idle context, describes it more accurately — only rehearses Stephen's concerns instead of producing something more definitive and substantial, the parables Stephen tells in each episode have to do with the relationship between history and representation. Despite this inability to achieve all that he sets out to do in either case — actually to complete his work, after all, is not really possible for the lazy idle schemer — Stephen questions the validity of conventional forms of intellectual labour, refuses to work to produce the authorized values sanctioned by the national imperative to work, and contributes to a process of the unworking of the Revival project that clears a space for the emergence of a modernist form of experimentation. The emergence of that more experimental type of representation is thematically registered by the character of Leopold Bloom and formally enacted by the ongoing process of autonomization (already apparent in the textual interruptions first encountered within 'Aeolus' and 'Scylla and Charybdis') that dominates the novel as soon as Stephen decides to 'cease to strive' at the end of 'Scylla and Charybdis'. Before *Ulysses* can be regarded as inaugurating the arrival of the Irish modernist novel, however, it must also be regarded as that text which negates those dominant values, motifs, and forms associated with the Revival in order to clear a conceptual space for something else. For this act of unworking to occur, the very role of the intellectual charged with the production of a national culture must be interrogated and dismantled.

4 'Almosting It': Stephen Dedalus and the Unworking of the Revival

I

The role of the lazy idle schemer depends upon the principle of negation. Frequently, this would-be intellectual celebrates innovation, and his emergence in Irish modernism indicates an implicit demand for new forms of representational labour. While he tends to be critical of the work achieved by those identified with the Revival, he never actually manages to propose an alternative. After all, he would no longer be lazy if he actually accomplished something concrete, like publishing his writing. To be a lazy idle schemer requires the performance of a role, however; Stephen Dedalus enacts an ongoing negation of the values and forms sanctioned by the Yeatsian intellectuals of the Revival. It is perhaps surprising to identify such a stance with the hero of *A Portrait of the Artist as a Young Man*, a novel that ends on one of the most affirmative and triumphant notes in all of Irish literature.

The climactic ending, in which Stephen famously sets off 'to forge in the smithy of my soul the uncreated conscience of my race' (P, 276), stems from a refusal. Stephen dramatically asserts to his friend Cranly, 'I will not serve' either 'my home, my fatherland or my church' (P, 268). Instead, he will commit himself to a new form of intellectual labour and '... I will try to express myself in some mode of life or art as freely as I can and as wholly as I can, using for my defence the only arms I allow myself to use — silence, exile, and cunning' (P, 269). Importantly, his declaration does not depend at this point upon a refusal to work. While he suggests that truly artistic work is not possible for him within prevailing circumstances, he asserts the desire for an innovative form of representational labour committed to an entirely different aesthetic realization of 'the uncreated conscience of my race' — or, in other words, a coherent sense of the national character. By committing himself to 'forge' some form of national consciousness, Stephen's declaration draws upon the different meanings of the word, meaning either 'to make' or 'to falsify'. But work in itself is still a necessary means to self-expression at the end of *Portrait*. Even if its essential irony is conceded, Stephen's idealization of art and his iconoclasm are in line with the tenets of modernism in general. The claims he makes for his own singularity are excessive.

Portrait, says Kiberd, 'offers one of the first major accounts in modern English literature of the emergence of a post-colonial elite'.[1] Though some of the students represented in the novel hope to find employment in the British civil service, many more became members of the new nationalist upper middle class — lawyers, journalists, doctors, and public functionaries. The historian Senia Paseta asserts that, 'due to its position as the primary Catholic university college in Ireland', Joyce's alma mater, University College Dublin, came increasingly to play the 'vital and organic' role in the nation, advocated in 1915 by Eoin MacNeill, the professor of early Irish history.[2] In his theorization of the social function of intellectuals, Gramsci distinguishes between 'traditional intellectuals' ('categories of intellectuals already in existence', who 'put themselves forward as autonomous and independent of the dominant social group'),[3] and 'organic intellectuals', who give every emerging group 'homogeneity and an awareness of its own function not only in the economic but also the social and political fields'.[4] As Ellmann's account of Joyce's university education demonstrates, he had many close friends who would later become organic intellectuals of the nationalist Catholic middle class.[5] While the specific positions of Joyce's friends — such as the militant republican George Clancy or the pacifist internationalist Francis Skeffington — may have differed, they collectively sought to provide a cohesive sense of identity for this emerging social bloc. Just as with the intellectuals of the Revival, whose position seems closer to what Gramsci identifies as that of the 'traditional' intellectual, the organic intellectuals of Joyce's generation sought to transform the disparate elements of the national character into a more canonical notion of the character of the Irish nation that would provide evidence of Ireland's suitability for modernity.[6] Though there was occasional conflict between these two intellectual formations — as in the riots inspired by J. M. Synge's *Playboy of the Western World* in 1907 or the various literary controversies contested by Yeats, John Eglinton, D. P. Moran, and others — they both relied upon the same imagery, expressed similar values, and ultimately shared a commitment to some form of autonomous statehood.

For someone of Joyce's background, becoming a traditional intellectual in the Gramscian sense would have meant the priesthood, a vocation Joyce explicitly rejected.

1 Kiberd, *Inventing Ireland*, 334.
2 Paseta Senia, *Before the Revolution: Nationalism, Social Change, and Ireland's Catholic Elite, 1879–1922* (Cork, 1999), 55. Paseta cites MacNeill's phrase from an article in *National Student* (May 1915), 11.
3 Gramsci, *Selections from the Prison Notebooks*, 7.
4 Gramsci, *Selections from the Prison Notebooks*, 5.
5 Ellmann, *James Joyce*, 61–64.
6 See Deane, *Strange Country*, 49–99.

Joyce and/or his fictional alter ego Stephen Dedalus have been described as Gramscian organic intellectual(s).⁷ But are such identifications appropriate for Joyce?⁸ In early critical polemics like 'The Day of the Rabblement' (1901), he sought to establish a distance from both his contemporaries and the writers of the Revival by idealizing individual isolation as a necessary stance via a reference to Giordano Bruno: 'No man, said the Nolan, can be a lover of the true or the good unless he abhors the multitude; and the artist, though he may employ the crowd, is very careful to isolate himself', and Joyce declares that the literary intellectual should not affirm popular values.⁹ To invoke yet another Gramscian concept, the values Joyce refers to here are precisely those of the 'national popular' — of those various groups and associations of the Revival era which, in one way or another, worked to establish the cultural, political, and economic character of the Irish nation. It is within those movements that one finds the organic intellectuals of early twentieth-century Ireland. It is perhaps more accurate to consider Joyce in terms derived from Bourdieu's theorization of the restricted field of literary production.¹⁰ If Yeats and the various other figures associated with the Revival represented something approximate to Bourdieu's notion of the 'consecrated avant-garde' — those writers, texts, and institutions which dominate the small literary scene committed to the production of highbrow art and to authorize its values — then Joyce presented an instance of that younger type of artist or intellectual who, while recognizing the achievement of the consecrated avant-garde, nevertheless sought to formulate a different type of aesthetic practice in the name of innovation. Joyce's remarks about Yeats in 'The Day of the Rabblement', which recognize the power of his writing but find fault with his growing alliance with the popular movements associated with the Revival, confirm such a reading.¹¹

Yet there is more to Joyce's rejection of the values of the Revival than a youthful pose of individual martyrdom in the name of art or a de facto rejection of what was then currently fashionable within Irish culture. He objected to the Revival's view of history, not to Irish nationalism as such.¹² To him the past was not an abstract source of tradition that would culminate in the nation-state. Instead, it was the basis for the 'mean influences',

---

7   Emer Nolan, *James Joyce and Nationalism*, 24, for example, takes Joyce's status as an organic intellectual for granted: Nolan's understanding of the concept seems to rely upon the social *position* of the intellectual rather than, as Gramsci has it, the social *function* of the intellectual.

8   See David Lloyd and Paul Thomas, *Culture and the State* (London, 1998), 27.

9   Joyce, *Occasional, Critical, and Political Writing*, 50.

10   See Bourdieu, *The Field of Cultural Production*, 121.

11   Joyce, *Occasional, Critical, and Political Writing*, 51: 'It is equally unsafe at present to say of Mr. Yeats that he has or has not genius. In aim and form, *The Wind Among the Reeds* is poetry of the highest order, and *The Adoration of the Magi* ... shows what Mr. Yeats can do when he breaks with the half-gods. But an aesthete has a floating will, and Mr. Yeats' treacherous instinct of adaptability must be blamed for his recent association with a platform from which even self-respect should have urged him to refrain.'

12   See, in particular, Nolan's *James Joyce and Nationalism*, which effectively corrects several generations of Joyce criticism through its detailed historical reading of the impact cultural nationalism made upon Joyce's writing.

the inheritance of 'a broken will', and 'servitude' (all phrases he uses in 'Day of the Rabblement') that characterize the squalid present. History was the source of the various material determinations that paralysed late colonial Irish society.

In 1904, Joyce wrote an autobiographical essay entitled 'A Portrait of the Artist', which he submitted to Eglinton's journal *Dana*, a publication that was not exactly opposed to the Revival but had a place for younger writers seeking to challenge some of its tenets. Eglinton's rejection of the piece inspired Joyce to start working on the autobiographical novel *Stephen Hero*, which eventually evolved into *A Portrait of the Artist as a Young Man*. The essay is hyperbolic, immature, and occasionally incoherent; yet it states a crucial concept that helps clarify both the role of the lazy idle schemer and, ultimately, his representation of temporality. Writing of the difficulty of representing childhood, Joyce says 'that we cannot or will not conceive the past in any other than its iron memorial aspect'. Thus narratives committed to the representation of memory are fictions that rely upon the formal structure of an a priori 'iron memorial aspect' of a past that has already been interpreted to confirm an understanding of the present. Similarly, in the project of cultural reclamation, elements of Irish history are interpreted and refashioned through an 'iron memorial' version of tradition in order to help form the collective national imaginary for the present. In contrast, since 'the past assuredly implies a fluid succession of presents, the development of an entity of which our actual present is a phase only', Joyce implies that his goal is to represent the past as it was first experienced. This involves a commitment to innovation and precision (not tradition) through a representational practice that 'seek[s] through some art, by some process of the mind as yet untabulated, to liberate from the personalized lumps of matter that which is their individuating rhythm, the first or formal relation of their parts'. Joyce's 'as yet untabulated' form of intellectual labour would strive to represent the social totality of a given moment in which various conditions of possibility become manifest.[13]

Joyce suggests that self-imposed isolation ('the first principle of artistic economy') and the arrival of socialism will create the conditions in which he might discover the artistic practice he seeks.[14] Ultimately, his observations about temporality in 'A Portrait of the Artist' anticipate his development of the formal technique of the epiphany in the stories of *Dubliners* and the structural organization of *Portrait* which seek to represent Stephen's past as 'a succession of presents', rather than as a diachronic narrative. But what is remarkable about the distinction between conceiving of the past through its 'iron memorial aspect' and regarding it as a series of presents, is how closely it resembles Benjamin's distinction between *Ehrfahrung* and *Erlebnis*. Just as the progressive narratives of *Ehrfahrung* no longer manage accurately to represent the temporality of modernity within capitalism, diachronic conceptions of the past arrived at through the 'iron memorial aspect' are conditioned by

13   James Joyce, *Poems and Shorter Writings*, eds. Richard Ellmann and A. Walton Litz (London, 1991), 210–11.
14   Joyce, *Poems and Shorter Writings*, 215.

the interpretative limits of the contemporary moment but fail satisfactorily to explain how it came about. Benjamin argues that the experience of time within modernity is more akin to the ongoing sense of *Erlebnis*, in which the past is knowable through an inventory of the traces history has deposited in the present. Joyce makes a similar claim; the present is only the latest phase in 'a fluid succession of presents'. Idleness, the opposite of the labour that drives development and one of the characteristic features of *Erlebnis*, is a condition that seeks to prolong the sense of the present. It becomes for Stephen the condition that allows the possibility of alternative ways of representing time.

Thus, Joyce claims, the past is not a repository of malleable material to be reshaped for a contemporary understanding of 'tradition'. Its distinctness, even recalcitrance, have to be acknowledged. But his speculations about the relationship between art and temporality brought him closer to Yeats than he may have wanted to admit. For Yeats, the contemplation of proper art produced a state in which the self blends into the timeless collectivity of what he would eventually call 'Spiritus Mundi'. Joyce sought for a different structure of feeling and a different form of collectivity in the workings of art.

In his 1903 Paris notebooks, he distinguishes between loathing and desire and terror, pity, and joy in a passage that would be integrated virtually unchanged into *Portrait*. Loathing and desire are the emotions created by improper forms of tragedy and comedy, while terror, pity, and joy are the affective consequences of proper forms of those respective genres. Loathing and desire are improper to Joyce because they inspire action in time. Terror, pity, and joy, however, produce something quite other:

> All art, again, is static for the feelings of terror and pity on the one hand and the feeling of joy on the other hand are feelings which arrest us. Afterwards it will appear how this rest is necessary for the apprehension of the beautiful — the end of all art, tragic or comic — for this rest is the only condition under which the images, which are to excite in us terror or pity or joy, can be properly presented to us and properly seen by us.

Rest — or, in other terms, the condition of idleness — is here presented as a rarefied state outside the flow of time; that condition in turn enables one to leave behind desire and other 'kinetic' attributes.[15] As with Wilde and Yeats, the achievement of the condition and value of disinterest is being tested. The problem for Joyce is that the tendency towards abstraction evident within his speculations about disinterest is incompatible with the materialist approach to temporality of the essay 'A Portrait of the Artist'. Ultimately, Joyce's materialism won out. Disinterest is an aesthetic concept but it is nevertheless an ideological value as well. Dedalus is the figure in whom Joyce begins his unworking of this central aesthetic commonplace of the Revival.

15 See Joyce, *Occasional, Critical, and Political Writing*, 102.

Ultimately, Stephen's idleness in *Ulysses* does not represent the rarefied form of contemplation advocated by Wilde and Yeats, but rather a repudiation of the social role of the literary intellectual: 'When we come to the phenomena of artistic conception, artistic gestation and artistic reproduction I require a new terminology and a new personal experience' (P, 227). The category of disinterest emerges in slightly reconstituted form as a central facet of Stephen's aesthetic philosophy. Aquinas allows him to articulate a specifically Catholic intellectual approach, but Stephen deflects it towards the aesthetic principle of disinterest. He makes a key distinction between 'kinetic' emotions such as desire or loathing aroused by 'pornographic or didactic' kinds of art, and 'static' emotions that are aroused in the contemplation of 'proper' art: 'The mind is arrested and raised above desire and loathing' (P, 222). The artist too achieves a disinterested distance from the work of art itself: 'The artist, like the God of the creation, remains within or behind or beyond or above his handiwork, invisible, refined out of existence, indifferent, paring his fingernails' (P, 233).

Both the creation of art and the contemplation of art — which mean, according to Stephen's understanding of Aquinas, the capacity to apprehend a given work of art's wholeness (*integritas*), harmonious integration of different elements (*consonantia*), and specific 'whatness' (*quiddatas*) that the mind perceives as that thing and no other (*claritas*) — take one away from the material, physical world into a universal realm in which disinterest is complete. Since different cultures perceive beauty according to different standards, the aesthetic emotions aroused by art will be conditioned by local particularities, 'these relations of the sensible' (P, 227). These allow for the possibility of national specificity in art. Just as in Yeats's understanding of an ultimately disinterested universal condition, arrived at through the creation and contemplation of specifically national motifs, the art Stephen speaks of will necessarily arise out of local conditions and qualities to arrive at a more universal 'aesthetic' condition. His grand ambition, after all, is 'to forge the uncreated conscience of *my* race' (P, 276; my emphasis). In his view, no specifically Irish work had yet achieved the universal condition of disinterest.

It is difficult to take the (ironized) details of Stephen's aesthetic seriously. Even his villanelle seems to contradict his initial statements about the inappropriate nature of the 'kinetic' emotions in relation to art. Once Stephen begins to stumble in his efforts, he revives his inspiration through the very kinetic act of masturbation. The artist, in this case, has done anything but refine himself out of existence. The dominant point of view (which passes from third person to the first-person observations of his diary at the close) inverts the progression from first person to third person that Stephen favours in his discussion of what makes proper narrative art. From its title to its narrative trajectory, almost everything about *Portrait* identifies it as an early modernist *Bildungsroman*. Usually in such a work, the mature protagonist is accommodated to the social order and the public sphere through the third-person point of view. But Stephen's musings are in the self-obsessed, first-person form of the diary.[16] The novel demonstrates that Stephen's aesthetic principles are unsustainable.

2

The central discussion about aesthetics in *Portrait* breaks off when Lynch notes the massive gap between Stephen's assertions and the social reality they both inhabit. 'What do you mean, Lynch asked surlily, by prating about beauty and the imagination in this miserable Godforsaken island? No wonder the artist retired within or behind his handiwork after having perpetrated this country' (P, 233). This objection provides a fundamental context for 'Telemachus', the opening section of *Ulysses*. Here history asserts itself with a vengeance. An overwhelming sense of the present prevails. In Benjaminian terms, a condition of *Erlebnis* marks the opening of *Ulysses* and not of the *Ehrfahrung* of the end of *Portrait*. As I have suggested, the characteristic turn-of-the-century Dublin *Erlebnis* is conditioned by the complicity between colonialism and capitalism. Many critics have noted the prominence within 'Telemachus' of a number of details that mark the experience of a young intellectual in a late colonial context.[17] What is less recognized is that Stephen consistently attempts to respond by returning to some of the aesthetic questions discussed at the end of *Portrait*.

At first, idleness appears to be a mark of privilege rather than a form of refusal. Stephen, after all, is the only resident of the Martello Tower who has to go to work, while Buck Mulligan, and Haines, his associate from Oxford, are committed to a day of idleness. But their idleness is not that of the lazy idle schemer. It is much closer to the sort of leisure (*Musse*) that Benjamin argues is distinct from *Mussiggang*, since it is complicit with the labour process by providing a brief respite of limited duration before the progressive temporality of the labour process continues. While the inactivity of Haines and Mulligan is characterized by a studied bohemianism and a calculated but ultimately safe iconoclasm, there is nothing recalcitrant about it. They play the colonial roles of (as Stephen puts it) 'conqueror and gay betrayer' (U, 14). In addition, Haines's knowledge of Irish, affection for the works of Douglas Hyde and other Revivalists, and habit of recording his observations of the natives identify him as an eager supporter of the Revival. Mulligan, by contrast, ridicules the Revival, but his enthusiasm for classical Greek culture, the poetry of Swinburne, and his taste for 'rebellious' clothing such as 'puce gloves and green boots' (U, 16, 17) mark him as a devotee of late nineteenth-century aestheticism. They remind Stephen of Wilde and Yeats respectively. His famous identification of 'the cracked

16   See Franco Moretti, *The Way of the World: The* Bildungsroman *in European Culture* (London, 1987), 3–13.
17   See Duffy, *The Subaltern* Ulysses, 23–52; Vincent Cheng, *Joyce, Race, and Empire* (Cambridge, 1995), 151–62; and Gibson, *Joyce's Revenge*, 23–37.

looking-glass of a servant' as 'a symbol of Irish art' (U, 6) has its origins in Wilde's 'The Decay of Lying', where life is declared to be an imitation of art.[18]

Stephen's declaration seems to suggest that the cultivated form of disinterest that Wilde finds in superior art has not been translated successfully into Irish terms, for the Revival does no more than reflect the sordid reality of one who must work for others. He generally dismisses the Revival out of hand (at least when speaking about it openly), but he demonstrates slightly more respect for Yeats in this episode than elsewhere. Notably, he remembers that he sang an arrangement of Yeats's poem 'Who Goes with Fergus?' in order to comfort his dying mother. Later, in his exchange with the elderly milk-seller about what obligation the artist has to the nation, he uses, perhaps mockingly, images from Yeats's recently produced *Cathleen ni Houlihan* ('Silk of the kine and poor old woman, names given her in old times. A wandering crone, lowly form of an immortal ...') (U, 14). All these examples emphasize the dominance of the lowly material world as against the forms of abstract disinterest Wilde and Yeats promoted in their aesthetic theories. In Stephen's response to Mulligan's exhortation to 'Hellenise' he associates Mulligan with his friend Cranly (U, 7), which in turn connects with Stephen's speculation about the relationship between male friendship and 'Wilde's love that dare not speak its name' (U, 49). Yeats's work provokes different associations. Stephen's thoughts about 'Who Goes with Fergus?' lead directly to his memory of the deterioration of his mother's body before her death. He resents that the milk-seller, emblem of Ireland, Cathleen ni Houlihan herself, appears to pay more respect to Mulligan and Haines than to him. This highlights the popular attraction of an art that converts woman into an abstract symbol that transcends material reality, and which would 'shrive and oil for the grave all there is of her but her woman's unclean worlds' (U, 14). But Stephen's thoughts and memories of Wilde or Yeats are entangled with his own torment that has, as a dominant element, a phobia regarding the material reality of the body, especially the female body. An aesthetic like his, predicated upon an avowed disinterest that is in actuality more like distaste or disdain, does not allow for the possibility of liberation, but rather serves to reinforce the depression, guilt, and misogyny that afflict Stephen periodically throughout *Ulysses*. Stephen's melancholy at the beginning conditions much of his behaviour throughout the day, and his laziness in later episodes retains this taint of misery.

Stephen tells Haines, 'you behold in me ... a horrible example of free thought' (U, 20), and complains that he is condemned to work as a 'servant' on behalf of the imperial British state, the Catholic Church, and/or the Irish nationalist movement. Yet the formulation of another innovative form of intellectual labour presents significant dangers for Stephen. In the middle of the conversation with Haines ('it seems that history is to blame', U, 20),

---

18 'I can quite understand your objection to art being treated as a mirror. You think it would reduce genius to the position of a cracked looking-glass. But you don't mean to say that you believe that Life imitates Art, that Life in fact is the mirror, and Art the reality?' (*CWW*, 982).

Stephen is ruminating at length about the sin of heresy. On the one hand, he considers that the Catholic Church is so powerful that even the British Empire pales in comparison and he imagines the damnation 'the brood of mockers' (U, 21) face for their respective heresies. Heresy is 'Idle mockery. The Void awaits surely all them that weave the wind: a menace, a disarming and a worsting from those embattled angels of the church, Michael's host, who defend her ever in the hour of conflict with their lances and their shields' (U, 21). Stephen will return to the concept of 'the Void' throughout *Ulysses*; it comes to represent much more than the hell of Catholicism. The privileged leisure of Mulligan is readily dismissed as a form of 'idle mockery' that will finally achieve nothing, despite its trendy iconoclasm; but a real danger faces those who strive to produce a new form of cultural expression. Yet Stephen's thoughts about heresy also imply — although much more subtly — that if innovation is ever to be possible, those 'weavers of the wind' must abandon established conventions. He imagines Palestrina's mass for Pope Marcellus playing in the background as 'the vigilant angel of the church militant disarmed and menaced her heresiarchs' (U, 21). That mass itself exemplifies how a work of art can signal the transition from heresy to innovation. It marks the precise moment in which polyphony, a form of musical composition previously considered impure and heretical by the Church, won favour with the papacy. But Stephen never arrives at a confident sense of what form innovation, arising out of his own heretical stance, might take. Yet, never to actualize one's potentiality in the formulation of a new aesthetic — to fall back upon one's impotentiality instead, for better or worse — is part of the point for the lazy idle schemer. The first move is to interrogate standard models of intellectual labour. Neither the Wildean nor the Yeatsian models provide him with the impetus to overcome the conceptual problems posed by the materiality and uncertainty of history. Although Stephen never manages to formulate a coherent theoretical response to these problems, Joyce himself does, through the stylistic shift that begins in the novel precisely after 'Scylla and Charybdis'. Before that shift occurs, we see Stephen improvise in response two different forms of intellectual labour, each of which involves virtuoso performances that mock and deride prevailing models of the literary intellectual. These performances do not constitute an account of an alternative, but they do provide a foundation for one. It is in 'Nestor' and 'Proteus' and in the remaining sections of the so-called 'Telemachiad' that he undertakes his initial critique. Notably, it queries the differences between work and idleness.

The relationship between work, temporality and history provides the focus of 'Nestor'. In this episode, Stephen teaches a curriculum that celebrates empire, with its focus on Roman history and Milton's *Lycidas*. The idea of Aristotle's theorization of potentiality preoccupies him, particularly the notion that *not* doing something provides the possibility of escape from an abject or dominated condition of being.[19] While teaching his students

19   See Agamben, 'On Potentiality', 179–81.

about the Battle of Asculum from the 'gorescarred' (U, 24) history textbook, Stephen thinks of events that have and that might not have happened:

> Had Pyrrhus not fallen by a beldam's hand in Argos or Julius Caesar not been knifed to death? They are not to be thought away. Time has branded them and fettered they are lodged in the room of infinite possibilities they have ousted but can those have been possible seeing that they never were? Or was that only possible which came to pass? Weave, weaver of wind. (U, 25)

He needs to construct a narrative that at once explains the differences between actuality and potentiality and that might evoke an alternative to 'the ruin of all space, shattered glass and toppling masonry, and time one livid final flame' (U, 24) that typifies history. Yet, the incantation to 'weave, weaver of wind' suggests, when considered in light of its earlier appearance in 'Telemachus', the possibility of heresy.

Stephen decides that it is through movement that potentiality becomes actualized — or, to put in terms more consistent with the episode, the process by which history occurs:

> It must be a movement then, an actuality of the possible as possible. Aristotle's phrase formed itself within the gabbled verses and floated out into the studious silence of the library of Saint Genevieve where he had read, sheltered from the sin of Paris, night by night ... Fed and feeding brains about me: under glowlamps, impaled, with faintly beating feelers: and in my mind's darkness a sloth of the underworld, reluctant, shy of brightness, shifting her dragon scaly folds. Thought is the thought of thought. Tranquil brightness. The soul is in a manner all that is: the soul is the form of forms. Tranquillity sudden, vast, candescent: form of forms. (U, 25–26)

Thinking about Aristotle, he remembers reading the *Physics* in Paris; this in turn leads him to confront, from the text itself and from his own vision of his past self, the question of his own potentiality. He envisages his own mind as a reptilian creature in the dark, caught in a state of immobile sloth. His thoughts, so entrapped, cannot be actualized (or so he thinks; the episode is full of such mirror effects). As the citizens of Dublin are paralysed, so Stephen is caught in a state of impotentiality, figured both as the metaphorical sloth of his mind and in his idleness throughout the rest of the day. Yet the question of how impotentiality in the form of idleness might acquire a more productive dimension becomes a crucial issue for him thereafter. It is a problem the lazy idle schemer has to face; 'Nestor' makes it abundantly clear that work will not provide an effective solution to his abjection. History — at least in its most dominant, oppressive form — is ineradicably associated with labour and the 'common sense' of work-logic; moreover, the obligation to work is even more dissatisfying than the idleness of sloth.

Everything about Stephen's job as a schoolteacher is stifling and depressing. His sense of personal inadequacy, arising from the sort of labour he must perform, his revulsion at the ignorance, misogyny and racism of his employer, his role within the ongoing reproduction of colonial ideology, and a general overriding sense of alienation, together make a sorry catalogue of woe. Mr. Deasy offers the 'common sense' of the imperative to work arduously and enthusiastically. The logic of work, as he understands it, is simple and expresses itself as money: 'Because you don't save, Mr. Deasy said, pointing his finger. You don't know yet what money is. Money is power, when you have lived as long as I have. I know, I know. If youth but knew. But what does Shakespeare say? Put but money in thy purse' (U, 30).

Mr. Deasy demonstrates a basic commitment to what Benjamin would have identified as a progressive historicist understanding of temporality, one in which 'all history marches towards one great goal, the manifestation of God' (U, 34).[20] Progress, racism, misogyny, the legacy of colonial rule and the conventional belief that one must inevitably work hard, generally in conditions not of one's choosing, are all implied, even explicit in some respects, in Mr. Deasy's advice to Stephen. This is the false form of *Ehrfahrung*, which justifies and attempts to disguise the abjection and stasis of the present. But for Stephen, work signifies repetition of the same form of misery over and over. It only reinforces the static condition of slothful abjection he has thought about in relation to the concepts of potentiality and impotentiality; he thinks to himself, upon receiving his wages, 'the same room and hour, the same wisdom: and I the same. Three times now. Three nooses around my neck here' (U, 30). In this sense of repetition, the alienation caused by work echoes that produced by history, in which brutality, conquest, violence and death recur over and over again. Thus Deasy's version of history is diachronic; Stephen thinks of it as the ongoing synchronic 'nightmare from which I am trying to awake' (U, 34). In other words, history is for him the *Erlebnis* of pain, misery, domination, and alienation; what he desires most is a form of representation that will allow him to escape from that condition, that does not reproduce the idea of temporality as an implacably progressive force of which the present is always the culmination.

Yeats and the Revivalists also desired a new form of *Ehrfahrung* that overcomes the *Erlebnis* of colonial modernity. But the Yeatsian intellectual ultimately ties representation to an ideal form of disinterest — a nationally particular, rather than universal, form of disinterest, but disinterest nevertheless — that attempts to transcend the materiality of immediate historical conditions without effectively registering their actuality. Moreover, the central value produced by the Revivalist imperative to do the work of the nation is the construction of an authorized conception of the Irish past in the form of tradition. As Stephen reflects in 'Telemachus', the images and rhetoric of the Revival do not correspond effectively to the actuality of the present. For his purposes, neither the employment

---

20   On Benjamin's critique of progressive historicism, see 'Theses on the Philosophy of History', in I, 260–61.

offered by Mr. Deasy nor the work of the Revival provide an understanding of temporality that would allow for the literary representation of late colonial Dublin.

3

Joyce provides a comprehensive anatomy of Stephen's abjection and slothfulness in 'Proteus'. It offers the first clues about how the lazy idle schemer will begin to discover an entirely new model of the modernist intellectual. The phrase 'morose delectation' (U, 47), Aquinas's term for the habit of dwelling upon evil thoughts, extends to the episode as a whole; its so-called 'male monologue' catalogues Stephen's feelings of guilt, sexual repression, threatened ambition, his unfulfilled desire for erotic love, guilt about his relationship with his dead mother, and extreme disappointment that he failed to achieve his artistic goals during his time in Paris. 'You were going to do wonders, what?' Stephen thinks, as he compares himself ironically to medieval Irish saints like Columbanus, and Duns Scotus (U, 42). The triumphalist/triumphant ending of Portrait affirms Stephen's sense that he could emulate such figures, but 'Proteus' suggests that his efforts have already failed. His inability to work as an artist — his slothfulness in respect to his creativity — continues to define his depression.

The understanding of history that predominates in 'Nestor' is vastly different from the sensation of time-in-flux that governs the structure of 'Proteus'. As Agamben argues, 'like time, whose essence is pure negation, history can never be grasped in the instant, but only as a total social process. It thereby remains at one remove from the lived experience of the single individual, whose ideal is happiness.'[21] At stake for Stephen is the question of representation: how can he begin to map the totality of history as a social process? He takes the materiality of the body as a starting point to ponder the relation between a broad conception of history and his own personal experiences. He is haunted by his own memories throughout the episode; he remembers his time in Paris, the details of his pretentious youthful literary ambitions, and the oscillation between erotic desire and revulsion towards the female body that structures his misogyny. He imagines the arrival several hundred years earlier of Viking invaders on the coast of Ireland and the native inhabitants they encountered ('a horde of jerkined dwarfs, my people'), then he reflects upon the legacy of medieval history: 'Famine, plague and slaughters. Their blood is in me, their lusts my waves' (U, 45). He understands that his personal history is part of a larger ethnic or racial history. That larger long-term understanding of history is attached to the 'paradise of pretenders then and now' (U, 45), the Ireland that periodically supported various doomed claimants to the British throne. Yet as the body bears history within it, as in Stephen's recognition of his corporeal descent from the ancient Irish, so its sheer materiality is the basis for the temporal progression of history.

21 Giorgio Agamben, *Infancy and History: Essays on the Destruction of Experience* (London, 1993), 99.

According to Stephen's Democritean understanding of molecular change, the body is composed of physical matter that is always becoming something else. The life of the body depends upon the ongoing flux of matter that allows it to persist through time; that matter, however, was something else before it became transformed into the living matter of the body, and it will go on to become something else after the corporeal changes that take place through a lifetime. He broods on the reports of a drowned body offshore:

> Bag of corpsegas sopping in foul brine. A quiver of minnows, fat of a spongy titbit, flash through the slits of his buttoned trouserfly. God becomes man becomes fish becomes barnacle goose becomes featherbed mountain. Dead breaths I living breathe, tread dead dust, devour a ruinous offal from all dead. (U, 50)

These imaginings have long been said to connect to the episode's Homeric correspondences or to the theme of metempsychosis.[22] Yet Stephen's thoughts also demonstrate a fundamental *irrelationship* between temporality and matter that makes the possibility of representation even more frail. Given the degree of abjection that characterizes Stephen's feelings about himself in this episode, he emphasizes the fact that all living matter, because it has lived before, is already dead, and that he himself is therefore already dead in some respect. Yet it is equally true in this sense that all dead matter is also already alive. Any measurement of temporality in this respect begins with the materiality of the body and its inevitable transformation through time. By implication, one can never awake from the nightmare of history if one is to go on living — or, to put it in the even stronger terms Stephen seems to be proposing here (and which look forward to the works of Beckett), if one is to go on dying. If matter does continue to exist and consistently becomes something else, then language, the means by which matter is classified in its specific form, is also consistently becoming something else. Earlier in the episode, while looking at the beach, Stephen reflects that 'these heavy sands are language tide and wind have silted here. And there the stoneheaps of dead builders, a warren of weasel rats ... Sands and stones. Heavy of the past' (U, 44). Here language presents the one seemingly reliable means of registering the particularity of matter within the forms that matter takes. Yet language cannot register previous incarnations of the same matter when it was something else; it can only speak to the current form matter takes, even if it is haunted by the possibility of what it once might have been in the past. To understand the passage of both time and history in so wholly materialist terms still leaves the problem of finding a form of representation for the processes involved, while still remaining faithful to Stephen's Aristotelian/Aquinian notion of an aesthetic practice that captures the

---

22 Joyce himself identified 'Primal Matter' as the Homeric correspondence to the sea-god Proteus as far back as the Linati schema of 1920, and such reflections upon the principle of transformation evident in Stephen's thoughts make that relationship clear. Meanwhile, Stuart Gilbert's *James Joyce's* Ulysses (New York, 1955), one of the earliest critical explications of *Ulysses*, notes that Stephen's thoughts here are dominated by the theme of metempsychosis.

'whatness', the defining individuality of each singular thing. Joyce himself, it might be said, does not really produce a potential solution to this representational quandary until *Finnegans Wake*. But in Stephen's case, the unresolvable tension between a materialist understanding of temporality and the impediments to representing it through language limit his explorations in aesthetic innovation. At least since the end of *Portrait*, Stephen has been looking for some form of aesthetic practice that would both represent and overcome the abject conditions of his personal life and of Ireland in general. Such an aesthetic practice would need to recognize the seemingly inevitable relationship between corporeality and a progressive temporality, postulate some form of innovative intellectual labour that could diagnose the reality of a given situation, and ultimately seek to transcend those conditions. Stephen's failure to successfully formulate just such an aesthetic in the period between his departure for Paris and the morning of 16 June is one of the sources of his dejection in 'Proteus'.

As 'Nestor' suggests, progressive notions of temporality are derived from work and therefore are ultimately complicit with forms of social domination. The brand of idleness celebrated by figures like Wilde and Yeats, the most prominent models of the literary intellectual Stephen considers throughout the 'Telemachiad', provide a stronger basis for the aesthetic possibilities he seeks. Such a practice would allow him to refuse conventional work in order to prolong a moment that does not pass into abeyance through time. Instead, it would create at least the possibility of attaining the condition of disinterest, in which both personal necessity and a reified conception of identity are overcome. In Wilde's and Yeats's formulations of it, idleness provides a context for the emergence of a superior form of abstraction committed to the goal of disinterestedness. However, as Stephen begins to realize in the opening episodes of *Ulysses*, the condition of disinterest is not really possible, given the inescapable features or limits of a materialist understanding of the body and history. Even those works by Wilde and Yeats he thinks about throughout this section of *Ulysses* lead him back towards the body, physical desire, and history.

In 'Proteus', Stephen continues to draw upon the influence of these role models for the young literary intellectual by fusing imagery, motifs, and values associated with Wilde and Yeats in a brief lyrical fragment. He muses about women in conventional terms as daughters of Eve in their passage from marriage to death: 'Bridebed, childbed, bed of death, ghostcandled. *Omnis caro ad te veniet*. He comes, pale vampire, through storm his eyes, his batsails bloodying the sea, mouth to her mouth's kiss' (U, 47–48). The initial image of the dying mother — like Stephen's memories of his own mother — acquires a gothic dimension. This image later inspires his brief lyric:

> On swift sail flaming
> From storm and south
> He comes, pale vampire,
> Mouth to my mouth.
> (U, 132)

A literary source can be glimpsed here. Douglas Hyde's translation of the anonymous lyric 'Mo Bhrón ar an Bhfarraige' ('My Grief on the Sea') is included in *Love Songs of Connacht*, the book Haines purchases later in the day. The original poem is a lament by a woman whose lover has emigrated. While he sails for America, she is left behind in a state of grief, which gives way to an erotic vision of him that takes her out of her misery into a condition of ecstatic union. In taking on the role of the grieving woman here, Stephen glosses his failed attempt to fly from Ireland and hints at the possibility of a passion that would momentarily allow him imaginatively to escape his present situation. Yet the gothic and homo-erotic dimensions of the poem suggest a connection to Wilde, made more explicitly when, on the very next page, Stephen mentions 'Wilde's love that dare not speak its name' (U, 49). But the connections go deeper; the figure of the vampire is associated with Wilde's youthful rival Bram Stoker rather than Wilde himself, but both writers had connections to a long-standing tradition of Anglo-Irish Protestant gothic writing.[23] The criminal history represented in that tradition, which still weighs on the present, returns as the incarnation of a dangerous yet alluring form of transgressive sexuality.

Taken together, both the Revivalist and gothic interpretations of the poem depend upon an aesthetic practice in which the speaker of the poem, trapped in a melancholy condition, begins to come to an understanding of history that does not depend on teleological narrative, but rather on the momentary juxtaposition of past and present. Yet the allure of that contradiction stops short of successful seduction. It does not ultimately help Stephen to overcome his own abjection, anxieties about the materiality of the body, or his frustration with life in a colonial context. The intertwined sexual frustration and loneliness is briefly countered by the attempt to enjoy the pleasure of aesthetic contemplation when Stephen turns to the imagery of Stéphane Mallarmé's 'L'Après-midi d'un faune', reflecting upon his hope that 'pain is far' (U, 49). But he is quickly reminded of a line from Yeats's 'Who Goes with Fergus?', which, in the 'Telemachus' episode, he had remembered singing to his mother. This in turn provokes the memory of the painful physical realities of her death. His attempt to distract himself by looking at his shoes reminds him that they once belonged to Buck Mulligan; that leads him back to his feelings of panic regarding the possibility that there may be a homo-erotic dimension to their friendship, echoed in the numerous references to Wilde. Thus the evocations of Yeats and Wilde remind him of his inability to escape a painful personal history and his anxieties about sexuality and the body, even though both those authors promoted a version of art as transcendence. For Stephen, it is impossible to overcome the materiality of the body and the progression of history. The Wildean and Yeatsian models of idleness

---

23 On the historical co-ordinates of the uses of the occult in Anglo-Irish Protestant writing up through the Revival, see Roy Foster, 'Protestant Magic: W. B. Yeats and the Spell of Irish History', in *Paddy and Mr. Punch: Connections in Irish and English History* (London, 1993), 212–32. For a more theoretical account of the relationship the Anglo-Irish gothic tradition has to history, see Margot Gayle Backus, *The Gothic Family Romance: Heterosexuality, Child Sacrifice, and the Anglo-Irish Colonial Order* (Durham, NC, 1999), 1–20, 109–43.

have to be inverted if they are to provide the possibility of an innovative, alternative form of intellectual labour. Stephen never overcomes the impasse he faces in 'Proteus'. His attempts to respond to the inevitability of a materialist relationship between the body and history expose the limitations of the Wildean and Yeatsian models.

In 'Proteus', Joyce first suggests that idleness might be the condition through which Irish modernism could be realized, rather than through aesthetic abstraction or an abject condition of sloth consequent upon the failure of ambition (as the representatives of bourgeois convention such as Mr. Deasy would argue and as the vast majority of the dissolute idlers of the novel demonstrate). Right from the very beginning of the episode, Stephen is preoccupied with the relationship between potentiality, actuality, and movement, as in walking along Sandymount strand: 'You are walking through it howsomever. I am, a stride at a time. A very short space of time through very short times of space' (U, 37). In the light of his earlier thoughts about potentiality in 'Nestor', movement in this instance is an experience of history as it happens, of the actual. But it also operates here as a motif for the conversion of creative potential into a representational practice, the actualizing. Physical activity and imaginative labour fold one into the other. Rather than pretending to escape materiality (whether of the body or of history), the aesthetic that derives from Stephen's walking on the beach relishes the physical and readily acknowledges the limits of a given reality. A transcendent form of disinterest would not arise from such an aesthetic, but the more Aristotelian/ Aquinian goals of '*Integritas, consonantia, claritas*' (P, 229), in which actuality is intensified rather than bypassed, would enable a dissenting view of the conventional versions of an endlessly progressive, eliminating history that is sponsored by colonial modernity.

This seems contrary to the otherwise relentlessly negative self-anatomization Stephen submits himself to in 'Proteus', but Joyce immediately undermines the suggested new form of aesthetic practice by re-introducing the principle of uncertainty. If Stephen's desire for a new aesthetic oscillates between the need for innovation and the fear of heresy, the timeless 'void' of uncertainty lingers in the background as the great obstacle to his formulating a new one. Immediately after contemplating the relationship between perception and movement in 'Proteus', Stephen ponders what might happen if he were to dwell upon uncertainty by closing his eyes: 'Am I walking into eternity along Sandymount strand? ... Open your eyes now. I will. One moment. Has all vanished since? If I open and am forever in the black adiaphane. *Basta!* I will see if I can see' (U, 37). Stephen has not disappeared into the void, for the material reality of space and time is inevitable and inescapable: 'See now. There all the time without you: and ever shall be, world without end.' His test puts him in a bind. On the one hand, history, the long nightmare from which he is trying to awake, will carry on regardless. Moreover, reproduction will continue; the very first image Stephen sees upon opening his eyes are the midwives who descend onto the beach from Leahy's terrace. Their appearance leads Stephen to consider his own anxieties about the body, corporeality, shame, and the various phobic details of his own misogyny.

The return of his relentless negativity concerning the body and history overwhelms any possibilities his ruminations regarding time, space, and movement might suggest. On the other hand, if he were to fall into the absolute state of uncertainty he calls 'the Void', he would be completely unable to act in the face of the unknown.

Whether attempting to appropriate models provided by Wilde and Yeats or working out a form of representation predicated upon the actualization of potentiality through movement, Stephen does not arrive at some new form of intellectual labour in 'Proteus'. Yet that is precisely the point for the lazy idle schemer. Though he may consider and attempt to supersede prior forms of representational practice, he will never finally actualize that potential through the elaboration of an effective alternative. To do so would mean the abandonment of idleness. He declares at one point in the episode, 'I am almosting it' (U, 47). This characterizes his role in *Ulysses* as a whole. Directed, purposeful movement signifies the actualization of potential. Yet the aimless, purposeless wandering of the *flâneur*, the sort of movement Stephen practises in 'Proteus', indicates a tendency to fall back on his impotentiality by almost—but not completely—coming to the articulation of a new form of aesthetic representation. Stephen's tendency towards 'almosting it' should not be regarded as evidence of a surrender to fate or a complete inability to keep working towards the possibility of a more effective type of aesthetic practice. As Agamben argues about the nature of impotentiality, to consider the act of doing something and then to choose not to do it constitutes an initial gesture towards the possibility of liberation — even if in 'Proteus' such a breakthrough is qualified by the frustration Stephen feels as a result of his lack of achievement.

Without question, Stephen's idleness, either in the 'Telemachiad' or throughout the rest of *Ulysses*, is neither a completely positive nor pleasant condition. It contributes to his abjection, which in turn leads to only more extensive bouts of idleness. Idleness stands in for all of the feelings of failure, guilt, and shame that typify his sensibility at the beginning of the novel, and it is a symptom of how deeply he is mired in the immobility of late colonial Irish society. Because it suggests the possibility of a life outside the dictates of responsibility, obligation or necessity and can often serve as the basis for enjoyment and pleasure, there is the great temptation to romanticize the joys of idleness. Yet idleness in *Ulysses* is a fundamentally paralysing fusion of both despair and innovation.

Stephen's performances in 'Aeolus' and 'Scylla and Charybdis' negate the values of the Revival and call into question the very process by which literary work produces abstract values useful to political or social agendas. Yet those performances go even further by responding to the questions about history that dominate the 'Telemachiad'. Stephen asks how he might effectively represent the *Erlebnis* of late colonial Dublin without resorting to narrative forms that only evade the social reality of its history. Agamben argues that

> the fundamental contradiction of modern man is precisely that he does not yet have
> an experience of time adequate to his idea of history, and is therefore painfully split

between his being-in-time as an elusive flow of instants and his being-in-history, understood as the original dimension of man.[24]

'Aeolus' and 'Scylla and Charybdis' stage precisely just such a distinction between being-in-time and being-in-history as Stephen experiments with new forms of representation. His inability to elaborate an aesthetic method that overcomes the impasse represented within the 'Telemachiad' underscores how idleness cannot by definition provide the possibility of an effective mode of innovation in itself, but also serves as the moment of negation necessary to the modernist practice that represents it.

4

Professional journalists played an important role in the Revival. Even though Yeats and others frequently railed against the popular media, they nevertheless often wrote for the newspapers.[25] In Joyce's representation of that milieu, the editorial office of the *Evening Herald* offers one of the 'laziest' locations in *Ulysses*. In 'Aeolus', Stephen rejects the opportunity to be a journalist, one among the many shabby-genteel idlers we find there. For many decades, Joyce criticism has focused primarily upon the form of the episode over and above anything else. There is an obvious reason for this; 'Aeolus' is the first episode of the book in which the style becomes visibly different, because of its use of newspaper headlines, which interrupt the text. Such a formalist approach has led to the neglect of the cultural politics of the episode.[26] Many of the headlines allude to both the material production of the newspaper and the labour involved ('GENTLEMEN OF THE PRESS', 'HOW A GREAT DAILY ORGAN IS TURNED OUT', 'WE SEE THE CANVASSER AT WORK', etc.).[27] However, in the editor's office, a variety of characters employed by the newspaper (although some have failed to turn up for work) spend their day in the sort of dissolute idleness we find elsewhere in *Ulysses*. Stephen, who arrives halfway through, represents an age group that has yet to make its impact upon Irish history. He arrives in the middle of a discussion about rhetoric, tradition and the past. An overly effusive speech, given the previous day by the moderate nationalist politician Dan Dawson, comes in for much ridicule. The classical scholar Professor MacHugh and the impoverished lawyer J. J. O'Molloy recall more effective forms of rhetoric.

---

24 Agamben, *Infancy and History*, 100.
25 Declan Kiberd discusses this fluidity in *Irish Classics* (London, 2000), 463–64.
26 Kevin Dettmar's reading of 'Aeolus' in *The Illicit Joyce of Postmodernism: Reading against the Grain* (Madison, 1996) is a case in point; his rhetorical reading of the episode as an instance of the Bakhtinian carnivalesque rather surprisingly fails to take into account the very prominent references to Irish cultural politics and neglects several matters that account for Joyce's politics. See 151–56, 183–85.
27 U, 116, 118, 119.

MacHugh alludes to a speech on behalf of the revival of the Irish language by the nationalist barrister and journalist John F. Taylor.[28] Taylor defended the preservation of the Irish language, citing the example of the ancient Jews and Moses in his support. Had Moses yielded to an imperial form of logic complicit with the ways of the conqueror 'he would never have brought the chosen people out of their house of bondage nor followed the pillar of cloud by day' (U, 143). Yet the shiftless MacHugh's retelling of the story is marked more by sentimental effusion that forthright resistance. It provokes in Stephen a reaction similar to James Connolly's to cultural nationalists: 'There is a danger ... they may only succeed in stereotyping our historical studies into a worship of the past, or crystallizing into a tradition — glorious and heroic indeed, but still only a tradition.' [29] To Stephen, Taylor's words sound like 'dead noise' (U, 143).

Other characters are more attuned to the possibility that innovation might be found in Stephen's generation. Myles Crawford invites him to become a writer for the *Evening Herald*:

> The editor laid a nervous hand on Stephen's shoulder.
> – I want you to write something for me, he said. Something with a bite in it. You can do it. I see it in your face. *In the lexicon of youth ...*
> See it in your face. See it in your eye. Lazy idle schemer. (U, 135)

Stephen's first response to Crawford's request is to recall the moment when Father Dolan beat him for appearing to be lazy.[30] He reminds Crawford of Ignatius Gallagher, a central character of the *Dubliners* story 'A Little Cloud'. Gallagher established his reputation with his account of the Phoenix Park murders by mapping locations in Dublin through the letters on a newspaper advertisement; implicitly, it is for Stephen a new and experimental form of representation. He eventually answers Crawford with a brief story. Two elderly and pious working-class Dublin women climb to the top of Nelson's Pillar (Stephen and the other characters are passing this local landmark as he tells the story) for a panoramic view of the city. Upon arriving at the top of the pillar, the women get only a brief glimpse before collapsing in exhaustion. The story ends as the women, staring at the statue of Admiral Nelson, eat a number of plums they have brought on their journey and spit the seeds towards the ground below. At that precise moment, as the group makes its way to Mooney's pub, the city's electric tram system short-circuits. The story recalls Joyce's early style in *Dubliners*.[31] The title is ironic: 'The Parable of the Plums, or a Pisgah Sight of Palestine' (U, 149). A Pisgah Sight of Palestine assured the dying Moses that the restoration of the nation of Israel to the ancient Hebrews was at hand; but such a

---

28 Though he considered Taylor something of a rival or even enemy, Yeats also expressed admiration for this speech in 'Reveries Over Childhood and Youth'; see A, 101.
29 James Connolly, *Collected Works* (Dublin, 1987), vol. 1, 304.
30 See P, 49–52.
31 Stephen even prefaces the story by thinking to himself, 'Dubliners'. See U, 145.

moment is very far off for Ireland. The 'Pisgah Sight' belongs to the ignorant natives of a colonized land, of a seemingly unfamiliar city dominated by the overwhelming image of the colonizer. Additionally, or alternatively, the story mockingly presents a large phallic symbol memorializing imperial conquest ejaculating seeds on to a barren, colonized city. Either way, it is a cynical and satirical response to the redemptive allegory of cultural nationalism of the John F. Taylor speech that MacHugh celebrates.

While the misogynistic details of Stephen's story provide yet another gloss on his general lack of maturity, the status of temporality in the parable is significant. There is no sense here, as in Taylor's allegorical use of Moses, of a progressive narrative of history leading towards the culmination of nationalist arrival. And the story is also unlike journalistic writing, which singles out specific events from the flow of time and invests them with a singular significance. Stephen's story offers an alternative narrative that breaks down the distinction between important and unimportant events. His story provides one of the better examples of how idleness could become an alternative form of intellectual labour. The bustle of the trams at the beginning of 'Aeolus' signalled the frenzied activity of the workday, the short-circuiting of that system concludes the episode by forcing the city into idleness and immobility. In a negative sense, the recognition of the stasis of Dublin provides a necessary precondition to any effort that would seek to eradicate the more abject qualities of idleness. Similarly, Stephen's idleness demands an alternative understanding of intellectual work in order to overcome the conditions and restraints that produce the idleness in the first place. Such an understanding would not reproduce a reified version of tradition that co-operates in a progressive historical narrative, but would rather represent the needs of the present in a radically defamiliarized manner.

The story is in an ironic register: what is important is the gap between the prophetic sense of assurance signalled in the biblical title and the central image of colonial/masculine domination in which virginal midwives with no work to do watch the seeds fall upon the sterile ground of the dominated city. The short-circuit of the tram system that coincides with the conclusion reinforces this sense of stasis — and since movement is a figure for Stephen's understanding of the passage of time, the suggestion is that history has come to a point of immobility as well. The form of the story is in part determined by the paralytic condition that he inhabits, as do the characters of *Dubliners*; the malaise of late colonial Dublin is so pervasive that it is difficult to conceive of how a narrative could be generated that could ever register change, the passage of time.

The headlines that interrupt the narrative reinforce both the novel's and the episode's connection to the world of journalism. They provide a wry commentary on the scene in the *Evening Herald* offices, but they could just as readily be understood as the subtitles to a silent movie (we recall Joyce's interest in film and his attempts to found one of the first cinemas in Ireland a few blocks away from the setting of the episode). Benjamin's theory of the dialectical image — a concept rooted in film but applicable in other media — provides a good analogy for the way the story produces a non-teleological account of history. The effects of history in the parable are overdetermined. Traces of the past are plainly evident, as in Nelson's Pillar. Yet its proximity to a memorial to Parnell that had been planned but not yet completed reminds us of an Irish Moses who died without seeing the arrival of some form of independence.[32] That drive for independence, meanwhile, began in the interim between the date in which *Ulysses* is set and the period in which Joyce wrote 'Aeolus' — and the General Post Office, the most important location identified with the Easter Rising, was next door to the offices of the *Evening Herald* and directly adjacent to Nelson's Pillar. Stephen's story registers the collision between a history of colonial domination, and an emerging contemporary Irish political condition, but without the standard romantic nationalist associations.

This does not necessarily mean that *Ulysses* provides some sort of critical counter-narrative to the Easter Rising. As Andrew Gibson has persuasively argued — and whatever an older Joycean critical tradition suspicious of *any* investment in the goals of cultural nationalism may have insisted — *Ulysses* demonstrates clear opposition to British rule in Ireland, even if it dissents from the customary rhetorical structures of Irish nationalism and the physical force tradition that was necessary to the struggle for independence.[33] The advantages of Stephen's representational method in 'Aeolus' stem from its objective account of the materiality of history embedded in the physical cityscape; nor does the central image of the parable become a vehicle for the kind of escape from material conditions that he considers and rejects in 'Proteus'. Instead, the parable actually reveals in microcosm an account of the manner in which Joyce provides a representation of history. Read as a particular narrative unit, which Joyce integrates into the novel, it encapsulates the truly innovative nature of Joyce's representation of temporality. Despite critical claims that 'any sense of historical movement is foreclosed' in *Ulysses* or that it betrays 'the absence of any hint of the political future', it is more precisely the case that evidence of the passage of time is repressed within the text and for the most part only visible through Benjaminian 'traces'.[34] The act of reading those traces reproduces a subterranean — but nevertheless importantly present — sense of the movement of history, difficult to recognize because it is so contrary to the teleological conception of temporality that underlies a Hegelian-Marxist understanding of history.

Post-colonial critics, from James Connolly to Frantz Fanon, have noted that the historical experience of imperialism and conquest produces different determinations within the colonized world; thus, it is necessary to produce an accurate account of the cultural

32 The recurring failure to complete monuments to national heroes in turn-of-the-century Dublin was something that apparently rankled Joyce. See *Occasional, Critical, and Political Writing*, 127. For Joyce, unbuilt statues provide a striking metaphor of a collective inability to come to terms with history. See also Robert Spoo, *James Joyce and the Language of History: Dedalus' Nightmare* (Oxford, 1994), 129–30.

33 See Gibson, *Joyce's Revenge*.

34 Brown, *Utopian Generations*, 37. See Luke Gibbons, '"Where Wolfe Tone's Statue Was Not": Joyce, Monuments and Memory', in Ian McBride, ed., *History and Memory in Modern Ireland* (Cambridge, 2001), 139–59.

specificity of each place.[35] A teleological understanding of history gives an enhanced role and prestige to the ideology of modernization, as Joyce suggests in the 'Telemachiad'. Stephen's idleness is an initial refusal of that process in which the passage of time, as he considers it in 'Nestor' and 'Proteus', is so closely tied thereby to the obligation to work. Yet 'The Parable of the Plums' demonstrates many of the shortcomings of the lazy idle schemer's position, as well as the formal possibilities of modernist innovation that Joyce increasingly began to deploy in the latter sections of *Ulysses*. In this sense, Stephen's narrative meets Crawford's demand to 'give something with a bite in it' (U, 135). His recitation of the story denies the central value of tradition that governed the speeches praised by his companions. Yet, within the text, 'The Parable of the Plums' remains inconsequential, even if it demands a form of reading that is necessary for recognizing the status of Irish history in the novel as a whole. It is, after all, a quickly forgotten tale, told to a group of dissolute layabouts; whatever his desire for a life committed to unalienated intellectual labour, Stephen remains a lazy idle schemer rather than the artist he affects to be. Through the representation of just such a literary type, Joyce exposes the role of the artist as consisting of nothing more than the false consciousness of an aesthetic ideology. 'The Parable of the Plums' encapsulates the viewpoint of one caught, as Agamben has it, within his being-in-time, without a suitably complementary understanding of his being-in-history, which could enable a more effective form of critique.

In 'Scylla and Charybdis', the last episode primarily devoted to Stephen, Joyce accounts for the status of being-in-history. The episode provides an exercise in the theory of interpretation that is appended to the formal experiments of 'Aeolus'. While the discussion in the editorial office of the *Evening Telegraph* showed Stephen in the world of journalism, one area appropriate for the would-be intellectual, 'Scylla and Charybdis' takes him into a more rarefied atmosphere of literature. Just as Stephen took the contrarian approach of insisting upon a literary approach to history in the previous episode, in 'Scylla and Charybdis' he conversely insists upon a historical approach to literature. The debate on Shakespeare in the National Library takes place because each of the participants is enjoying a moment of idleness. The writer and journalist George Russell is momentarily away from his duties at the *Irish Homestead*, while the head librarian T. W. Lyster, the literary critic W. K. Magee (better known as John Eglinton) and the philologist Richard Best are all enjoying a temporary break. Stephen has earlier delivered Mr. Deasy's letter on foot-and-mouth disease to one newspaper editor, and has now sought out Russell for the same purpose.

In 'Scylla and Charybdis', sailing between two dangerous points of opposition is an action elaborated by Joyce as a choice between noted pairings (Aristotle and Plato, dogma and mysticism, Stratford and London).[36] A number of additional pairings linger in the

---

35 On this, see Cleary, *Outrageous Fortune*, 58–84.
36 See Kenner, *Dublin's Joyce*, 226–27, for a synoptic version of the schema.

background, including Yeats and Wilde. Yeats was a good friend of Russell, while Best, a devotee of late nineteenth-century aestheticism, repeatedly demonstrates his enthusiasm for Wilde; the form of the episode even resembles the structure of the Platonic dialogues Wilde used in his critical writing, providing a metafictional dimension to Best's concluding comment to Stephen regarding his theory about Shakespeare.[37] Andrew Gibson argues that Joyce's choice of Shakespeare as topic for discussion recalls earlier debates between Yeats and the Anglo-Irish intellectual Edward Dowden, thus intimating the further tensions between Irish and English forms of cultural nationalism and the competing values of localism and cosmopolitanism.[38] The last of these oppositions involves questions on the role of the literary intellectual in the present. In that sense, 'Scylla and Charybdis' provides one of the more detailed cartographies in the novel of what Bourdieu would identify as 'the literary field of production' of the Revival. Claire Hutton is correct to insist that the Revival itself was in no way a monolithic affair, and that Joyce's representation of the scene in the National Library demonstrates the relative religious and ideological diversity of the movement, as well as the need to rethink literary periodization in terms of the institutions that enable the production and dissemination of the literary positions of the time.[39] The group of people assembled in the National Library represents the humanist branch of the Revival. Russell was famous for his financial support of young writers (including both the fictional Stephen and the actual Joyce), whether or not he agreed with their viewpoints, while Eglinton was the editor of *Dana*, a journal defined by its insistence upon diversity of opinion.[40] Yet even liberal pluralism has its limits; some principle of exclusion inevitably contributes to the aesthetic ideology of a given cultural movement. In Bourdieu's terms, figures like Russell and Eglinton stand as members of a 'consecrated avant-garde', which inhabits a position of dominance within a given cultural field. By virtue of their position, which stems from their control of the important literary institutions of the field, they contribute to the promotion of the chosen values idealized by the Revival. Stephen, on the other hand, represents that emerging splinter group of younger would-be artists who define themselves in opposition to the values of the consecrated avant-garde. Like Stephen, they are excluded from the key institutions.

---

37 'Are you going to write it? Mr. Best asked. You ought to make it a dialogue, don't you know, like the Platonic dialogues Wilde wrote.' (U, 214)

38 See Gibson, *Joyce's Revenge*, 60–80.

39 See Claire Hutton, 'Joyce and the Institutions of Revivalism', *Irish University Review: A Journal of Irish Studies*, 33, 1 (2003), 117–32.

40 The initial editorial manifesto of *Dana* declares: 'We would have our magazine, however, not merely a doctrinaire but a literary, or rather a humanist, magazine; and we would receive and print contributions in prose and in verse which are the expression of the writer's individuality with greater satisfaction than those which are merely the belligerent expression of opinion.' See Deane, ed., *The Field Day Anthology of Irish Writing*, vol. 2, 976.

Stephen's position becomes apparent early in the episode. As Russell departs from the library, a brief conversation regarding an impending literary evening at the house of George Moore takes place around the uninvited Stephen:

> Listen.
> Young Colum and Starkey. George Roberts is doing the commercial part. Longworth will give it a good puff in the *Express*. O, will he? I liked Colum's *Drover*. Yes, I think he has that queer thing, genius. Do you think he has genius really? Yeats admired his line: *As in wild earth a Grecian vase*. Did he? I hope you'll be able to come tonight. Malachi Mulligan is coming too. Moore asked him to bring Haines. Did you hear Miss Mitchell's joke about Moore and Martyn? That Moore is Martyn's wild oats? Awfully clever, isn't it? They remind one of Don Quixote and Sancho Panza. Our national epic is yet to be written, Dr. Sigerson says. Moore is the man for it ... James Stephens is doing some clever sketches. We are becoming important, it seems. Cordelia. *Cordiglio*. Lir's lonliest daughter. (U, 192)

The conversation refers not only to the young writers (such as Padraic Colum, James Starkey, and James Stephens). who are Stephen's contemporaries and committed to the Revival, but also to the commercial framework for the Revival's productions (George Roberts published and marketed many of its important works), to their critical reception and interpretation (Ernest Victor Longworth was a literary critic and editor of the conservative *Daily Express*; Susan Mitchell was an essayist for the *Irish Homestead*; Dr. George Sigerson was a scholar of Gaelic literature), and to the central 'consecrated' authorities that stand as the dominant figures in the field (Yeats, and to a lesser extent, George Moore, Edward Martyn, and Russell himself). This moment demonstrates the gap between Stephen's aspiration to become a successful writer and his current condition as a lazy idle schemer who lacks access to the literary field of turn-of-the-century Ireland. Stephen's grudging awareness of the conversation that takes place around but does not include him, is an example of literary revenge, a notion that pervades his discussion of Shakespeare. Stephen's identification with *King Lear*'s Cordelia indicates his exclusion. He identifies with her because he also refuses to pay false obeisance to one of the primary and social values of the Revival.

An idea of tradition dependent upon a reified idea of the peasantry and rural Ireland is the fake authority he refuses. Such was the power of this motif that even a writer as cosmopolitan and 'modern' as Moore could produce a work as firmly grounded in this ideal as *The Untilled Field*. Yeats and Eglinton held very different ideas about what exactly should constitute a national literature, but both considered the authority of the past as an imperative for contemporary Irish culture (even if Eglinton had his doubts about some of the more conventional trappings of the Revival).[41] It is not so much a repudiation of the content of tradition that places Stephen outside the Revival's framework of value, as it is his reluctance to consider tradition in sacrosanct terms. His refusal to prioritize tradition as a defining value becomes especially apparent in his interpretation of *Hamlet*. Eglinton asks him at one point, 'Do you mean to fly in the face of the tradition of three centuries?' (U, 190). That is exactly Stephen's intention. Russell's argument on behalf of tradition is more consistent with the ethos of the Revival:

> 'I mean when we read the poetry of *King Lear* what is it to us how the poet lived? As for living, our servants can do that for us, Villiers de l'Isle has said. Peeping and prying into the greenroom gossip of the day, the poet's drinking, the poet's debts. We have *King Lear*: and it is immortal.' (U, 189)

According to Russell, literature has an autonomous status as the bearer of traditional eternal truths — a position that Eglinton and Best share with him. The problem with tradition considered in such terms is that it tends to force interpretation to conform to the dominant values of a given society. Joyce himself took a somewhat different position in his essay 'A Portrait of the Artist'. There he suggested that 'the iron memorial aspect' that conditions the consideration of the past — in other words, the framework of tradition that identifies and interprets the value of the supposedly timeless qualities of what is found within it — actually destroys the understanding of the 'fluid successions of the present', which constitute the experience of history. What was needed was 'some process of the mind as yet untabulated', which could account for 'the individuating rhythm' that identifies a text with its moment of production and also enables its relation to the conditions of the present in a manner that did not reproduce a conventional notion of tradition.[42] Yet the specific texts that comprise a tradition retain clues and fragments — or, in Benjaminian terms, traces — which might provide the basis for an alternative understanding of history. In an echo of his formal approach to a literary representation of the past in 'Aeolus', in 'Scylla and Charybdis' Stephen attempts to formulate an interpretative method that regards as primary the relationship between art and the material context in which it appears, rather than reproduce the 'timeless' qualities of Russell's understanding of tradition. Just as in 'Aeolus', the results are mixed.

Idleness, as Wilde declared in 'The Soul of Man under Socialism', was the luxury of the privileged and thus depended upon an unjust social formation. Such a conception of idleness was not problematic for Yeats. And the disinterested form of indolence referred to by Russell is much different to the more ambiguous and unstable condition

---

41 The various debates in question were later collected in the volume edited by Eglinton, *Literary Ideals in Ireland* (London, 1899).

42 See Joyce, *Poems and Shorter Writings*, 211.

of the lazy idle schemer. Though the possibility that an idealized form of idleness might enable a transcendent condition of disinterest that would allow escape from the realities of the material world certainly appeals to Stephen, throughout the day he comes to the conclusion that such an opportunity is not really available to him. Though his background, education, and social circles are resolutely middle class, his current condition in *Ulysses* is not. He will 'fly in the face of centuries of tradition' in his interpretation of Shakespeare in order to construct a theory of intellectual labour hostile to the values of his audience. For him, lazy idle scheming in 'Scylla and Charybdis' requires a head-on confrontation with, rather than an evasion of, the material consequences of history. Just as in 'Aeolus', Stephen's contrarian approach is presented through a spoken parable of sorts rather than a written text. The energies of the virtuoso who fulfils the role of the lazy idle schemer are performative in nature.

Stephen's reading of Shakespeare presents a disavowal of the authorized values of the Revival, although his conclusion is problematic, in that it does not completely break with the assumptions about the nature of literary work that he queries. But he at least suggests a template for an 'unworking' of the standard version of the literary intellectual. At the end of the episode, when pressed by Eglinton, Stephen disclaims his own speculation. Of course he cannot believe the truth of his statements about Shakespeare, as he knows that he has untruthfully manipulated and repressed certain kinds of factual evidence. But it is not his goal to produce a definitive reading of Shakespeare; he is actually more concerned with a larger allegorical theory of the relationship between intellectual labour and history. In his theory, the certainty of external material reality and history is inevitable and inescapable. The actuality of specific historical circumstances always creates the conditions of possibility for the potentiality of literary creation. Stephen's theory suggests that art does not transcend history. Instead history explains art (and vice versa). Art in itself does not provide a teleological record of history in process, but rather a synchronic inventory of the given moment in which it is produced.

Stephen likens the praxis of intellectual labour to fatherhood (though he will ultimately insist that it does not have to do with the specificity of gender), and his early discussion of Shakespeare's literal fatherhood allows him to shift into a discussion of the creative process in general. He first suggests that the creation (the 'son', or by implication, literary creation) is 'consubstantial' (of the same essence) as the father (the writer). His assertion does not have to do so much with the traits that the son has inherited from the father as — just as he had thought earlier in the day in 'Proteus' while thinking about the nature of molecular composition — with their shared composition of living matter:

> As we, or mother Dana, weave and unweave our bodies, Stephen said, from day to day, their molecules shuttle to and fro, so does the artist weave and unweave his image. And as the mole on my right breast is where it was when I was born, though

all my body has been woven of new stuff time after time, so through the ghost of the
unquiet father the image of the unliving son looks forth. (U, 194)

The 'weaving' of the artistic creation out of the raw material of the author's experience
allows for some distance between the creator and the created. Stephen alludes to the
heretical beliefs of Sabellius, who also believed in the equivalence between creator and
created by arguing that 'the Father was Himself His Own Son' (U, 208), in order to invoke
St. Thomas Aquinas's refutation of that heresy through his insistence on the necessary
distinction between father and son (or, to continue in the terms of Stephen's allegory,
between author and text). To Aquinas, there must be some necessary form of mediation
between author and text even if they spring from the same source. Stephen's allegorical
term for this mediation is paternity, an equivalent to intellectual labour. Just as one can
perceive the son and find evidence of the father, despite the fundamental uncertainty of
that relationship, one can also read the facts of society and find evidence of the human
soul/mind that embarked upon praxis — or, for Stephen's purposes, one can read a literary
text like *Hamlet* and find evidence of the actual existence and experiences of the author.
Because no author actually lives in the timeless repository of value that both Russell and
Eglinton regard as the ideal imaginative location of art, the specific conditions in which
the writer lives provide an inevitable determination for the text. Conversely, as the product
of human praxis, the text will have an effect upon history.

Stephen's theory challenges the conventional positions of the Revival in at least two
ways, by arguing against the timelessness of art and the value of disinterest. He insists
upon a necessary relation between art and the circumstances in which it was produced.
As his close reading of the relation between the details of Shakespeare's writing and
the supposed facts of his biography suggests, the events of a writer's personal life
make an impact upon his work. Yet he is aware his 'facts' are picked from a variety of
not entirely reputable sources. But there is a larger point to be made. He refers to the
subject of his argument at one point as 'Rutlandbaconsouthamptonshakespeare' (U, 208),
identifying him as a composite of the various different historical figures who allegedly
wrote Shakespeare's plays and poems (or some of them). This suggests that the actual
biographical identity of the writer in Stephen's theory of intellectual labour is not as
important as his greater claim that it is through material history in general that literature
comes into existence. In refusing the 'timeless' qualities of art, Stephen also rejects the
value of disinterest that lurks behind Russell's argument; the contemplation of art does
not remove one from the body and history, but rather reiterates a deeper knowledge of
those material realities.

Underlying Stephen's theory, as Ellmann has argued, is the Viconian position that man
makes the human world by transforming one's own potentiality (located in the self)

into the facts of society and the actuality of history.[43] This position is also at the basis of Marx's understanding of the relationship between praxis and history. Stephen explains it in reference to contemporary European literature:

> Maeterlinck says: *If Socrates leave his house today he will find the sage seated on his doorstep. If Judas go forth tonight it is to Judas his steps will tend.* Every life is many days, day after day. We will walk through ourselves, meeting robbers, ghosts, giants, old men, young men, wives, widows, brothers-in-love. But always meeting ourselves. (U, 213)

One does not find in art (or anywhere else), a more general sense of the external world but a more refined sense of one's own self. Personal interest is reaffirmed, not transcended. According to Stephen's argument, alienation — as described in 'Scylla and Charybdis' — is the biggest problem facing the would-be intellectual. No matter how much he desires to create an innovative literary form that will respond to the primary attributes of colonial *Erlebnis* he has been thinking about all day, Stephen can only assume a place within the established field, and thus actually become a conventional, rather than lazy idle, schemer. It is precisely this form of alienated intellectual labour that Stephen eventually addresses in 'Eumaeus', when Bloom argues that there must be an acceptable place for Stephen within the literary field of the Revival. Stephen refuses it as a possibility, stating, 'count me out!'

In 'Aeolus', Stephen remains a figure of potentiality; at the end of 'Scylla and Charybdis', he is at least partially aware of this continuing state, as in his avowal to himself that he will now 'cease to strive' (U, 218). His parable about the relationship between authorship and history is problematic. Fatherhood — even in the mystical terms of the Holy Trinity that Stephen draws upon in order to explain creativity — is not a very serviceable metaphor, for in the end there can be no son without maternity as well. Moreover, Stephen's theory is very much predicated upon the centrality of the figure of a solitary genius/author.[44] At the end of his performance, Stephen drops his insistence upon paternity by suggesting that intellectual labour finally depends upon a divine form of androgyny in which every artist is both male and female at the same time — even if his entire discussion depended up to that point on a normative masculine model in order for him to develop his analogy. But the move is too little, too late — and as Buck Mulligan's satirical ripostes to the argument indicate, Stephen's metaphor ends up looking like a masturbatory version of male self-indulgence, rather than a truly androgynous unification of separate gendered categories. Ultimately, gender lurks as the great impediment to the various models of intellectual labour discussed in 'Scylla and Charybdis'. Joyce carefully constructs the institutionalized space of the Revival (symbolized by the location of the National Library) from which

---

43 See Richard Ellmann, *Ulysses on the Liffey* (Oxford, 1972), 84–85.
44 See Joseph Valente, 'The Perils of Masculinity in "Scylla and Charybdis"', in Devlin and Reizbaum, eds., *Ulysses: En-Gendered Perspectives*, 111–35.

women are absent. Despite the actual historical reality, that a number of women played major roles within the Revival, the scene in the library is fundamentally homo-social. The instances of homosexual panic that occasionally emerge in Stephen's private thoughts throughout the episode reinforce the sense of the overwhelmingly male atmosphere in which he presents his argument. Joyce's depiction of the intellectual context of the Revival foregrounds one of the primary limitations of the lazy idle schemer. Despite his challenges to a number of assumptions about the literary intellectual in his argument, masculinity remains a category that Stephen never interrogates. The lazy idle schemer may present a significant challenge to the role of the literary intellectual within 'Scylla and Charybdis', but nevertheless the assumed gender of the artist is taken for granted.

Stephen's assumptions about the inevitable masculinity of the intellectual are connected to his characterization of the artist as a transcendent God-like figure, although thoughts contrary to that position had emerged in 'Proteus'. He is unable to break with this primary component of aesthetic ideology, which he ultimately shares with figures like Eglinton and Russell. It also demonstrates a structural deficiency evident elsewhere in the episode. As Eglinton notes at the end of the episode, 'You have brought us all this way to show us a French triangle' (U, 213). Despite the ostensible iconoclasm and interpretative twists of Stephen's theory of the intellectual, it does not manage to break with pre-existing structural forms (especially ones that might be considered as banal and clichéd as the French triangle). Unlike 'The Parable of the Plums', which at least manages to achieve a degree of formal innovation in its representation of history, even if it does not allow for the possibility of an explicit narrative that would make that history entirely legible, Stephen's parable about Shakespeare and the nature of intellectual labour invokes the necessity of understanding a historical context without including the possibility that it could be presented through an innovative literary form.

Stephen's tendency to fall back upon safe, familiar structural forms in his argument in order to make his various points about intellectual labour is a consequence of his fear of uncertainty, the main thing preventing him from finally committing himself once and for all to an innovative practice that would supersede the efforts of the lazy idle schemer. In 'Telemachus', he considers that banishment to 'the Void' of uncertainty is the eternal punishment for heretics, but also that would-be innovators must risk the consequence of heresy if they are to bring about artistic change. While the void represents everything he fears, he must risk it if he is to achieve anything as a writer, since innovation might become the basis for the dominant art forms of the future. In 'Scylla and Charybdis', he returns to this problem and compares it to the basis of faith necessary for belief and spirituality in his primary allegory of creative labour. According to Stephen, there is a necessary relationship between the Father/creator and Son/created, but it is a relationship that is 'mystical' because it depends upon a form of faith in spite of uncertainty (unlike the closer relationship between mother and child, which is a physical certainty):

> Fatherhood, in the sense of conscious begetting, is unknown to man. It is a mystical estate, an apostolic succession from only begetter to only begotten. On that mystery and not on the madonna which the cunning Italian intellect flung to the mob of Europe the church is founded and founded irrevocably because founded, like the world, macro- and micro-cosm, upon the void. Upon incertitude, upon unlikelihood. (U, 207)

That fundamental uncertainty, upon which both the Church and the universe are founded, is an instance of 'the Void' — that which lies just beyond what can be known for certain. The role of the mystery of imaginative labour, just as with that of faith in Stephen's very Catholic metaphor, is to provide a bulwark of reassurance, which affirms some sense of certainty against the frightening uncertainty of the void. Ideally, innovative forms of art risk the uncertainty of the void and provide the means to go on existing in spite of it.

The problem with Stephen's argument is that rather than risk the void through a closer engagement with the fundamental sense of uncertainty that lies at the basis of existence itself, he relies upon a familiar structural methodology that attempts to fix all of the elements of his position with as much certainty as possible. Consequently, Stephen attempts to deny the threat of uncertainty through safe and familiar forms (such as the 'French triangle', which structures his reading of Shakespeare), rather than risk the danger of the void through the elaboration of a new aesthetic practice that will fundamentally break with the inheritance of tradition. Stephen's desire for certainty (despite the fact that he knowingly represses information contrary to his argument over the course of the episode) in his discussion of the relation between the surmised events of Shakespeare's life and his writing demonstrates an obsessive commitment to the fixity of knowledge. Although the inevitability of temporal and material flux, the image of movement as a metaphor for both idle *flânerie* and for the circulation of knowledge, and the inescapable presence of uncertainty in any theory, are all positions that Stephen entertains both here and earlier in the novel, his argument refuses these possibilities through a strict insistence that everything can be accounted for in an absolutely certain manner. *Ulysses* as a whole valorizes the very principle of uncertainty that Stephen is attempting to repress at all costs. After all, coincidence, displacement and ambiguity are crucial and indispensable facets of the narrative, and for all of the strides Stephen takes against literary convention in 'Scylla and Charybdis', the textual form of the novel once more demonstrates how Joyce's modernist writing goes one step further in its approach to creative labour than the lazy idle schemer is capable of at this point.[45] Ultimately, Stephen is just as guilty as the Revivalists of possessing the desire for an a priori narrative of *Ehrfahrung*, in which all questions are answered, despite the fact that he is more aware of the prevailing condition

---

45 See Colin MacCabe, 'The Voice of Esau: Stephen in the Library', in Colin MacCabe, ed., *James Joyce: New Perspectives* (Sussex, Harvester, 1982), 111–28, 115.

of *Erlebnis*, which characterizes late colonial Ireland. The lazy idle schemer thus presents an initial point of opposition to the customary role of the intellectual within a literary field dominated by the Revival, but he does not completely break with that position in order to suggest a feasible alternative. In the words he uses to characterize the apparent aimlessness of his own wandering in 'Proteus', Stephen's interpretation of the relationship between intellectual labour and history in 'Scylla and Charybdis' presents a classic case of 'almosting it'.

But if Stephen were to actually do anything more, he would no longer be a lazy idle schemer. As a figure of negativity as well as impotentiality, the lazy idle schemer does not yet provide a viable alternative to all of the various models of the intellectual Stephen has interrogated throughout the day. By the end of 'Scylla and Charybdis', this process comes to a halt as Stephen resolves to 'cease to strive' (U, 218). This statement is ambiguous. On the one hand, it presents a refusal to work any more, which reaffirms his commitment to idleness; on the other hand, it demonstrates a sense of futility that suggests he never will actually produce any work that could take its place alongside, and in juxtaposition to, the publications of the Revival. Stephen sees two plumes of smoke coming from nearby chimneys, which remind him of the closing lines of *Cymbeline*. As Colin MacCabe notes, the allusion is important, for it refers to a moment in Shakespeare's *oeuvre* in which a British national allegory of sorts concludes with an accommodation to imperial power.[46] The suggestion here implies that despite all of the talk of Irish national allegories at the beginning of the episode, the efforts of the Revival will not ultimately overcome some form of complicity with British rule, and Stephen, whether he finally manages to work as an intellectual or not, can do nothing about that. Stephen's performative interventions throughout the rest of *Ulysses* no longer press against the conventions of intellectual life in Ireland as they did in the earlier episodes. By 'Oxen of the Sun', another episode that places him in close proximity to an important bourgeois group comprised of intellectuals (in this case, medical students, who, like the Oliver St. John Gogarty, the model for Buck Mulligan, would eventually go on to become influential doctors), Stephen consistently takes the most conservative and orthodox Catholic positions possible in yet another discussion of paternity and maternity. He no longer seems willing to risk the heresy of innovation in his apprehension of the void and instead demonstrates the more dissolute indolence of the majority of the idlers represented in *Ulysses*, rather than the distinct behaviour of the lazy idle schemer.

Stephen's brief encounter with Bloom at the end of 'Scylla and Charybdis', immediately prior to his thoughts about *Cymbeline*, suggests another version of idleness. Blanchot's concept of *désoeuvrement* is often translated as 'unworking', a term I have been using throughout this chapter to denote the process by which Stephen undoes many of the values promoted by the intellectuals of the Revival. But *désoeuvrement* can also be translated

---

46 MacCabe, *James Joyce: New Perspectives*, 122.

as 'idleness', and in a formal sense derived from Blanchot, it astutely characterizes the various stylistic transformations that take place in *Ulysses* in all of the episodes that follow 'Scylla and Charybdis'. The formal shift evident in the latter episodes would ultimately have as great an impact upon the aesthetic experimentation of the Irish modernist writing that followed Joyce as the figure of Stephen Dedalus would have as a representative version of the post-Revival literary intellectual who would be emulated in a number of subsequent texts.

Désoeuvrement is a difficult concept to grasp precisely because, in the words of one of Blanchot's critics, it 'denotes neither a concept in itself nor some positive aspect of art that might accordingly be defined, made present, or recuperated as some supersession of an obsolete problematic'. It refers in a sense to that which is absent in a text — that which looms as a ghostly shadow signifying the labour never completed in an artistic work that aspires to a greater sense of totality and finality. To quote the same critic, 'among other possibilities of meaning, the term indicates a process by which all forms of art and literature constantly aspire to the stature of the Work only to fail by succeeding (or vice versa)'.[47] Another way to understand it would be to consider it as a mark of incompletion; no matter how many allusions a work may contain, no matter how great its gesture towards the representation of totality, something must inevitably be left out for the work to be completed. Yet the work is never really complete because something is inevitably missing; in this case, the work could more properly be said to be an ongoing work-in-progress because that which it lacks gestures towards the 'unworking' of its own totality. Blanchot's very modernist concept has a clear analogue in the form of *Ulysses*. The styles that increasingly proliferate and dominate create its encyclopedic illusion of totality, and the elaborate structural co-ordinates, ranging from the Homeric correspondences to all of the different attributes from episode to episode accounted for in documents like the Linati schema, create a sense of methodological fixity, in which everything falls into an orderly place. But if the fixity of meaning was really as dominant a force in the novel as such details initially suggest, it would be Stephen's work, not Joyce's, and the abundance of styles only disguises the innumerable possibilities that Joyce never made use of. Joyce raises the stylistic and technical stakes of the novel only to allow for crucial moments of the narrative in which the structure does not *work*. To give one very significant example drawn from the Homeric correspondences, perhaps the most important of these — the slaughter of Penelope's suitors and the restoration of Odysseus as patriarch — never actually occurs in *Ulysses*. The *désoeuvrement* evident in the episode is precisely that fundamental sense of uncertainty that characterizes the novel as a whole.

It is in this sense that Leopold Bloom, the embodiment of uncertainty who has his own idle tendencies (even if he is more markedly committed to the value of hard work), becomes

---

47 Shershow, *The Work and the Gift*, 193, 165. I am deeply indebted to Scott Shershow for introducing me to this concept and helping me to understand its difficulty.

a crucial complement to the lazy idle schemer. Stephen provides a point of juxtaposition against which to measure the conventional types of intellectual who participated in the Revival. His idleness signals a refusal to work on behalf of the values of the Revival, and his performative interventions in the novel offer a negation of the aesthetic ideology of that movement. His interventions, however, generate yet another aesthetic ideology, which mistakenly insists upon the certainty of knowledge. The problem with a fixed, unyielding conception of meaning is that, in its inflexibility and its need to categorize, it creates the conditions of possibility for a rigid conception of identity premised upon the necessity of exclusion. Stephen has little in common with the various forms of exclusion that Bloom encounters throughout the day; nevertheless, rigid conceptions of identity that are at the basis for perceptions of Bloom's otherness are just as fixed in their certainty as Stephen's methodology in 'Scylla and Charybdis'. Yet the stability of Bloom's identity is anything but certain. Bloom is a figure in which identity unworks itself. If the formal characteristics of the novel demonstrate Blanchot's notion of *désoeuvrement*, then the presence of Bloom exemplifies Nancy's political extension of 'unworking'. Despite the efforts of various characters to classify Bloom's identity according to their own prejudices, Joyce takes great steps to demonstrate that he is beyond classification. Bloom is, in Nancy's words, that 'which, before or beyond the work, withdraws from the work, and which, no longer having to do with either production or completion, encounters interruption, fragmentation, suspension'.[48] As such, he is the mark of incompletion necessary for a more egalitarian form of community than is otherwise possible in *Ulysses* and which was still a work-in-progress in the newly independent Ireland that coincided with the publication of the novel. Just as the stylistic proliferation provides evidence of the aesthetic *désoeuvrement* of *Ulysses*, Bloom's centrality to the narrative registers the unworking of fixed forms of identity. Though both Blanchot's and Nancy's formulations of idleness are very different to the idleness of the lazy idle schemer, all are necessary for an Irish modernist project that will constitute an epistemological break with the Revival.

Even if it does not ultimately measure up to Joyce's achievement in *Ulysses*, Stephen's lazy idle scheming has considerable consequences for the Irish modernist moment that began after the publication of the novel in 1922. No matter how abject Stephen's idleness appears in Joyce's representation of it, it nevertheless presents an attempt to live in opposition to the primacy of a temporal progression derived from the rhythm of work, which, in the Irish version of modernization, unfolds towards the grand redemptive moment of national independence. Such an approach to temporality provides a point of connection between Stephen and Benjamin's conception of the idler as someone who rejects the progressive drive of modernity through resistance to the imperative to work. If Yeats classified one facet of the labour of the intellectual as 'creation without toil', then Joyce depicts Stephen as a would-be intellectual who toils without creation, at least in the

---

48 Nancy, *The Inoperative Community*, 210.

sense that the values that define Stephen's work are not the socially recognized values of the Revival. Because of his inability to get anything actually done, it is difficult to identify Stephen as a viable model for the actual modernist literary intellectuals that would emerge after Irish independence and who are the subjects of the rest of this study. As a *representation* of the dissident literary intellectual unable to work according to dominant social values, Stephen became a textual model for the later lazy idle schemers that inhabit the works of modernist Irish writing after *Ulysses*. But Joyce's materialist transformation of the motif of idleness found in the works of Wilde and Yeats had an impact that went beyond the creation of subsequent lazy idle schemers in later novels. Eimar O'Duffy, Samuel Beckett, and Flann O'Brien each seized upon the interpretative positions about the relation between idleness and intellectual labour found in *Ulysses* and situated the motif of laziness in the fields of economics, philosophy, and politics respectively. By extending the ramifications of idleness into those particular areas, each of these writers provided incisive critical observations about the course of decolonization in independent Ireland. If Joyce's writing first suggested the possibility that laziness enabled a political understanding of issues evident in the culture of post-colonial Ireland, ranging from the role of the literary intellectual to the temporality of modernization, the way in which these later writers made this motif a central facet of their own writing indicates the degree to which idleness had become one of the hallmark characteristics of Irish modernism.

5 Eimar O'Duffy, Heroic Idleness, and the Leisure State

I

Ulysses had already acquired notoriety by the time it was published in 1922. Yet, for all the controversy in Britain the United States and France about the book's alleged obscenity, it met with a quieter reception in the more socially conservative Irish Free State. Despite the state censorship, the book was never banned in Ireland, though it was difficult to obtain and Joyce's reputation as a dangerous and lascivious writer persisted long after 1922.[1] It is difficult to find critical assessments of Ulysses in Irish literary journals and newspapers in the first decade or so after publication. The various writers associated with the Revival, now coming into their own as the literary establishment of a newly independent nation, had little to say about it. Yeats confessed that he had been unable to get beyond the first few episodes, though he strongly defended Joyce's freedom of expression and his tendency towards literary experimentation.[2] Those early discussions that did appear were in marginal, modernist avant-garde publications. In 1924, Beckett's close friend Con Leventhal, under the name Lawrence K. Emery, founded a journal called The Klaxon, which, with its 'whiff of Dadaist Europe' and vorticist-inspired prints, aspired in its editorial manifesto 'to kick Ireland into artistic wakefulness'; Leventhal included a lengthy essay of his own devoted to Ulysses.[3] The Klaxon ran for only one issue. The absence of Ulysses from the numerous cultural discussions that accompanied the emergence of

---

1   Brian Fallon, An Age of Innocence: Irish Culture 1930–1960 (Dublin, 1999), provides a compressed summary of the Irish reception of Ulysses; see 67–69.
2   On Yeats's inability to finish reading Ulysses, see Ellmann, James Joyce, 531.
3   Con Leventhal, 'Confessional', The Klaxon (Winter 1923–24), 1, 'The Ulysses of Mr. James Joyce', 14–20. Leventhal was inspired to found The Klaxon when his essay on Joyce was rejected by the much more conventional Dublin Magazine. See Allen, Modernism, Ireland and Civil War, 89–90.

post-colonial Ireland should not be attributed either to a malevolent or even a benign indifference to Joyce's achievement. Instead, *Ulysses* served as a limit text; it could not be understood in terms of the dominant values of the Revival. Like Stephen's exclusion from the conversation about George Moore's literary salon in 'Scylla and Charybdis', the relative indifference towards *Ulysses* suggested an inability upon the part of the literary establishment even to consider a genuinely revolutionary literary work.

Yet there is at least one interesting exception to the critical neglect of Joyce within the mainstream Irish literary journals and newspapers of the period. Eimar O'Duffy, an aspiring writer who had recently written a realist novel about the Easter Rising entitled *The Wasted Island*, was one of the first Irish critics to recognize the innovative qualities of *Ulysses*.[4] In a review for the *Irish Review*, written in late 1922, O'Duffy suggested that *Ulysses* should reconfigure the conventional hierarchies of the literary field as they had existed during the Revival, arguing:

> It is time for Ireland to realize that in James Joyce she has produced a great artist — perhaps the greatest artist in English prose now living; and that in *Ulysses* it has produced a very great work ... Its bulk alone should have secured it attention in a land where a hundred poetasters have built up reputations on the strength of slim volumes that do not contain between their covers as much thought or beauty as can be found in one of eight hundred pages of *Ulysses*. The book is, in conception and execution, magnificent. It is also unique. It is an epic — *the* epic of modern Ireland.[5]

Beginning with Eliot's influential essay 'Ulysses, Order, and Myth', which famously drew upon certain hermeneutical clues that Joyce provided himself, early criticism of *Ulysses* generally accounted for Joyce's allusions to Homer to some degree.[6] Therefore, O'Duffy's emphasis on the 'epic' qualities of the novel initially does not seem surprising. Yet O'Duffy's review was written almost a year before Eliot's brief essay; it shows no awareness of a Homeric mythic structure. Instead, his use of the word 'epic' seems to indicate a foundational text for 'modern Ireland', rather than a specific ancient literary genre. Unlike Eliot, or other modernists such as Ezra Pound in 'James Joyce et Pécuchet' and Virginia Woolf in 'Modern Fiction', O'Duffy's assessment of *Ulysses* is not primarily concerned with the experimental formal characteristics of the novel (though O'Duffy demonstrated enthusiasm for those elsewhere).[7] Instead, he considers the meaning of *Ulysses* within the immediate cultural

---

4   *The Wasted Island* (Dublin, 1919). This novel was one of the first literary representations of the Easter Rising.

5   'Reviews', *Journal of Irish Literature*, 7, 1 (1978), 12–13. (Hereafter, 'Reviews'). The review was originally published in the *Irish Review*, 1, 4 (1922), 12–13.

6   T. S. Eliot, 'Ulysses, Order and Myth', *The Dial* (November 1923), 480–83.

7   Ezra Pound, 'James Joyce et Pécuchet', *Mercure de France*, 1 (June 1922), 307–20; Virginia Woolf, *Times Literary Supplement*, 10 (April 1919). O'Duffy praises the experimental breakthrough Joyce made within the form

and political context of the independent nation that had come into being only weeks before
the book's publication — thus anticipating a historicist critical approach that would not
become prominent until much later.[8] To O'Duffy, *Ulysses* offered an alternative expression
of Irish singularity that did not correspond to the fixed categories of the nation advocated
by the most influential proponents of the struggle for independence:

> The gunman and the political theorist have so long claimed the monopoly of
> patriotism in this unhappy island, that it is time a case was made for less obtrusive
> practitioners of the virtue ... there is one whose love of country excels that of the
> common man, and receives even less recognition. This is the artist, who loves her
> for herself alone, apart from all political theories or conception of duty.[9]

Though *Ulysses* embodied a negative representation of 'the bleak, shiftless, sordid, soulless
Ireland that came to an end catastrophically in 1916', its innovative qualities provided an
important formal model for an effective response to what had occurred since the Rising.[10]
For O'Duffy, it was still possible to represent the recent history of Easter 1916 through a realist
aesthetic, as in his own novel *The Wasted Island*. Yet the instability and social fragmentation
that characterized the period of the civil war demanded new representational forms.
During this period, seventy-seven anti-Treaty members of the Irish Republican Army were
executed by their former comrades in the forces of the Irish Free State — including the
notable republican Liam Mellows and three others, the day before O'Duffy's review was
printed. O'Duffy feared that this culture of violence would prevent the actualization of any
of the possibilities offered not only by *Ulysses*, but by the Irish revolution in general.[11] He
wryly noted in his assessment of the novel, 'there would now be no Beatrice but for her
poet; who knows that certain Irishmen may yet get their way, and leave to posterity nothing
of Ireland but what is enshrined in the pages of *Ulysses*'.[12]

Still, O'Duffy asserts that a modernist work of literature like *Ulysses* does not come
into being according to 'political theories or conceptions of duty' — or, in other words,
according to the dominant values that define more conventional forms of writing such as
the works of the 'hundred poetasters' of the Revival. It is, rather, the result of an alternative
form of intellectual labour. This Joycean position provided a rationale for what O'Duffy
hoped to achieve in his subsequent writing. The formal process of autonomization — that

of the novel in a review of a collection of Eugene O'Neill's plays; see 'Reviews', *Journal of Irish Literature*, 7,
1 (1978), 9–11; the review was originally published in *Irish Review*, 1, 2 (1922), 22–23.

8   See, for example, Duffy, *The Subaltern Ulysses*, which provides a month-by-month analysis of the events of
the Irish struggle for independence in relation to Joyce's composition of the novel.

9   'Reviews', 12.

10   'Reviews', 13.

11   For a discussion of the events leading to Mellows's execution, see J. J. Lee, *Ireland 1912–1985: Politics and
Society* (Cambridge, 1989), 66.

12   'Reviews', 12.

quality inherent to modernism and typified by *Ulysses*, in which discrete and increasingly smaller sections of the text develop their own unique formal qualities — became for O'Duffy an exemplary anti-Revivalist achievement. One consequence was the Cuanduine trilogy of *King Goshawk and the Birds*, *The Spacious Adventures of the Man in the Street*, and *Asses in Clover*, perhaps the first instance of a self-consciously experimental form of Irish fiction after *Ulysses*. Just as the Easter Rising had served as a point of departure for O'Duffy's earlier writing, the civil war presented one of (admittedly many) motivations for the more explicitly modernist works of the Cuanduine trilogy. However, O'Duffy's marginal status suggests how unsuccessful he was in his aspirations.

He was little known during his life, and quickly forgotten after his death in 1935.[13] On the outbreak of World War I, he became permanently estranged from his family, resisting the pressure they put on him to enlist in the British army. Instead, he rebelled by joining the Irish Republican Brotherhood and eventually became a captain in Pearse's Irish Volunteers. O'Duffy's radicalism intensified during the 1920s; he eventually aligned himself with the Social Credit movement theorized by Major C. H. Douglas in the pages of A. R. Orage's cultural and political journal the *New Age*.[14] Eventually, O'Duffy founded and wrote pamphlets for a Social Credit discussion group called the Leisure Society, though this venture collapsed not long after his death.[15] By the time he died early at the age of forty-two from chronic duodenal ulcers, he had written two plays, one lengthy economic work, one collection of poetry, and ten novels. Yet by 1946, only eleven years after his death, Vivian Mercier could state with confidence in an essay in the influential Irish journal *The Bell* that 'O'Duffy's work is unknown outside a small circle of friends and "fans"'.[16] Published between 1926 and 1933, the Cuanduine trilogy begins in the not-too-distant future of the 1940s, but in *King Goshawk and the Birds* (1926) takes a critical view of the recent past by anticipating a dystopian future. In this novel, Dublin is half destroyed after yet another civil war; the rich live in palaces protected from the masses, while the poor live in shanty towns that have been erected upon the ruins. All political discussions in Ireland are dominated by a schism between the Yallogreen party and the Greenyallo party, two political groups that trace their origins to the recently concluded war. Despite their opposition they are mirror images of one another. The political stalemate reflects the fact that Ireland's fate is inevitably tied to global capitalism. This loss of national specificity is the consequence of nationalism and of modernization. This diagnosis lies at the heart of the Cuanduine trilogy. Power in *King Goshawk and the Birds* and *Asses in Clover*

13 The brief biography that follows draws upon John Cronin's *The Anglo-Irish Novel: Volume Two: 1900–1940* (Belfast, 1990), 100–01, and Robert Hogan's *Eimar O'Duffy* (Lewisburg, 1972), 14–19.

14 See Francis Hutchinson and Brian Burkitt, *The Political Economy of Social Credit and Guild Socialism* (London, 1997). On Orage and the interrelationship between literary modernism and the Social Credit movement, see Wallace Martin, *The New Age under Orage: Chapters in English Cultural History* (Manchester, 1967), 266–93.

15 See John L. Finlay, *Social Credit: The English Origins* (Montreal, 1972), 132.

16 Vivian Mercier, 'The Satires of Eimar O'Duffy', *The Bell*, 12, 4 (1946), 325–36.

(1933) belongs to capital, and the monopoly capitalists, who run the world by effectively re-creating a modern form of feudalism, are its true villains. Most powerful of all is Goshawk the Wheat King, who controls most of the world's food production. In a parody of the beginning of the *Táin Bó Cúailgne*, Goshawk seduces his bride, Guzzelinda, by promising to buy her all the birds and flowers in the world for her own private enjoyment. An elderly would-be intellectual in Dublin called the Philosopher of Stoneybatter — a sort of prior form of the lazy idle schemer, now grown old and ignored by the masses — hears of Goshawk's purchase and, suitably offended by this crime against nature, conspires to free the birds and flowers of the world. After a series of misadventures, the Philosopher manages to bring Cuchulainn back from Tír na nÓg in order to fight Goshawk and the forces of capitalism. This is not the Cuchulainn of Yeats and Pearse. He proves to be comically unsuited to the task at hand. Frustrated with the modern lack of respect for archaic forms of heroism, he renounces his mission and returns to eternity. Before he does that, however, he agrees to father with his lover Thalia (the rebellious daughter of Boodleguts the Tripe King) a half-mythological, half-human hero called Cuanduine who will continue the struggle against Goshawk. The remainder of *King Goshawk and the Birds* and *Asses in Clover* tell of Cuanduine's attempts to depose Goshawk and free the birds. Meanwhile, *The Spacious Adventures of the Man in the Street* (1928) presents an interlude in this longer narrative. While visiting the planet Earth, Cuchulainn borrows the body of a typical working-class Dubliner named Robert Emmet Aloysius O'Kennedy, whose soul in turn journeys to an alternative universe in order to visit a planet called Rathé. The description of O'Kennedy's journey allows O'Duffy to produce a narrative that at times serves as an extensive clarification of his utopian economic views and at other times as a modernist reworking of Swiftian satire, which functions by exaggerating the gruesome qualities of modernity in order to denaturalize it.

Mercier's generally positive assessment of the Cuanduine trilogy presents the first of three attempts to recover the critical reputation of O'Duffy's writing (though Mercier is very dismissive of most of O'Duffy's works, aside from the trilogy). In addition to Mercier, Robert Hogan devoted a special issue of the *Journal of Irish Literature* to O'Duffy and contributed a volume to a series of monographs covering the lives of Irish writers in the 1970s.[17] More recently, both Marguerite Quintelli-Neary and José Lanters have included chapters concerning the Cuanduine trilogy in analyses of fantasy and satire in Irish writing.[18] Aside from these scattered examples of criticism, there are at present virtually no other critical works that contain any prolonged consideration of O'Duffy. He has a scant presence in broad overviews of twentieth-century Irish writing and is usually

17   See *Journal of Irish Literature*, 7, 1 (1978); see also Hogan's *Eimar O'Duffy*. The monograph was part of Bucknell University Press' 'Irish Writers Series'.
18   See Marguerite Quintelli-Neary, *Folklore and the Fantastic in Twelve Modern Irish Novels* (Westport, CT, 1997) and José Lanters, *Unauthorized Versions: Irish Menippean Satire, 1919–1952* (Washington, DC, 2000).

cited as yet another example of a given recurring tendency in Irish writing.[19] Mercier and Hogan shared a central motivation in their efforts to revive O'Duffy's reputation. Both felt that O'Duffy's writing, and the Cuanduine trilogy especially, provided evidence of a persistent, frequently comic, experimental tendency within the Irish writing of the 1920s and 1930s. In this sense, O'Duffy can be seen as the intergenerational novelistic link between a Joycean moment and the later experimentalism of Beckett and Flann O'Brien. I agree with this assessment. Yet both Mercier and Hogan are ambiguous in their assessment of O'Duffy. I want to suggest that what they take issue with — the political nature of O'Duffy's writing — provides precisely an ideal point of entry for a contemporary re-evaluation of it.

It must be conceded that some of O'Duffy's fiction, apart from the Cuanduine trilogy and a few other works, is of such poor quality that it is difficult to retrieve from obscurity. He had limited success in Ireland or elsewhere. In order to make some sort of a living, he resorted to both tabloid journalism and the authorship of lowbrow romantic comedies and pulp thrillers. Unfortunately, he clearly hated popular fiction (though he would also incorporate popular forms into the Cuanduine trilogy in an impressive manner), and seemingly put little effort into writing it. Consequently, he never achieved any mainstream success either. A bitter and often hostile sarcastic tone inflects much of his writing, even when it is at its most impressive.

Critical objections to O'Duffy oscillate between a mistrust of the political and economic dimensions of his writing and anxieties about his appropriation of popular forms. Mercier, for example, suggests: 'O'Duffy lacked the style and constructive power necessary for the full development of his original conception. His style wavers between the epic and the commonplace, and his imagination falters; *Asses in Clover* ... bogs down in expositions of capitalist fallacies and monetary reform.' [20] Hogan also finds fault with *Asses in Clover*, arguing that O'Duffy was unable to transcend the difficult historical context of the moment into a pure modernist realm of aesthetic autonomy: 'the book was written when the world was in the throes of a great economic depression, and the intensity of O'Duffy's feelings about the Depression keep breaking out into overt statement'. Leaving aside for the moment Hogan's questionable suggestion that there is something inherently wrong with an overtly political mode of modernist writing, it is important to note that the critical objection has to do with O'Duffy's mix of popular and more experimental techniques. Hogan takes issue with O'Duffy's representation of American capitalism in *Asses in Clover*, arguing that 'his America ... hangs between the America of Bertolt Brecht and the America

---

19   See Vivian Mercier, *The Irish Comic Tradition* (Oxford, 1962), 202. John Wilson Foster similarly considers O'Duffy part of a 'fabulist' tradition of minor Irish writers; see his *Fictions of the Irish Literary Revival* (Syracuse, 1987), 288–90. See also Seamus Deane, *A Short History of Irish Literature* (Notre Dame, 1986), 200, and Terry Eagleton, *Crazy John and the Bishop* (Cork, 1998), 233.
20   Mercier, *The Irish Comic Tradition*, 205.

of Al Capp'.[21] If it is indeed the case that works like *Asses in Clover* — and by extension, the other novels of the Cuanduine trilogy — juxtapose a style that resembles high modernist formal autonomization with the characteristics of a popular comic strip, it seems that O'Duffy's writing presents an example of a textual *désoeuvrement* or 'unworking' of the text for explicitly political purposes.

While such writing might seem scandalous to a theorization of modernism that takes for granted (in Andreas Huyssen's phrase) 'the great divide' between high and low culture within self-consciously modernist cultural activity, O'Duffy's trilogy, like *Ulysses*, is another example of a specifically Irish version of modernism in which the opposition between high and low is absent.[22] In a conceptual sense, the simultaneity of all of the elements of the past, present, and future — for there is a utopian facet to O'Duffy's writing that tries to imagine a better tomorrow even if it never really comes to pass in the trilogy — contribute to a unique form of Benjaminian *Erlebnis* in which the traces evident within the text evoke a history that has been largely forgotten. Formally speaking, the juxtaposition of these different traces requires montage as a narrative principle, something which Luke Gibbons suggests is a symptomatic condition of Irish culture in general. Since the violence and trauma of colonization mediated the modernization of Ireland, the fragmentary characteristics of the Cuanduine trilogy register the uneven, non-synchronous nature of that modernity.[23] As Gibbons and others insist, such a history contributes to a singular conception of modernity within Ireland. Irish modernism takes on a particular form — or, at the very least, those textual characteristics identified with modernism in general acquire a specifically politicized meaning in an Irish context. If this means, as in the case with the Cuanduine trilogy, the stylistic juxtaposition of the traditional and the contemporary as well as the high and the low, then that seems to me a crucial justification for a reconsideration of O'Duffy's writing.

I have argued so far, a form of idleness that has political connotations is one indicator of Irish modernism. In *Ulysses*, while the motif of idleness denotes the negative, inactive situation of pre-revolutionary Ireland, it also suggests the need for alternative forms of intellectual labour that would transform Irish culture and society more dramatically than the conventional kinds of work sponsored by cultural nationalism. O'Duffy's writing goes one step further; he straightforwardly suggests that the pleasures of laziness anticipate the utopian daily life of a non-capitalist future. The 'Leisure State', the name O'Duffy gives to a polity devoted to the cultivation of idleness, depends upon a fundamental redefinition of conventional notions of progress. The Cuanduine trilogy presents one of three variants of idleness, as it is figured in Irish modernist fiction after Joyce. Beckett's *Murphy* addresses the status of idleness in a philosophical sense and Flann O'Brien's *At*

---

21 Hogan, *Eimar O'Duffy*, 77.
22 Andreas Huyssen, *After the Great Divide: Modernism, Mass Culture, Postmodernism* (Bloomington, 1986).
23 See Gibbons, *Transformations in Irish Culture*, 165–69.

Swim-Two-Birds brings a modernist conception of idleness to bear upon politics; O'Duffy understands idleness in economic terms. Ultimately, just as Brecht proposed that his dramatic plays of the 1930s were 'learning plays' in which one might come to inhabit an ideological position outside capitalist common sense, O'Duffy's novels present a pedagogical form of modernism that strives to create the conditions in which idleness can be regarded as a social necessity.

O'Duffy's project in the Cuanduine trilogy is twofold. On the one hand, it involves the exposition of the economic theories he formulates in *Life and Money* (1932) through the representation of a utopian future in which a decentralized state does nothing more than insist upon the social priority of idleness. In terms of the structure of the trilogy itself, he develops this facet of his work primarily in *The Spacious Adventures of the Man in the Street*. Though he states repeatedly that his writing is first and foremost an economic intervention, it gains a political dimension through its implicit juxtaposition of the utopian Leisure State with the actual post-colonial state that emerged in Ireland after 1922. On the other hand, O'Duffy's writing is equally committed to the critique of the dystopian near-future that he anticipated in Ireland, given the emphasis placed upon modernization — however modestly expressed at times — by the nationalist movement in general and the state in particular. This dimension of the trilogy is most evident in *King Goshawk and the Birds* and *Asses in Clover*. Cuanduine is not exactly a lazy idle schemer along the lines of Stephen Dedalus or the other characters I discuss here, though at times he gives a virtuoso performance as the literary intellectual. Yet he stands as an embodiment of the clash between the pre-modern values identified with his father and the ethos of modernity. Of the various traces of a repressed past no longer feasible within a capitalist world order, the most crucial is the sense of 'heroic indolence' referred to by Marx and Benjamin. The representation of 'heroic indolence' in the face of a dehumanizing modern socio-economic order suggests exactly why the utopian value of idleness is so valuable and necessary. Since the economy of the Leisure State is so crucial to the understanding of the Trilogy, it is necessary to examine it first, even though it means considering the individual novels out of their chronological order.

2

O'Duffy's advocacy of a state-form that would ensure the right to idleness echoes Wilde's promotion of socialism as a political possibility that would allow intellectuals and artists to devote themselves to cultural production and to the life of the mind. Bertrand Russell's essay 'In Praise of Idleness'[24] and Joyce's early socialism share a certain sentimental idealism that is echoed and extended in O'Duffy's economic writings. His ideas originate in the Social Credit movement, which attracted him in part because of the possibilities that

24 See Bertrand Russell, *In Praise of Idleness* (London, 1996), 1–15.

it could offer intellectuals. O'Duffy had very little success in his efforts to become a writer; it seems that he regarded his failure as symptomatic of the condition of intellectual labour in capitalist modernity. He writes of 'our present competitive civilization' in *Life and Money*:

> Its richest rewards are for the grasping, cunning, acquisitive type, and it affords a modest livelihood to a certain proportion of the dull, patient, plodding type. To every other type it is fiercely intolerant. For the poet and philosopher it has no use at all; for the man of letters it cares only so far as he can market his talent; for the man of science, only so far as his discoveries have 'commercial value' (sometimes, on account of its lack of imagination, not even then). If men such as these are not to starve, they must prostitute their gifts, or crush them out of mind and undertake some routine occupation; and even these are increasingly hard to get. (LM, 209)

O'Duffy's complaint is not as elitist as may appear from this quotation, since he proceeds to affirm the needs of the 'common' worker, 'who dislikes being tied to somebody else's stool' as well. Social Credit seemed to him and many other modernist writers the means to discover a non-alienated form of intellectual labour.[25] Pound's strenuous espousal of Social Credit principles and his failure to distinguish between it and Fascism have given it a reputation over the years as authoritarian and anti-Semitic.[26] In fact, it was neither. O'Duffy never supported Fascism. In *King Goshawk and the Birds*, he even produced a critical parody of Fascism as early as 1926 through his representation of the villainous Italian dictator 'Nervolini'.

The Social Credit movement advocated the abolition of money in the form of hard currency and a system of exchange in goods or services, the primary form of which would be credit, which the state (rather than private banks) would create and restrict according to the volume of available goods in circulation. This would restrict the accumulation of excessive private wealth. The credit created each year would be distributed equally by the state; one would not be required to sell one's labour in order to subsist. 'By "decommodifying" the worker and separating income from work ... the "new economics" enables the economic actor to take account of values which lie outside the market mechanism.'[27] For O'Duffy, idleness provided just such an alternative value. At stake was

---

25 The most famous association between modernism and Social Credit is Pound's, but such modernists as William Carlos Williams, Herbert Read, Aldous Huxley, Sybil Thorndike, and Charlie Chaplin, among others, were associated with Social Credit at one point or another. A. R. Orage's journal *New Age* was both an important 'little magazine' for the initial publication of many modernist works, as well as the primary site for the exposition of Major C. H. Douglas's theorization of Social Credit. See Hutchinson and Burkitt, *The Political Economy of Social Credit and Guild Socialism*, 167–69, and Martin, *The New Age under Orage*.

26 On Pound's understanding of the relationship between economics and cultural politics, as well as his erratic oscillation between Fascism and Social Credit, see Leon Surette, *Pound in Purgatory: From Economic Radicalism to Anti-Semitism* (Urbana, 1999), esp. 92–107.

27 Hutchinson and Burkitt, *The Political Economy of Social Credit and Guild Socialism*, 2.

an understanding of the temporality of progress. In capitalism progress depends upon technological development, the expansion of the market, and an emphasis on the dignity of work. But the system ultimately serves to better the condition only of those who do not need to sell their labour. Ultimately, progress comes at the cost of personal freedom. Development undeniably benefits a privileged few. O'Duffy notes:

> All of these civilizing influences we have to leave to the so called idle rich, whom we smugly censure while secretly envying them ... Many of us, even, are so rushed that we have no time to linger over our toilet, to enjoy or digest our meals, or attend to the calls of nature, and our health and appearance suffer in consequence. Probably it has never occurred to you that there is a connection between constipation and currency reform; but it is a profound truth notwithstanding. (LM, 74–75)

Real progress lay in recognizing how technology had already contributed to a world in which one did not have to work:

> Every human invention ever made, from the Paleolithic flint to the latest electrical apparatus, has been designed to save labour and create leisure, or else to make leisure more enjoyable. We have definitely set ourselves to do away with labour, and we are continuing to do away with it. Any attempt, therefore, to 'create employment' is running directly contrary to that process, and it is simply futile and ridiculous to try and run both policies concurrently. One or other should be stopped. (LM, 200)

For O'Duffy, Social Credit provided just the sort of disruptive potential that would value idleness — more than work. Both *Life and Money* and the Cuanduine trilogy offered more prolonged versions of this guiding principle.

Life and Money presents a prolonged attack on capitalism, a theorization of his understanding of Social Credit theory, and most importantly, a valorization of the Leisure State as the most utopian possibility available to modern humanity. O'Duffy had some success with *Life and Money* — it went into three editions. But it is not a major theoretical intervention. While his willingness to write a major economic work without any training as an economist is in some respects impressive — in fact, he makes a virtue of being an amateur and argues he is able to see through the fallacy of capitalism precisely because he has not been indoctrinated by the 'natural' laws of economics — O'Duffy's understanding of finance capitalism was not exactly nuanced, and can appear completely outlandish from the perspective of contemporary economic theory. Key parts of his theory, such as his understanding of credit or the commodity form, are flawed even to those sympathetic to his critique of capitalism and his valorization of leisure. Nevertheless, *Life and Money* provides an important insight into the political values O'Duffy sponsored in the Cuanduine trilogy, and the flawed or possibly impractical nature of some of the positions expressed does not discredit his attempt to unite his dissident stance on economics with an experimental literary technique. *Life and Money* interrogates the relation of work and idleness to the state. O'Duffy wrote the first two volumes of the Cuanduine trilogy and *Life and Money* in the first decade after independence. The first edition of *Life and Money* appeared in January 1932, only weeks before the election victories of Eamon de Valera and Fianna Fáil, previously insurrectionary enemies of the Free State. By the time the third edition appeared in October 1935, the de Valera government had begun to draft a new constitution designed to reorganize the government. In the interim, the government had withstood and overcome the brief prominence of more extreme political movements of the right (the vaguely Fascist Blueshirts) and the left (the Republican Congress) that opposed the status quo. An interest in alternative forms of state and society in post-colonial Ireland was thus not unusual in this period, and O'Duffy's enthusiasm for Social Credit registers the longing for a more radically different society than that achieved by the Irish Free State. In tying that alternative form of the state to idleness —both as a utopian condition and as a persistent remainder of a pre-colonial past resistant to the ideology of modernization — O'Duffy brought a more explicitly political dimension to the modernist break with the Revival than any of the other writers discussed in this book, whatever his literary shortcomings may have been.

O'Duffy saw a connection between work as a dominant social value and the power of the state. For him, the problem of modernity was the centrality of the state, for the only forms of rule possible within capitalism were examples of the 'work-state', defined as a 'state in which the claim of an individual to a livelihood is based on the performance of a certain amount of work, and which enjoys compulsion in one form or another to induce its citizens to work'. In the 'Capitalist' state, for instance, the 'multitude of unpropertied men and women are lashed into the service of the wealthy by the invisible whip of starvation' (LM, 197). In societies governed by work-states, the social control that results from the inculcation of a subservient, obedient desire for work discipline is just as important as the commodity produced through labour-power. O'Duffy calls the underlying philosophy of the work-state 'Sisyphism', after the Greek myth of Sisyphus, in which repetitive, inevitable, and ultimately meaningless forms of obligatory work are regarded as the central goal of existence.[28] Sisyphism characterizes not only de Valera's Ireland, but every form of the modern state.[29] O'Duffy claims there is the possibility of escape from modernity's 'iron cage', in Weber's phrase for the transposed Puritan work-ethic.[30] Idleness is not completely missing from a Sisyphist social order, for it exists negatively as unemployment for the poor and in a positive form as leisure for the rich:

---

28 See LM, 40–47.
29 'When Mr. De Valera said that Ireland had been well served by the civil war of 1922 because the repairing of the damage done would give employment to the workers, he was talking the language of pure Sisyphism.' LM, 42
30 See Max Weber, *The Protestant Ethic and the Spirit of Capitalism* (New York, 1930), 181.

'if a man has money, it does not worry him to be unemployed. He does not even call his idleness unemployment: he calls it leisure — and uses it for good or ill according to his quality' (LM, 73). The problem with both capitalism and socialism to O'Duffy is a shared Sisyphist insistence on the creation of more work to eradicate unemployment. Yet idleness is not a social problem in itself. Instead, the problem lies in the fact that the powerful and affluent hoard idleness as an additional form of wealth to the detriment of the rest of humanity. In a passage that underscores his desire not to work too rigorously, even in the development of his own argument, O'Duffy argues that Sisyphism cannot be overcome and a just society created until idleness, in its positive manifestation of leisure, is redistributed equally for all:

> There is no need to labour the point. Leisure is obviously a prime human necessity, following immediately upon food, warmth, and shelter. Without it we can be neither healthy nor wise, and therefore cannot be really wealthy either. Like the other necessities it is available in plenty, only awaiting distribution. (LM, 75)

Towards this end, O'Duffy posed the utopian possibility of the Leisure State. Unlike the almost Foucauldian work-state, the Leisure State governs a society in which work is optional:

> It [i.e. the Leisure State] declares that there is no virtue in work as such, and insists on the right of the citizen as to a free choice whether he shall work or not. It rejects the idea that justice requires that everybody shall do his share of the world's work, and replies that the world's work will be done best by those most competent to do it, who should be highly paid in return. Finally it declares that freedom and leisure are essential to the spiritual evolution of the race, and demonstrates that they are economically possible. In a word, the policy of the Social Credit state would be 'maintenance' simply, without any condition as to work. (LM, 198–99)

This does not mean that work would be abolished in the Leisure State, as 'maintenance' itself involves a certain amount of work. The difference between Sisyphist work and the utopian labour of the future depends upon the presence or absence of alienation, a condition that Marx had argued was inherent to the capitalist division of labour itself. While capitalist work is dehumanizing, soul-destroying and dependent on the dictates of others, the non-alienated labour process of the Leisure State exemplifies the expression of a given skill or creative capacity. O'Duffy does not describe a utopian future specifically, nor does he explain the political form of the state in such a society. Instead, his gestures towards a utopian future are redolent of Wilde and Morris.[31] To the greatest

---

31 O'Duffy's description of life in the Leisure State is worth quoting in full: 'The continuance of the Work State is, then, not only not favourable to human evolution, but decidedly inimical to it. Religion and science

extent possible, difficult or unpleasant types of work will be done by machines, and all of humanity will benefit from a fundamental liberation of intellectual labour: 'Above all, people will have time to think, and thus we shall revive a fundamental human function which our present civilization has very nearly killed' (LM, 210).

While O'Duffy frequently argues that the implementation of Social Credit will, in an economic sense, contribute to the construction of the utopian Leisure State, he is remarkably vague about the political means necessary to construct it. At no point in Life and Money does he explain the practical strategy that will bring this society into being; it was the absence of such a pragmatic approach to the political changes that led Hogan and Mercier to dismiss O'Duffy as a 'crank'. Yet, as Oscar Wilde had asserted a few decades earlier, an insistence upon political practicality is often just another way to dismiss radical possibility. In this case, it stifles the recognition of the greater work of ideological demystification in all of O'Duffy's writing. At the end of Minima Moralia, Adorno argues that one cannot begin to imagine the possibility of a more utopian future without first taking a position that is seemingly impossible to begin with:

> The only philosophy which can be responsibly practiced in the face of despair is the attempt to contemplate all things as they would present themselves from the standpoint of redemption ... Perspectives must be fashioned that displace and estrange the world, reveal it to be, with its rifts and crevices, as indigent and distorted as it will appear one day in the messianic light.[32]

The principle of distortion that Adorno refers to here characterizes not only the rhetoric of Life and Money, but is also the link it has to the formal qualities of the Cuanduine trilogy.

In a brief section near the end of Life and Money entitled 'Educate for Leisure', O'Duffy provides some suggestion of how one can at least anticipate the formation of the Leisure State: 'if the people are going to get the full benefit from their leisure and build up a real new civilization, we shall have to educate them with that end in view; which means that education must be conducted on principles very different from those that form its basis at present' (LM, 210–11). While O'Duffy does provide a few concrete examples of

---

unitedly demand the institution of the Leisure State, that it, a state in which the world's work will be done by a comparatively small number of highly paid and highly skilled mechanics and by handcraftsmen working for the mere love of their jobs (there will be no "competition" to kill them, since there will always be enough money to buy whatever is produced). The "dirty work" will all be done, as far as possible, by machinery, and any that may have to be done by men will be paid at the highest possible rate, instead of the lowest as at present. Those whose work is not required will use or abuse their leisure according to their natures, but since most are sensible and decent, I presume that it will generally be used profitably. Apart from the simple pleasures of domestic life, there will be books to read, music to listen to, knowledge to acquire, sports to enjoy, and the thousand and one hobbies that are usually far more interesting and useful than the "work" which now snatches us from them to sit in somebody's office.' LM, 210

32 Theodor Adorno, Minima Moralia: Reflections from Damaged Life (London, 1974), 247.

possible educational reforms that might help hasten the arrival of the Leisure State, the greater implication is that intellectuals who desire a utopian version of the future should work to demystify the concept of idleness by celebrating it as a necessary human value. As an economic treatise, *Life and Money* itself provides one straightforward example of this pedagogical version of intellectual labour. More importantly for discussions about the trajectory of Irish writing, the Cuanduine trilogy provides a more prolonged, experimental formulation of modernist writing as an alternative form of intellectual work that serves a politicized, didactic purpose. *The Spacious Adventures of the Man in the Street* offers a clear example of just such a pedagogical modernism. It departs from the primary narrative of the Cuanduine trilogy in order to represent Robert Emmet Aloysius O'Kennedy's experiences in the alternative world of Rathé, a planet like Earth. Part of O'Duffy's purpose is to satirize the official, state-sanctioned values of post-colonial Ireland by comic exaggeration — particularly what he felt to be the problematic relationship of a very conservative form of Catholicism to the state. He resented the way the Church intervened in Irish secular politics, especially about matters concerning sexual morality.

In *The Spacious Adventures of the Man in the Street*, Ratheans enjoy completely open sexual relationships; marriage and monogamy are considered the terrain of an idealistic, cultish minority, and sexual guilt does not exist. O'Kennedy, who is constantly troubled and aroused by the 'immodest' dress of the Ratheans, is completely shocked by such a state of affairs and worries whether committing acts that would be considered sinful in Ireland but harmless in Rathé will affect his standing in a Catholic afterlife. Yet Ratheans have the same relationship to eating that Irish people do to sex. Based on the advice of a 'mathematician' (the Rathean equivalent of a priest), who 'scientifically' calculates what is proper, Ratheans choose one type of food that they enjoy eating and remain faithful to that only for the rest of their lives. In this 'monophaguous' society, eating happens in private; it is considered obscene to speak openly about food. Even the language used to describe it is controversial, as any reference to the pleasures of eating must focus on the emotion identified with food rather than physical need: 'they never mentioned the word Hunger, for instance, but the word Taste was never out of their mouths' (SMS, 129). An idealistic bohemian movement devoted to 'Free Eats' (largely based in the rabidly gluttonous cities of Israp [Paris] and Donlon [London]) is especially notorious, and the most scandalous avant-garde literature reveals a distressing obsession with food.[33] At a

33 In one of his better parodies, O'Duffy writes of a Rathean version of Joyce's *A Portrait of the Artist as a Young Man*: 'It was called A Picture of My Youth, and gave a horribly detailed description of the effect on a clever and imaginative boy of all this suppression, and thwarting, and confusion with guilt of a perfectly healthy appetite. It was a painful, and in places a disgusting, revelation, but, I have no doubt, quite true to life. I made an attempt to discuss it with Mr. Juicewit, but the mere mention of the book drove him into a fury. It was a foul and filthy concoction, he said: thoroughly morbid, and the product of a diseased mind. It ought to be burnt publicly in the market place. As for the notion that children suffered from hunger — pooh! He waved it aside with a comprehensive gesture. It was mere theorizing, and morbid at that'. (SMS, 133)

more sordid level, some vice-obsessedRatheans 'indulge themselves irregularly at illicit eating-houses, ruining their constitutions with the corrupt and unnatural food supplied there' (SMS, 129). While most other descriptions of Rathean life in *The Spacious Adventures of the Man in the Street* positively describe the utopian possibilities of life in the Leisure State, O'Duffy is obviously less prescriptive here, for he does not suggest in this extended parody that the 'monophaguous' habits of the Ratheans should be replicated on Earth. Instead, he exaggerates the rigorous morality of Catholic Ireland to such a degree that the conservative social policies that indicate the Church's influence on the Irish Free State — like censorship and the prohibition on divorce — seem as ridiculous as the Ratheans attempts to police nourishment. Just as *Life and Money* repeatedly asserts that egalitarian social change can only occur once the masses realize that capitalism is not really 'natural' or permanent but only presents itself as such, so too does the Cuanduine trilogy call into question the oppressive qualities of the new state.

  O'Duffy's narrative also expounds on how a theoretical understanding of Social Credit can provide the basis for the utopian society governed by the Leisure State. In Rathé, O'Kennedy travels between a utopian society governed by the Leisure State and a different country committed to a particularly dystopian form of capitalism. Despite the horrors O'Kennedy witnesses in this nightmarish delineation of capitalism, he is most comfortable with those characteristics of Rathé that are most similar to life on Earth and most troubled by those details that are economically heretical. In Althusserian terms his 'imaginary relationship to the real conditions of his existence' is mediated by the conservative developmental ideology of the Irish Free State.[34] In the nightmarish dystopia of Harpaxe, O'Duffy shows a grotesque, violent form of the work-state. Most work in Harpaxe is performed by a caste of impoverished dwarves called Outlanders who are too brainwashed to imagine how they might escape from their plight. The Outlanders are not born as dwarves; at any early age the lower portions of their legs are removed so that they never grow beyond a certain height. The rationale for the shortening of the Outlanders is that their houses would be too small for them to inhabit if they were to grow to full size. The ruling class of Harpaxe has no desire to commit resources to the construction of bigger houses or the alteration of a system that seems to work so well. The Outlanders also mutilate other parts of their bodies in order to make use of standardized consumer goods they are provided with (all of the Outlanders' clothes come in only one size), and O'Kennedy's admiration for the Outlanders' resourcefulness demonstrates O'Duffy's ironic condemnation of the way in which the working class alters its needs and desires in accordance with the supposedly unchangeable dictates of the market: 'Altogether the Outlanders had shown a most reasonable spirit of compromise in grappling with the problems of a highly industrialized civilization, and a praiseworthy readiness to adapt themselves to the conditions of the age which had produced them' (SMS, 313).

34 See Louis Althusser, *Lenin and Philosophy* (New York, 1971), 162.

Outlanders who take jobs in domestic service suffer especially severe mutilation; they are lobotomized by their masters so that they may become perfect servants. O'Kennedy meets a young woman who has undergone this procedure, and he observes that she 'is in consequence virtually an automaton, devoid of emotion and reason, and responsive only to such stimuli as I had seen him apply; and that she was, of course, perfectly insensitive to pain. By this process, he said, they had at last solved the servant problem' (SMS, 326). In an especially grotesque touch, the Harpaxean ruling class grafts the excised brain tissue of the lobotomized Outlanders on to the brains of their favourite pet dogs. The dogs, who are 'sent to special schools where no expense was spared to give them the best education procurable', then become a special class of animal. Though O'Kennedy's interview with J. Towser — an advanced dog that feels anxieties regarding his background similar to a member of the nouveau riche — provides one of the funnier moments of the novel. O'Duffy's satirical condemnation of a society in which the rich treat their pets much better than their servants is fierce.

Yet despite this critique of capitalism — and it is the business of the other two novels to launch an even more thoroughgoing attack on it — the primary focus of *The Spacious Adventures of the Man in the Street* is on the utopian qualities of the rest of Rathé. O'Kennedy spends most of his time on Rathé in the city of Bulnid, an idealized version of Dublin. His picaresque adventures in Bulnid provide an almost anthropological description of the life and culture of the Ratheans. For example, in matters of religion, the Ratheans are committed Satanists, and the diabolical creed of Beelzebub (which reads like a parody of the sorts of motivational pamphlets that were popular with salesmen in the 1920s) commands them to obey their individual competitive desires and earn as much money as possible. Just as on Earth, however, most Ratheans worship without really thinking about their professed beliefs, and fail to live according to the message of their gospel; consequently, their society exemplifies a collective form of benevolent socialism with no competition and very little private property. Other aspects of Rathean life provide O'Duffy the opportunity to represent a detailed fictional version of the sort of society he calls for in *Life and Money*. The Rathean understanding of work and leisure presents just such an example of his more prescriptive approach, and presents one of the clearest formulations of idleness as a key cultural value. Since there are almost no social hierarchies on Rathé, all Ratheans are paid the same (in the form of credit, no other form of money exists on Rathé), whatever their job. They do not sell their labour; their work affirms their creative capacities. Consequently, in most cases Ratheans really enjoy their work 'because they think one job's as good as another so long as it's done right, and you have to take the job you're fitted for' (SMS, 105).

Certain kinds of work, like the production of goods, bear a strong resemblance to the utopian propositions of Morris; groups of artisans collectively own their shops and produce beautiful things. Other kinds of work, such as the immaterial labour of teachers, artists, and other intellectuals, are done for their own sake. Though Ratheans work as little as possible and devote most of their time to the idle cultivation of their interests, laziness is not a completely unproblematic condition. The neglect of that social role one is best suited to is one of the few serious crimes in Rathé and is considered worse than murder. Yet there is a loophole for the aspiring Rathean idler as well. Since certain people are particularly skilled in the practice of idleness, they are best suited to the occupation of idler and are not punished; on the contrary, these 'charming idlers' are treated as minor celebrities (SMS, 79). 'Charming idlers' do not contribute to the limited work that enables the upkeep of an organized, egalitarian society, but they have already reached a more highly evolved condition. The most advanced part of Rathé is a tropical location called the Isles of the Blest. When O'Kennedy arrives there, he discovers that the highly evolved inhabitants of this region spend almost all of their time in the absolute idleness of philosophical contemplation. The Blest can be said to be working, but their labour is of a purely intellectual nature.

Such a fantastic image presents the most explicit connection between intellectual labour and idleness to be found anywhere in the Cuanduine trilogy — or, for that matter, within any of the other works discussed here either. The value of 'heroic indolence', which presides in the other two volumes of the trilogy, is all that is left of a social order that had become outmoded by the twentieth century. This version of *otium* that O'Kennedy encounters in the Isles of the Blest provides a Benjaminian trace that both invokes that history which abolishes idleness as an acceptable social possibility and marks the conceptual limit of a world free of the ideological assumptions of capitalism. O'Duffy dramatizes how the supposedly natural qualities of modernity can be queried and other, more egalitarian possibilities considered; it is in these that the radical potential of the Irish revolution could be realized.

3

The Spacious Adventures of the Man on the Street recalls an older Swiftian sort of narrative. By contrast, the other two novels of the Cuanduine trilogy bear a clearer resemblance to Joycean modernism. The narrative of *King Goshawk and the Birds* oscillates between different styles ranging from naturalism to fantasy, from the Wildean comic drama to tabloid journalism. The stylistic variety recalls the later episodes of *Ulysses*; and the narrative of *King Goshawk and the Birds* similarly exemplifies the autonomization of the text, which Jameson identifies as the primary formal characteristic of modernism. Though it is not as carefully constructed — O'Duffy was severely ill and in dire financial straits when he wrote it — *Asses in Clover* displays similar formal tendencies and makes the social and political positions of *Life and Money* and *The Spacious Adventures of the Man on the Street* more explicit. As his earlier review of *Ulysses* indicates, O'Duffy believed formal innovation was needed to represent the rapidly changing political conditions Ireland faced after 1922. A longing for historical narratives other than those of heroic, pre-colonial Gaelic tradition celebrated in the Revival reveals a problem Lloyd suggests is familiar to Irish writers, critics, or historians who must come to terms with the restrictive and oppressive qualities of a post-colonial state that idealized tradition:

> The problem, then, is twofold: on the one hand, to fragment the canons of verisimilitude which stabilize the various elements that constitute the ideological self-evidence of the modern state formation; on the other hand, the longer and more arduous project of inventing other modes of narrative, of historicization, of representation, which might counter the extraordinary weight of self-evident truths without stabilizing or fetishizing alternative formations into fixed oppositional locations.[35]

Regardless of whatever ideological differences the writers of the Revival and the empowered politicians of Cumann na nGaedheal might have had over certain issues — Yeats's opposition to the ban on divorce comes to mind — the cultural imaginary of the Revival in large part provided the 'self-evidence' of the Irish Free State.[36] During that period, the 'canon of verisimilitude' that Lloyd writes of centred upon a fixed notion of a sacrosanct pre-colonial past that had been revived to justify the political needs of the present. The political consequence of the valorization of tradition that had occurred during the Revival proved to be problematic for O'Duffy, since a tragic conception of heroic martyrdom had justified bloodshed and continued to disguise the violence of state formation.

Rather than reproducing the legendary tales of Cuchulainn as fruitful period pieces within twentieth-century Dublin, as Yeats and others had done, O'Duffy, in *King Goshawk and the Birds* and *Asses in Clover*, depicted an out-of-touch and befuddled Cuchulainn on holiday from the afterlife in Tír na nÓg, walking the ruined streets of a half-destroyed Dublin of the near future. Some have suggested that O'Duffy's introduction of canonical traditional material into a dystopian future that draws upon the most repressive features of the Irish Free State shows that he celebrated the nostalgic qualities of a heroic Irish tradition as a solution to his dissatisfaction with early post-colonial Ireland — but he is doing the opposite.[37] O'Duffy takes the more radical step of demonstrating the almost

---

35 Lloyd, *Ireland after History*, 63.

36 Not long after the emergence of the Irish Free State, the Abbey Theatre became a state-subsidized National Theatre; the enthusiasm for the Abbey demonstrated by Free State leaders like Desmond Fitzgerald and Ernest Blythe provides one index of the importance placed on the symbolic cultural values of the Revival by the new government. Lionel Pilkington suggests that the plays chosen and celebrated by the Abbey directors Yeats, Lady Gregory, and Lennox Robinson during this period corresponded to the ideological values of the Free State despite the fact that Yeats objected to a number of its specific policy decisions; see *Theatre and the State in Twentieth-Century Ireland: Cultivating the People* (London, 2001), 86–111.

37 Quintelli-Neary, *Folklore and the Fantastic in Twelve Modern Irish Novel*, 116, argues that in O'Duffy's writing 'the only hope for the world is in a return to traditional Irish heroic values, some of which include the romantic notions of bravery, loyalty, and justice, in the code of Cuchulainn and his warriors'. See also, Mercier, *The Irish Comic Tradition*, 202.

complete insufficiency of traditional symbols and images to address the needs of the present. Traditional heroes like Cuchulainn or Cuanduine, the half-mythological, half-modern son who gives his name to the trilogy, are comically unsuited to the demands of modernity. Even when Cuanduine seems to defeat the forces of big business through legendary feats of heroism, global capitalism reorganizes itself quickly enough to triumph in the end — although it is a pyrrhic victory, as the developmental narrative of capitalist progress leads inevitably to the extinction of the universe. Like many Irish literary works, the Cuanduine trilogy ultimately reproduces what Deane identifies as the national paradigm of apocalypse. Unlike most of those narratives, however, in which apocalypse is 'also the prelude to a final regeneration in which the national character and national history would ultimately be redeemed and the experience of oppression and colonial subjection overcome', O'Duffy's has no future after its apocalypse.[38]

Yet, as destroyed fragments of Rathean art are deployed by newer artists to produce something that speaks to the needs of the future, certain aspects of Irish tradition do suggest utopian possibilities that could be reclaimed for the present to counter the state's monopoly on tradition. O'Duffy faced the trap Lloyd warns of, by which alternative points of resistance might be stabilized into fixed oppositional roles. His solution to this problem avoids the perils of identity and fixes upon common practices — hospitality, free and equal relations between men and women, collective ownership, and most of all, the 'heroic indolence' of idleness. These are in themselves, and are harbingers of, the alternative values that will emerge with the arrival of the Leisure State.

In the Convolute on idleness in The Arcades Project, Benjamin notes, 'in bourgeois society, indolence — to take up Marx's word — has ceased to be "heroic". (Marx speaks of the "victory ... of industry over a heroic indolence")' (AP, 800). The quote Benjamin refers to (which, in its English translation, uses slightly different wording for the term Faltheit) focuses upon the revolutions of 1648 (in England) and 1789 (in France):

> In these revolutions the bourgeoisie gained the victory; but the victory of the bourgeoisie was at the same time the victory of a new social order, the victory of bourgeois property over feudal property, of nationality over provincialism, of competition over the guild, of the partition of estates over primogeniture, of the owner's mastery of the land over the land's mastery of its owner, of enlightenment over superstition, of the family over the family name, of industry over heroic laziness, of civil law over privileges of medieval origin.[39]

In short, Marx's discussion refers to that violent moment of transition that separates traditional society from the modernity of capitalism when all of the latter terms in

---

38 Deane, Strange Country, 147–48.
39 Marx, The Revolutions of 1848: Political Writings: Volume 1, 192–93.

Marx's list of antagonisms become obsolete upon the triumph of the bourgeoisie. 'Heroic laziness' refers to those pre-modern forms of enjoyment in which one could rigorously *not* work in a manner that was socially acceptable and even valued. In its heroic form, this type of idleness does not concern usefulness or propriety. 'Heroic indolence' can be further clarified, once understood through the very same Irish mythological material that was so important in the Revival.

Yeats and Pearse helped construct the symbolic imagery of the Easter Rising and its aftermath by establishing the heroic values of necessary violence and the inevitability of self-sacrifice as traditional. Less valued were all of the attributes of heroism in ancient Ireland that *did not* involve violence or the completion of epic tasks: the bacchanalian feasting, leisurely pursuits like sports or music, even the act of story-telling itself, all of which required a general collective commitment to idleness. In O'Duffy's hands, the heroic indolence of ancient Irish society anticipates the utopian values of the Leisure State of the future. Yet such behaviour is no more possible in modern conditions than the ancient aggressive forms of heroic combat Cuchulainn attempts to use in *King Goshawk and the Birds*. The inability of Cuchulainn and, to a lesser extent, Cuanduine (though he has more success than his father) to achieve anything substantial through heroic violence suggests that the role of the individual hero is inappropriate for modernity. On the other hand, the practice of heroic indolence — for, when not entering into combat, Cuchulainn pursues leisure — marks a utopian form of the past opposed to the values of modernity, far outside the common sense of capitalism.

King Goshawk and the Birds opens in a post–civil war Ireland dominated by the bitterly antagonistic but virtually identical Greenyallo and Yallogreen parties. For O'Duffy, the disagreements that led to the Irish Civil War are not really relevant; indeed, his fictitious civil war occurs because the two sides, having given up on national sovereignty, cannot agree on the best way Ireland might rejoin the British Empire (against the wishes of Britain). What is more problematic for O'Duffy is that national sovereignty, however worthy a political ambition, needs the state, 'paternal government', as he calls it, to be realized. In the future of global capitalism, O'Duffy suggests, every form of government will be oppressive and predicated upon the logic of censorship:

> Political and social stability were preserved by the same means; there being in every country a law forbidding the speaking or writing of any word declaring, implying, or insinuating that the legislative, executive, or judicial system of that country was not the best conceivable for that country. Thus in one country it would be forbidden to criticize plutocracy disguised as monarchy; in another to criticize plutocracy disguised as republicanism; and in Ireland it was high treason to condemn the system of flamboyant posters, mean-little hand bills, and dirty language. (KGB, 85)

In these novels the primary purpose of the state is to prepare its citizens into a subservient position in which supposedly natural and unchangeable material conditions are never questioned. The nameless political system that O'Duffy identifies with Ireland might lack more stable forms of state and civil society, but it certainly does not lack repressive characteristics. The 'paternal government' of Ireland is dedicated to the absolute repression of pleasure, intoxication, sexuality, and any cultural activity that refers to blasphemous or forbidden activities or is critical of a sanctified national tradition; it has also severely restricted women's rights and destroyed two-fifths of the world's literature. O'Duffy's exaggeration is designed to make repression appear ludicrous; yet some of the measures that seem ridiculous (such as the unyielding ban on divorce and contraception, the intensification of state censorship, and the exclusion of married women from any publicly funded job) were actually implemented in the decade after the publication of *King Goshawk and the Birds*.

No state, not even the 'paternal government' of Ireland in *King Goshawk and the Birds*, is as powerful as the forces of global capital; the role of the state, in O'Duffy's sketch of the future, is to ensure that the economy operates without restraint. Monopoly capitalism has re-created feudal conditions on a global scale. The hierarchy among the global capitalists is complex, but the most powerful among them is Goshawk the Wheat King. The novel is centred on Goshawk's purchase of all of the birds in the world in order to fulfil a wedding promise to Guzzelinda, an act of privatization in which all of the governments of the world acquiesce. Eventually he purchases all of the flowers in the world as well, and everyone is obliged to travel to Castle Goshawk (located in upstate New York; Goshawk and Guzzelinda usually live in the Grand Palace of Manhattan) and pay exorbitant sums of money to see the birds and flowers. The 'Philosopher of Stony-Batter takes great offence at the commodification of nature and begins scheming as to how he might free the birds. Though he vaguely resembles a medieval Irish bard in appearance (and philosophical outlook), he lives in a working-class section of twentieth-century Dublin that is 'not a place prolific in philosophers, for the reason that the folk there are too busy picking up half a living to have time for the cultivation of wisdom. The Philosopher himself could only make time for it by giving up the food scramble entirely' (KGB, 7). In this sense, the Philosopher inhabits a specific moment, but is not of it; the marker of difference is his commitment to what the people around him consider mere idleness, a condition once favoured by ancient philosophers and medieval bards alike, but now outmoded in a modern world defined by the discipline of work. Given that the novel is set in the future, the Philosopher may be regarded as an older echo of the figure of the lazy idle schemer who never did get around to formulating an alternative form of intellectual labour. However, he is apparently the only intellectual in Ireland who sees beyond the impasse either of nationalist political debate maintained by the Greenyallo and Yallogreen parties, or of global capitalism. When he tries to express his opposition to King Goshawk's purchase of the birds, he is immediately set upon by an angry mob that throws him into the Liffey.

O'Duffy's comic representation of the Philosopher's early attempts to resist King Goshawk indicates the rather grim prospects intellectuals face. As the general disapproval of the Philosopher's idleness expressed throughout by 'the man in street' suggests, he cannot find sympathy or employment in a system predicated upon values he opposes. Yet the Philosopher's marginal social status allows him to call into question the seemingly unchangeable nature of dominant society. What appears to be mere idleness in the conventional eyes of the mob actually involves a rigorous, socially unrecognized form of intellectual labour:

> He began, therefore, to ponder how man might be redeemed from the course of wickedness and folly by which he was travelling to destruction; and to that inquiry he devoted the full labour of his mind for a period of thirty days; at the end of which time he came to the conclusion that the task was beyond the power of mortal man, and would be accomplished only by one returned from the life beyond. (KGB, 23)

Unfortunately, the Philosopher's powers prove limited; he can argue against global capitalism, but cannot do anything to replace it.

The Philosopher possesses special powers of meditation that enable him to travel into the supernatural world of the afterlife. This narrative conceit allows O'Duffy to address the work of retrieval so favoured during the Revival. By the 1920s, Cuchulainn had become a hallowed figure. Yet in *King Goshawk and the Birds* he appears ridiculous. As he travels around Ireland, in a confused and disenchanted condition, he shows himself to be useless, practically speaking, in this world that he comes to hate. His liking for wine, women, and song quickly gets him into trouble with the Censors, a special police force devoted to the enforcement of the morality of Irish paternal government, and the Philosopher constantly has to intervene to make sure no one is harmed because of Cuchulainn's tendency readily to resort to violence. He simply does not fit into modern Ireland; his incongruity is emphasized in formal terms in chapters that stylistically parody the popular forms of the tabloid newspaper and the romance novel. Despite his ineffectiveness, Cuchulainn's 'ancient' values retain a utopian dimension. They include an open approach to sexual relationships, the legal and social equality of men and women, a sacred conception of artistic creation and official position for the artist, the collective enjoyment of nature and, most of all, the affirmation of idleness. Taken together, they contribute to a general notion of the heroic indolence Marx argues was lost as a consequence of the triumph of the industrious bourgeoisie. What is clear in O'Duffy's representation of Cuchulainn, however, is that heroic violence will not help to restore those values of the past.

If twentieth-century Irish writing is often predicated upon a dialectical relationship between the archaic and the modern, as Joe Cleary argues, then O'Duffy's characterization of Cuchulainn demonstrates the insufficiency of that contradiction in itself as the basis for a critique of post-colonial Ireland.[40] What is needed, in other words, is a more flexible type of schemer than either the Philosopher or Cuchulainn. O'Duffy's solution lies in the introduction of Cuanduine, the central character of the trilogy (though he only actually appears in roughly half of it). Disgusted by the repressive aspects of modernity, Cuchulainn decides to leave humanity to its inevitable ruin and to return to his afterlife in Tír na nÓg. Before leaving the planet, however, he eventually fathers the half-mythological, half-human child named Cuanduine ('hound of the people'), who will eventually overthrow King Goshawk and liberate the birds and flowers of the world. Cuanduine is close to being a paradigmatic lazy idle schemer. He represents, however fitfully, the post-colonial Irish embodiment of heroic possibility: like his father, he retains archaic values that have a revolutionary potential in the context of modern capitalism but, unlike his father, he understands the need for a coherent plan that will bring about an alternative modernity.

After a childhood in which he is tutored in ancient customs by his father and educated about capitalist modernity by the Philosopher, Cuanduine sets forth as 'the new evangel' who will bring a subversive, anti-capitalist message to Ireland (KGB, 192). Though he makes a great initial impression upon his audience, the Irish people flatly reject him as a dangerous rabble-rouser. His reputation as a dangerous political activist attracts the attention of the aristocratic newspaper magnate Lord Cumbersome, who invites him 'to come amongst us and apply your saving doctrines to our desperate case' (KGB, 216). Of course, as one of King Goshawk's lackeys, Cumbersome has no intention of promoting social change, but he thinks that Cuanduine's notoriety will arouse public interest in England and increase newspaper sales. In this section of the trilogy, Cuanduine follows a path opened earlier by Wilde and George Bernard Shaw, both of whom negotiated between stereotypes of Irishness and Englishness in attacking the system that created such stereotypes in the first place. O'Duffy specifically alludes to Wilde and Shaw at several points in this section — one chapter is even written as a parody of a one-act Wildean or Shavian comedy of manners. O'Duffy frequently suggests that the influence of literary intellectuals is seriously limited, however; the references to Wilde and Shaw are a reminder of how initially radical cultural positions can become muted through their co-optation by the dominant status quo. His prediction is that Shaw, despite the radical reputation he had in 1926, would be misremembered as a conservative:

> No less than five millionaires, with a choice collection of politicians, soldiers, archbishops of all denominations, vivisectionists, and other scientists, a couple of the leading sportsmen of the day, and a sprinkling of fashionable novelists had all assembled to do honour to the memory of this great Artist and Moral Teacher. (KGB, 249)

---

40 Cleary, *Outrageous Fortune*, 70.

All of these typical butts of Shavian humour have either completely failed to understand the nuances of his irony or have never read any of his works, referred to here as 'an imperishable monument to Britain's glory' and 'an imperial asset'; Shaw is called 'England's greatest moral teacher' and 'an apostle of work and efficiency' (KGB, 249, 251, 252, 253). Despite such an absolute misreading of virtually everything Shaw ever wrote, he has become a canonical figure in the England of *King Goshawk and the Birds*. While this episode serves as a brief ironic commentary on the lack of irony or cultural capital among the powerful, it also demonstrates how a dominant system appropriates dissidents for its own purposes. In spite of Shaw's rebellious or controversial political views, he had become a respectable man of letters by the 1920s. This example has clear implications for Cuanduine's attempts to write as a radical journalist while working for the highbrow newspaper of record. After all, rebels who work within the system ultimately face a dilemma: they must risk assimilation by the dominant power structure, or they must break with the system completely in open rebellion and thus potentially lose the possibility of public support.

Cuanduine learns that subservience itself is rooted in the labour process. At one point, while working as a journalist, Cuanduine meets a worker who is so reduced that he is barely sentient. Cuanduine asks this 'flat-faced fellow with hunched shoulders and vacant eyes' a series of questions; each time he receives the response, 'ninety-nine'. The man is a worker in one of Goshawk's factories, and for his entire life has been engaged in making 'part ninety-nine' of some product:

> Whatever it is [i.e., 'part ninety-nine'], he's been making it ever since he was a kid. He can make it to perfection, but he can make nothing else. By this time he can think of nothing else. That's Goshawk's policy: one man one job, and get it Right. He's hardly got it going properly in this country yet; but, by Jove, you should see how it works in America. They've whole towns there that can only say one word, like our friend here. Think of that! A whole town in which every blessed man, woman, and child is making, or is being trained to make, Part Umpty-um of some blasted thing they've never seen entire, or even heard the name of. That's progress for you. (KGB, 244)

When Cuanduine finally attempts to lead the rebellion against King Goshawk, he combines his rhetorical skills, derived from his work as a journalist, with his father's flair for dramatic heroic action, by attempting to incite the masses against Goshawk on the day of the annual Gold Cup race at Ascot. However, the only response he receives from the crowd outside the royal box is, 'Cheese it, Paddy. Get off the course' (KGB, 305). In Goshawk's world, the possibility of rebellion is subordinate to the culture of distraction and momentary enjoyment. If Cuanduine is to find any success against Goshawk, it will be based upon a critique of the division of labour itself, through an inquiry into the relationship between work and idleness.

Cuanduine increasingly comes to view the pressure of the modern idea of work as the primary source of humanity's subservience to capital. *Asses in Clover* is a more frustrating narrative than the earlier two novels of the trilogy — it is much more digressive, with the result that roughly only half of it is devoted to Cuanduine's struggle against King Goshawk to liberate the birds. The resolution finally begins halfway through the novel, when one of the birds manages to escape from Guzzelinda's private aviary in upstate New York and flies to the west of Ireland. The people of Ireland, who had forgotten the sound of birdsong, are immediately enamoured of the bird:

> Thereafter, the people came running from all parts to hear the song of the bird, which poured forth the joy of its heart in fullthroated melody so that all the men of Eirinn were enchanted with it; and they forgot their sorrows and their hatreds, and mingled like brothers upon the green slopes of Royal Teamhair. (AC, 168)

The song of the bird is natural; the contemplation of such beauty, we gather, animates a sense of collectivity that O'Duffy associates with ancient Irish civilization in which the natural retained much of the force and appeal since lost. Dramatically, all work stops in Ireland as people rediscover the joys of idleness in their contemplation of the song of the bird. The Philosopher writes a manifesto justifying the right of the people to the collective enjoyment of the bird's song, and he demands the freedom of all of the birds as well as for a world in which 'people stopped working for a time' (AC, 177). Such a turn of events is especially galling to King Goshawk and the other capitalist kings; at their behest every other nation of the world dispatches its airforce to attack Ireland with bombs and chemical weapons for its refusal to work. Cuanduine, who has married and is himself living a heroically indolent life in a magical valley, is visited by the ancient Irish war goddess Badb and persuaded to protect his native land.

Cuanduine returns to Ireland and single-handedly defeats the approaching airforce through the aid of a magical aircraft called Poliorketes (though his efforts are briefly threatened by a dispute among the Irish people concerning the best way to fight, another echo of the divisions of the Irish Civil War). Cuanduine then flies to New York to confront King Goshawk directly; Goshawk dies from fear at Cuanduine's approach, and, as Cuanduine contemplates the best way the birds of the world might be repatriated to their lands of origin, the whole system of capitalism is threatened. Unfortunately, he spares Slawmy Cander, Cuanduine's chief financial adviser and the most powerful person during Goshawk's reign ('Goshawk ruled the world; but Mr. Slawmy Cander ruled Goshawk') (AC, 4). Cander convinces Cuanduine to let him serve as his foremost consultant on the most practical, economic way to free the birds. The forces of capitalism thus symbolically reorganize themselves immediately after a revolutionary change.

Through the debate regarding the birds, O'Duffy announces that the most nefarious quality of modern capitalism is its endless adaptability. The mass media and the economists of the most prestigious universities — both effectively managed by Slawmy Cander — argue strenuously against the liberation of the birds. Underlying their argument is the fear that idleness will replace work as a central social value — for, as the events in Ireland demonstrated, people might quit working in order to enjoy the song of the birds. Since they would enjoy the birds without having to pay for the privilege, they would have no incentive to work — and the possibility of not having to work is too dangerous an idea to be entertained. Earlier in the novel, Cuanduine encountered a group of unemployed men who work without pay; they cannot bear the unnatural feeling of not working. For Slawmy Cander and the system he represents in the dystopian world of the trilogy, such a condition is crucial for the preservation of capitalism. Cuanduine, for his part, argues for the liberation of the birds precisely because they might encourage the pleasures of idleness. The denaturalization of a social compulsion to work becomes the central aim of Cuanduine's opposition to capitalism. Idleness, according to Cuanduine, signifies a (non) practice that enables the imagination of a better world; not surprisingly, it recalls O'Duffy's discussion of the Leisure State in *Life and Money*:

> What do you think you live for? Is it to toil with pick and spade, to serve in shops, to pull the levers of machines, and to sit on office stools? Or rather is it to live comfortably or adventurously, according to your choice, to laugh and to love, to enjoy sunshine and flowers and the song of birds, and to give glory to your heavenly Father? Then if these things can only be had in return for work, well and good: do the work that lies at hand to produce them. But if the work can be done by machines, better still: you will have more time to live. (AC, 268)

But the argument falls on deaf ears, as a character named Mac ui Rudai (a pathetic modern everyman) answers for humanity by responding: 'Sure, if we've got nothing to do, we'll all go to the devil entirely' (AC, 270). Filled with nihilistic disgust at humanity's refusal of a utopian form of social living, Cuanduine performs the last heroic act of the trilogy by finally opening the birds' cages so they might fly free. 'The birds, however, were so accustomed to captivity that they would not stir, and pecked him viciously when he tried to shoo them forth' (AC, 271). The birds' refusal to fly free serves as one final metaphor for the triumph of capitalism in the trilogy. Just as humanity cannot conceive of life outside of the Weberian cage of the obligation to work, Goshawk's birds cannot imagine a world outside of a more literal form of that cage. Cuanduine finally abandons his mission and leaves the world behind, his attempt to re-create the role of traditional Irish hero just as ineffective in a modern context as his father's had been. As the trilogy ends, monopoly capitalism is as dominant as it had been at the beginning of the novels — that is, until O'Duffy represents the final annihilation and extinction of mankind in the final pages of *Asses in Clover*.

While movements devoted to Social Credit had some success in a local sense in various parts of the British Commonwealth (most notably in western Canada), the sort of economy and society favoured by O'Duffy had a negligible impact upon Irish politics. In the year *Asses in Clover* was published, the Irish people voted Eamon de Valera's Fianna Fáil into office, thus establishing precisely the sort of conservative nationalist 'Work-State' O'Duffy had warned against in *Life and Money*. Whatever utopian hopes for an independent Ireland and a post-capitalist future he may have held in his earlier works had dissipated by the end of *Asses in Clover*. As his hopes for the possibility of a future society devoted to idleness diminished, the quality of his writing arguably declined as well. In the work of later writers like Beckett and Flann O'Brien idleness became thematically as important in Irish modernism as formal experiment was in both *Ulysses* and the Cuanduine trilogy, but it lost the utopian dimension of O'Duffy's writing. Yet, a comparison with another notoriously grim assessment of capitalism clarifies the importance of idleness in the Cuanduine trilogy. In *Minima Moralia*, Adorno momentarily breaks off from his own bleak assessment of post-war capitalism in order to offer a brief conception of utopia in which society has 'grown tired of development':

> A mankind which no longer knows want will begin to have an inkling of the delusory, futile nature of all the arrangements hitherto made in order to escape want ... Enjoyment itself would be affected, just as its present framework is inseparable from operating, planning, having one's way, subjugating. *Rien faire comme une bête*, lying on water and looking peacefully at the sky, 'being, nothing else, without any further definition and fulfilment', might take the place of process, act, satisfaction, and so truly keep the promise of dialectical logic that it would culminate in its origin. None of the abstract concepts comes closer to fulfilled utopia than that of eternal peace.[41]

There is a remarkable degree of similarity between Adorno's description of the inactivity of 'eternal peace' and O'Duffy's representation of the highly evolved form of life on the Isles of the Blest in *The Spacious Adventures of the Man in the Street*. Just as Adorno suggests that once utopia has been realized, the future need no longer be planned for, in the Cuanduine trilogy the Leisure State is a condition in which the relentless drive for progress has finally come to a stop. Neither Adorno's nor O'Duffy's descriptions of a better future are practical, according to a worldview conditioned by the labour process. But in their identification of precisely what is outside the realm of possibility for any period longer than the brief temporal unit of 'free time', their respective accounts of the importance of doing nothing but existing and thinking, gesture towards a more optimistic conception of a future alternative to that of capitalism. As Benjamin too argues, heroic indolence

41 Adorno, *Minima Moralia*, 156–57.

was one of the casualties of development. The Cuanduine trilogy is unique in its radical commitment to an alternative form modernization and in allying this with a commitment to answering innovations in fictional form.

6   Samuel Beckett and the Philosophy of Idleness

I

In 1931 Samuel Beckett found himself at a crossroads. In mid-1930, he had returned from post-graduate studies in Paris to take a job as lecturer in French at Trinity College, Dublin. As soon as he had accepted the position — indeed before he even arrived to begin the school year — he had serious misgivings about returning to Ireland and his family. In a letter of July 1930 to his close friend Thomas MacGreevy, Beckett states that 'the acceptance of this thing makes flight and escape more and more complicated, because if I chuck Dublin after a year I am not merely chucking Dublin — definitely — but my family, and causing them pain. I suppose I may as well make up my mind to be a vegetable.'[1] The self-deprecating remark is telling; in the following decade he often associated intellection with a vegetative condition. As the school year went on, he wrote to MacGreevy, noting that 'looking vaguely round college there is nothing but loneliness', of how 'wilful seclusion is a natural measure of protection' for him, and how 'nothing is so attractive anyhow as abstention' from the duties of his job.[2]

In December 1931 he resigned his post. He claimed that 'I want to do nothing more than lie on my back and fart and think about Dante'.[3] The brief lyric 'Gnome', written in 1934, outlines his alienation from the academy in a more poetic manner:

1   Martha Dow Fehsenfeld and Lois More Overbeck, eds., *The Letters of Samuel Beckett: Volume 1, 1929–1940* (Cambridge, 2009), 32. (Hereafter, *Letters I*).
2   *Letters I*, 49, 61, 88.
3   See Kiberd, *Inventing Ireland*, 452. Beckett's authorized biographer, James Knowlson, notes that in actuality Beckett was deeply concerned with the disapproval of his parents upon his resignation and that the decision was far less cavalier than the famous quote would suggest. See Knowlson, *Damned to Fame: The Life of Samuel Beckett* (New York, 1996), 141–42.

> Spend the years of learning squandering
> Courage for the years of wandering
> Through a world politely turning
> From the loutishness of learning.[4]

The poem foreshadows the direction Beckett's writing would take in the 1930s. 'Wandering' may well have been the only course of action available to him, although his ability to do that or anything else remained open to question. By the mid-1930s, he had developed severe problems with depression, held deep anxieties about his habitual laziness, and underwent a long course of therapy with the celebrated psychoanalyst W. R. Bion at the Tavistock Clinic in London. Aimless wandering, of course, became a central action in his writing. Furthermore, 'Gnome' draws a distinction between the inner world of the university and the larger world outside its gates; Beckett's early novel *Murphy* echoed the distinction through its portrayal of the inner world of idle intellectual labour and the outer world of activity. It is certainly not difficult to connect Beckett's justification for resigning from Trinity College to one of the most obvious motifs in his writing; John Harrington notes, 'indolence, inertia, and, of course, waiting, are conditions central to all of Beckett's work'.[5]

Beckett's representation of the lazy idle schemer dates from his first published work of fiction: Belacqua Shuah, 'the indolent bourgeois poltroon' at the centre of Beckett's *More Pricks than Kicks*, stands as a quintessential lazy idle schemer who manages to become more idle than his obvious role model Stephen Dedalus by lacking any ambition whatsoever.[6] Belacqua was also the name of a lazy lute-maker in Dante's *Purgatorio* who deferred his repentance until the last possible moment, and was condemned to spend a time in Purgatory equal to the time he spent procrastinating. Belacqua Shuah lives up to his name in his inability to work or do anything productive until his death in the penultimate story 'Yellow', though he does spend a great deal of time in pubs, at literary parties, in assignations with young women, and (like his creator) in thinking about Dante. Though Belacqua never attempts to write, nor does he identify himself as an artist, his preoccupations mark him as a would-be literary intellectual obsessed with the need for some form of aesthetic or philosophical autonomy. But he is perhaps no more than a parody.[7] He might be more accurately described as a lazy idle schemer who never even

4   Samuel Beckett, *Collected Poems in English and French* (New York, 1977), 7.
5   John P. Harrington, *The Irish Beckett* (Syracuse, 1991), 56. See, for example, Lidan Lin, 'Labour, Alienation, and the Status of Being: The Rhetoric of Indolence in Beckett's *Murphy*', *Philological* Quarterly, 79, 2 (2000), 249–71, for another account of idleness in *Murphy*.
6   Samuel Beckett, *More Pricks than Kicks* (New York, 1972), 161. The collection (a reworked version of Beckett's unpublished first novel *Dream of Fair to Middling Women*) was first published in 1934.
7   Seán Kennedy argues that parody is precisely the point in *More Pricks than Kicks*, and that one source of a historical understanding of the collection's engagement with post-colonial Irish society has to do with its satire of the Anglo-Irish performance of identity after independence; see Kennedy, '"Yellow": Beckett and

gets around to scheming. Beckett's great contribution to the genealogy of the lazy idle schemer came instead in the novel Murphy.

Kiberd notes that 'for Beckett's early heroes (if that is the word), the most prolonged crucifixion of all is the necessity to earn a living by the sweat of their brows'; he argues that figures like Belacqua and Murphy resist and satirize the Protestant work-ethic, which was a defining feature of the Anglo-Irish upper middle class.[8] But although Belacqua is identified in More Pricks than Kicks as 'a dirty low-down Low Church Protestant high-brow' and seems to have been a student at Trinity College, Murphy's identity is notably vague.[9] Yet certain biographical factors do help in understanding Beckett's comic response to the glorification of work, and more specifically his representation of intellectual labour, which he first experienced at Trinity College, then enduring its most difficult period as a university.[10] Beckett remarked in a letter to MacGreevy how distant he felt from his faculty colleagues because of their enthusiasm for things British.[11] Trinity professors had been involved in debates on the nature of a national culture up through the Revival; yet that collective participation in Irish society had diminished considerably by 1922.[12] While Trinity held representation in the Dáil, these positions were of a symbolic nature (and the legal reforms enacted by de Valera's Constitution of 1937 would limit their influence). Trinity had no role in the national work of decolonization comparable to University College Dublin, or University College Cork. Trinity academics were increasingly detached from social and political matters.[13] The historian F. S. L. Lyons, graduate, professor and ultimately provost of the college, described the 1930s as a period in which

the Performance of Ascendancy', in Ruth Connolly and Ann Coughlan, eds., New Voices in Irish Criticism 5 (Dublin, 2005), 177–86.

8   Kiberd, Inventing Ireland, 456.

9   Beckett, More Pricks than Kicks, 172.

10   See Brown, Ireland: A Social and Cultural History, 90.

11   See Letters I, 55: 'How long it will drag on, my dear Tom, I have no idea ... The room is full of bastards talking about war films and the National Anthem — having ideas — et quelles idées — à toute vitesse. And making little jokes — the kind that dribble into subtle smiles.' It was greatly disputed during the 1920s and 1930s whether Trinity College should continue to raise the Union Jack, officially toast the health of George V, and recognize 'God Save the King' as the official national anthem. These quarrels indicate the degree to which the university regarded itself as separate from the newly independent country. See R. B. McDowell and D. A. Webb, Trinity College Dublin 1592–1952: An Academic History (Cambridge, 1982), 433–34.

12   On Trinity College's prominence as an intellectual centre in the nineteenth century, see Terry Eagleton, Scholars and Rebels in Nineteenth-Century Ireland (Oxford, 1999). One of the formative moments of the Revival was a debate concerning Irishness between the nationalist writer D. P. Moran and the Trinity academics Stopford A. Brooke and T. W. Rolleston in the nationalist newspaper The Leader in 1900; for a selection of the positions in this debate, see Deane, ed., The Field Day Anthology of Irish Writing, vol. 2, 969–75.

13   One example is Professor of Romance Languages T. B. Rudmose-Brown, who was close to Beckett during his time there (Beckett parodied him through the character of 'the Polar Bear' in More Pricks than Kicks). Rudmose-Brown had helped introduce contemporary French literature into Ireland and had encouraged experimental Irish writing; he was also a politically engaged nationalist (something not appreciated by his colleagues at Trinity) and freethinker. By the 1930s, however, his work consisted mainly of ponderous and pedantic reviews of books about French culture; a review in Dublin Magazine of George Cronyn's popular

the world had changed overnight and too many Fellows were too set in their ways to change with it. The result was that though individual scholars of repute were still in evidence, the Twenties and Thirties rank among the darkest periods of the College's history — it was poor, the buildings became steadily more dilapidated and a great tradition of learning seemed destined for extinction.[14]

Lee uses the term 'Trinity sloth' to characterize the ethos of the college at that time.[15] Yet, while the predominantly Catholic National Universities had deeper connections to Irish society at large than Trinity during this period, they were not marked by a high quality of intellectual achievement either.[16] According to Lee, Trinity sloth had its roots in the inability of a residual elite, which once had had a monopoly on leisure, to recognize it no longer played an important part in Irish society. Trinity sloth should not be mistaken for a refusal to work. Trinity sloth was neither a product of the various strains of anti-intellectualism evident during this period, nor was it a mode of resistance towards socially empowered forms of Catholicism or nationalism. Rather, it indicated an inability even to recognize the existence of the organic intellectuals of post-colonial Ireland as organizers of a new culture. To put it in the Cartesian terms favoured by Trinity's philosophy department and later parodied by Beckett in Murphy, as an intellectual institution Trinity resembled a self-absorbed mind that had finally reached a state of detachment from the body of the rest of Ireland.[17] Yet that detachment was something of a ruse; the cultural capital acquired by Trinity during its earlier period of high academic achievement was a benefit deriving from its central position in a society founded on colonialism. It did not participate in the construction of the new civil society that had superseded the colonial province, which it had helped build and maintain; it failed (at least at this point in its history) to offer alternatives to post-colonial Ireland by remaking itself in light of recent events.

In rejecting Trinity sloth in his resignation from the faculty of the university, Beckett rejected the values of colonial elitism. But this did not mean that he rejected sloth in

---

historical novel *The Fool of Venus: The Story of Peire Vidal* provides a good example. See *Dublin Magazine*, 10, 3 (1935), 73–77; the repetitions, genealogical obsessions, and comically meticulous, yet irrelevant, details of Beckett's *Watt* do not look so unusual after reading the book reviews of Rudmose-Brown.

14 F. S. L. Lyons, 'The Minority Problem in the 26 Counties', in Francis MacManus, ed., *The Years of the Great Test* (Cork, 1967), 99. For a slightly contrary take on the condition of Trinity College in the 1920s and the 1930s, see Pauric Dempsey, 'Trinity College Dublin and the New Political Order', in Mike Cronin and John M. Regan, eds., *Ireland: The Politics of Independence, 1922–49* (London, 2000), 217–31.

15 Lee, *Ireland 1912–1985: Politics and Society*, 621.

16 See Lee, *Ireland 1912–1985: Politics and Society*, 616. On the other hand, Brian Fallon argues that 'in the Thirties it was UCD that produced the bulk of the writers and intellectuals, while Trinity could only point to Beckett … The remarkable generation of Brian O'Nolan, Denis Devlin, Mervyn Wall, Donagh MacDonagh, Brian Coffey, Charles Donnelly, Liam Redmond, Cyril Cusack, had no real equivalent in Trinity at the time.' See Fallon, *An Age of Innocence*, 181.

17 On the status of Descartes at Trinity College during Beckett's time as a student there, see Richard Kearney, 'Beckett: The Demythologizing Intellect', in Kearney, ed., *The Irish Mind: Exploring Intellectual Traditions* (Dublin, 1985), 267–93.

itself; to become a full-time literary intellectual he needed to discover alternative forms of laziness. Nor did it mean that he rejected elitism completely; like an increasing number of Irish aspiring literary intellectuals of his generation, he found a model for such productive forms of laziness in Joyce and his circle in Paris, which by the 1930s had become one version of modernism's 'consecrated' avant-garde.[18] Even before the end of Beckett's career as an academic, he had developed a friendship with Joyce; he assisted him briefly in the composition of *Finnegans Wake* and regarded him as the ideal literary intellectual.[19] The writer Samuel Putnam's memory of 'certain young Irishmen, friends and admirers of Joyce' distinguishes between the inactivity of such Irish literary figures as MacGreevy, Beckett and George Reavey and the work-ethic of other members of the avant-garde, noting that 'Beckett and Reavey were often seen on the Boulevard du Montparnasse, while Eugene Jolas and his American associates very seldom, for they were workers rather than café sitters'.[20] Despite being a 'café sitter', Beckett did manage to produce a number of critical essays and reviews during this period, in addition to his earliest creative writing.

In an essay entitled 'Dante … Bruno … Vico … Joyce', written for a collection of critical essays devoted to the 'Work in Progress' that would eventually be published in its entirety as *Finnegans Wake* ten years later, Beckett celebrated the alternative reading practices demanded by the linguistic experimentation of Joyce's latest writing:

> And if you don't understand it, Ladies and Gentlemen, it is because you are too decadent to receive it. You are not satisfied unless form is so strictly divorced from content that you can comprehend the one almost without bothering to read the other. The rapid skimming and absorption of the scant cream of sense is made possible by what I may call a continuous process of copious intellectual salivation. (D, 26)[21]

In conventional terms, the text serves as the medium for the transmission of a straightforward message. The problem with such a utilitarian approach is that it can easily be appropriated by a social order premised upon the necessity of work and consumption. To Beckett, the distorted language of 'Work in Progress' puts an end to that process of appropriation, as the formal difficulties prevent the text from working in the usual way:

> Here form is content, content is form. You complain that this stuff is not written in English. It is not written at all. It is not to be read — or rather, it is not only to be

---

18 See Bourdieu, *The Field of Cultural Production*, 115–25. While *Ulysses* offered a thoroughgoing challenge to the 'consecrated' values of the Revival upon its publication, by the 1930s it had already been 'consecrated' through its admission and centrality to the canon of international modernism. On this, see Lawrence Rainey, *Institutions of Modernism: Literary Elites and Public Culture* (New Haven, 1999), 42–76.

19 See Knowlson, *Damned to Fame*, 104–11.

20 Quoted by Harrington, *The Irish Beckett*, 11.

21 The essay was originally published in Paris in 1929 in a collection called *Our Exagmination Round His Factification for Incamination of Work in Progress*.

read. It is to be looked at and listened to. His writing is not *about* something; *it is that something itself.* (D, 27. Emphasis in original.)

Reading 'Work in Progress' demands a new form of intellectual labour. Its alternative temporality reinforces the structural model of the book (one of the chief concerns of Beckett's essay): a Viconian theory of cyclical history that contrasts with the more conventional linear narratives of progressive historicism, which, as Benjamin suggests, typify the homogenous empty time of modernity.[22]

Written in 1931, Beckett's monograph on *Remembrance of Things Past* was his first notable publication since his resignation from Trinity College. Marcel Proust is governed by an interest in the possibility of a modernist form of writing directed towards problems of temporality.

Here is no escape from the hours and the days. Neither from tomorrow nor from yesterday. There is no escape from yesterday because yesterday has deformed us, or been deformed by us … We are not merely more weary because of yesterday, we are other, no longer what we were before the calamity of yesterday.[23]

Proust disrupts the inevitable flow of time and allows for the recovery of lost experience through involuntary memory. For Beckett, heavily influenced by Arthur Schopenhauer in his interpretation of Proust, such an aesthetic goes beyond the recovery of lost time to a moment of rapture that stands outside of the inevitability of temporality altogether: 'time is not recovered, it is obliterated'.[24] Like the act of reading 'Work in Progress', the act of reading Proust poses for Beckett the problematic relationship between representation and temporality as a basic structural principle of the narratives; his interest in modernist writing's innovative approach to the possibility of alternative temporalities acquires a political resonance when transplanted into the Irish literary field he left by moving to Paris.

But Beckett does not really address the writing of Joyce or Proust in any obviously political sense in either essay. His preference for a rarefied, aesthetically autonomous avant-garde, typical of the modernist coteries of Paris in the 1930s, stands out in both more clearly than any sort of sociopolitical argument. His readings of Joyce and Proust do have implications for the cultural politics of post-colonial Ireland; that became more evident in an essay entitled 'Recent Irish Poetry', written around the time he began to

---

22 Benjamin, 'Theses on the Philosophy of History', in I, 261.
23 Samuel Beckett, *Proust and Three Dialogues with Georges Duthuit* (London, 1965), 13.
24 Beckett, *Proust*, 75. On the Schopenhauerian dimension, see Rupert Wood, 'An Endgame of Aesthetics: Beckett as Essayist', in John Pilling, ed., *The Cambridge Companion to Beckett* (Cambridge, 1994), 1–16, esp. 3–7.

write *Murphy*.[25] In that essay, Beckett presents a brief theoretical description of how Irish writers of the 1930s worked as intellectuals. This provides some important clues to his representation of intellectual work — and non-work — in *Murphy*. Since it was written under the pseudonym 'Andrew Belis' for an 'Irish Number' of the journal *The Bookman* in 1934, and was not brought back into print until the publication of Beckett's early criticism in *Disjecta*, fifty years later, it does not have an especially prominent place in his writing. Arguably it was not even the most important contribution by Beckett to that particular issue of *The Bookman*; the same issue also contains his early short-story 'A Case in a Thousand' (published under his own name). Nevertheless, 'Recent Irish Poetry' is crucial evidence for the Irish dimension in *Murphy* or in his other early writing.[26] He begins by discussing the nature of perception after the emergence of high modernism:

> I propose, as a rough principle of individuation in this essay, the degree in which the younger Irish poets evince awareness of the new thing that has happened, or the old thing that has happened again, namely the breakdown of the object, whether current, historical, mythical or spook. The thermolaters — and they pullulate in Ireland — adoring the stuff of song as incorruptible, uninjurable, and unchangeable, never at a loss to know when they are in the Presence, would no doubt like this amended to the breakdown of the subject. It comes to the same thing — rupture of the lines of communication. (D, 70)

As examples of works of art that take into account the 'rupture of the lines of communication', Beckett cites Eliot's *The Wasteland* and the experimental painting of his friend Jack B. Yeats. Despite the differences in medium, both artists make use of distortion to register the inability of the individual subject to situate itself in relation to the lived present ('current'), to a sense of inhabiting a temporal process ('historical'), to abstract forms of belief that contribute to a national culture ('mythical'), or to the supernatural ('spook'). All four objects of literary representation are central to the Revival; even though it was written in the early 1930s, Beckett's essay shows how the values of the Revival persisted. W. B. Yeats and his followers seem to be the primary 'thermolaters' of Beckett's essay. Like the machine Beckett alludes to — a thermolater heats molten plastic so that it

---

25 On the composition of *Murphy* and its historical relation to Beckett's other writing, see John Pilling, *Beckett before Godot* (Cambridge, 1997), 121–23, 125–48.

26 Much of the criticism that explores the Irish dimension of Beckett's writing refers back to 'Recent Irish Poetry', and its importance to Irish Studies is perhaps best symbolized by its inclusion in *The Field Day Anthology of Irish Writing*, vol. 3, 244–48. Beckett wrote another piece for *The Bookman* entitled 'Censorship in the Saorstat' (published in D, 84–88) that gives a very definite sense of his relation to Irish cultural politics, though the essay was never published by that journal. For important recent assessments of 'Recent Irish Poetry' and its relation to the polarities of the literary field, see Sinéad Mooney, 'Kicking against the Thermolaters: Beckett's "Recent Irish Poetry"', *Samuel Beckett Today/Aujourd'hui*, 15 (2005), 29–42, and Pascale Casanova, *Samuel Beckett: Anatomy of a Literary Revolution* (London, 2006), 33–36.

can be shaped into identical moulds — the literary intellectuals who 'pullulate' in Ireland insist upon a proper form of literary practice that reproduces the Yeatsian belief in the privileged position of the poet in constructing a meaningful historical narrative that renders events into what Beckett terms 'the stuff of song as incorruptible, uninjurable, and unchangeable'. Beckett suggests that a Yeatsian intellectual would argue that the problem facing younger Irish writers is their inability to live up to such lofty roles of literary practice. For Beckett, given the breakdown of the object, or the inability of the literary intellectual to work straightforwardly due to the breakdown of the subject, the primary effect is that by the 1930s it has become impossible for Irish writers to write poetry or produce any other form of art according to canonical notions of literary value. Moreover, as Beckett suggests, the most troubling characteristic of contemporary Irish poetry is that most writers continue to hold to precisely those canonical values.

According to him, the primary remnant of value from the Revival was a sacrosanct concept of tradition that signified the triumphant progression of an Irish national culture through time. Most Irish writers worked to reproduce that idea of tradition; 'these are the antiquarians, delivering with the altitudinous complacency of the Victorian Gael the Ossianic goods' (D, 70). The problem with the 'antiquarians' was that their work constituted 'a flight from self-awareness, and as such it might perhaps be described as a convenience' (D, 71). The antiquarians hold themselves hostage to a sterile formalism that merely reproduces 'segment after segment of cut-and-dried sanctity and loveliness' (D, 71). Ultimately, such a project ceases to be interesting:

> What further interest can attach to such assumptions as those on which the convention has for so long taken its ease, namely, that the first condition of any poem has an accredited theme, and that in self-perception there is no theme, but at best sufficient *vis a tergo* to land the practitioner into the correct scenery, where the self is either most happily obliterated or else so improved and enlarged that it can be mistaken for part of the *décor*? None but the academic. And it is in this connection that our lately founded Academy may be said to meet a need and enjoy a function. (D, 71)

The endless reproduction of tradition as a dominant cultural value makes for a conventional form of intellectual practice that is acceptable to the institutions of society at large. Beckett's reference to the Irish Academy of Letters is important. Founded in 1932 by Yeats and later dominated by younger prose realists like Sean O'Faolain and Frank O'Connor, the academy sought to represent the position of literary intellectuals in regard to social and political issues like censorship and the suppression of civil liberties. It represented the liberal side of Irish writing to a greater degree than the nativism of Daniel Corkery and his followers.[27] Yet, in a manner that Bourdieu might recognize, Beckett regards the

27 On the foundation of the Irish Academy of Letters, see Fallon, *An Age of Innocence*, 45–46.

academy as a social institution devoted to the reproduction of the values that define the proper manner in which one works as a literary intellectual. Moreover, while members of the academy such as Yeats, O'Faolain, and O'Connor might vociferously oppose some of de Valera's political policies (such as increased censorship or the growing influence of the Catholic Church in affairs of the state), their valorization of a form of intellectual labour premised upon the celebration of a distinct Irish tradition only served to help legitimate the political entity governed by de Valera, since it continued to assert a cultural notion of Irishness that justified the existence of an Irish nation-state.

After this polemical opening, Beckett spends the rest of 'Recent Irish Poetry' enumerating as many contemporary Irish writers as possible (he refers to thirty in all), rather than appraising how far their work demonstrates the antiquarianism of the Revival. Much of the humour of the essay lies in his lazy refusal to participate in the conventions of aesthetic evaluation:

> Mr. Francis Stuart is of course best known as a novelist, but he writes verse. So does Mr. R. N. D. Wilson. So does Mr. Leslie Yodaiken when his politics let him. So I am sure do Mr. Frank O'Connor and Mr. Sean O'Faolain — also best known as novelists of course. And I know that Mr. Sean O'Casey does, having read a poem of his in Time and Tide. (D, 75)

But at the beginning of his essay he celebrates poetry that refuses to do the antiquarian work of the Revival, and instead takes into account the now unstable, ruptured, or distorted relationship between writer as perceptive subjective and the object of representation:

> The artist who is aware of this may state the space that intervenes between him and the world of objects; he may state it as no-man's-land, Hellespont, or vacuum, according as he happens to be feeling resentful, nostalgic, or merely depressed ... Or he may celebrate the cold comforts of apperception. He may even record his feelings, if he is a man of great personal courage. (D, 70)

Whether through a principle of distortion or a self-reflexive sense of the impossibility of expression — Beckett's favoured approach in Murphy and much of his later work — both kinds of writing seek to enact alternative forms of intellectual labour by refusing to concede to conventional notions of the central importance of Irish tradition and the privileged position of the literary intellectual as an author of a national culture.

Beckett celebrates those emergent modernists who seek to enact alternative forms of intellectual labour in their writing. He singles out Denis Devlin, Brian Coffey and, to a lesser extent, his friend Thomas MacGreevy for praise. Though he notes that their work is still somewhat derivative of Artur Rimbaud, Jules Laforgue, Paul Éluard, Eliot, and Pound, they have nevertheless achieved a real breakthrough: 'What matters is that it does not proceed from the *Gossoons Wunderhorn* of that Irish Romantic Arnim-Brentano combination, Sir Samuel Ferguson and Standish O'Grady, and that it admits — stupendous innovation — the existence of the author' (D, 76). He is not celebrating the autobiographical dimension to be found in the works of Devlin and Coffey here — one finds an autobiographical dimension in many of the 'antiquarians' he cites as well — but the self-reflexive manner in which these younger modernists examine the nature of their role as writers. He suggests that the writing of Devlin and Coffey questions whether it is even possible to regard an object of representation as the embodiment of an abstract value, given the breakdown of the relationship between the writer as subject and the object of representation. In admitting 'the existence of the author' as a type of intellectual who labours to represent something, Beckett implies the inherent impossibility of that work.

While he went on to theorize a form of intellectual work predicated upon the impossibility of intellectual labour more explicitly in subsequent critical reflections like the 'Letter to Axel Kaun' and *Three Dialogues with George Duthuit*, 'Recent Irish Poetry' provides early evidence of this characteristic of Beckett's aesthetic practice.[28] Nevertheless, one must be careful not to overstate the revolutionary qualities of this essay; its brevity and its publication under a pseudonym must also be taken into account. Perhaps Beckett did not wish to offend several of the writers — many of them prominent members of the Irish Academy of Letters — published in the same issue of *The Bookman*.[29] Harrington argues that Beckett's critique of antiquarianism in opposition to the Revival, and his positive references to Devlin and Coffey's Anglo-American and continental influences, serve as evidence of a modernist cosmopolitanism that began to appear in Ireland despite the nativism of intellectuals like Corkery.[30] Many critics take for granted the assumption that Beckett is best identified as a cosmopolitan. While Harrington and Phillip Weisberg disagree strongly about the relevance of Beckett's relationship to Irish cultural history, both critics routinely refer to Beckett as 'cosmopolitan'.[31]

Yet it is questionable whether 'cosmopolitan' is the best identification one can make of Beckett's position in 'Recent Irish Poetry', as well as in his other writing of the 1930s. 'Cosmopolitan' was a description then most often used to identify the cultural politics of O'Faolain and other liberal writers opposed to the repressive, nativist conservatism

---

28 See D, 51–54, 138–45. In the 'Letter to Axel Kaun', Beckett states: 'Let us hope the time will come, thank God that in certain circles it has already come, when language is most efficiently used where it is being most efficiently misused' (D, 172–73). The letter was written not long after Beckett completed *Murphy*, so 'Recent Irish Poetry' and the 'Letter to Axel Kaun' might be regarded as theoretical bookends to that novel.

29 See Knowlson, *Damned to Fame*, 180–81. The 'Irish Number' of *The Bookman* also included pieces by Stephen Gwynn, Lennox Robinson, Frank O'Connor, and Sean O'Faolain, all members of the Irish Academy of Letters.

30 See Harrington, *The Irish Beckett*, 33: 'By attacking antiquarianism, Beckett did not relinquish his own involvement in local culture. Instead he joined a dissenting faction of impeccable credentials that has been an important feature of modern Irish literature in all but its crudest revival forms or most exigent aims.'

31 For example, Harrington, *The Irish Beckett*, 56–57, and Phillip Weisberg, *Chronicles of Disorder: Samuel Beckett and the Cultural Politics of the Modern Novel* (Albany, 2000), 176.

typified by Corkery's literary criticism and practised by de Valera's government. Beckett's essay 'Censorship in the Saorstat' is completely consistent with O'Faolain's virulent opposition to censorship. Yet O'Faolain's sense of cultural politics is firmly grounded in an aesthetic devoted to the representation of Irish life in as realistic a manner as possible. If Corkery felt that a realist aesthetic should represent those qualities (Catholicism, rural life, nationalism, the Irish language) that could contribute to a sense of Irish cultural difference, O'Faolain opposed that position on the grounds that it was incomplete. O'Faolain's alternative realist aesthetic asserted that nothing should be left out of the literary representation of Ireland, including those political, sexual, or anticlerical facets of daily life in Ireland that proved troubling to de Valera's censors. Whatever the merits of the cultural politics of either Corkery or O'Faolain, both have their basis in assumptions about the feasibility of a realist aesthetic completely at odds with Beckett's formulation of the breakdown of the subject as writer and the object of representation. If Corkery and O'Faolain characterized the nativist and cosmopolitan positions, respectively, within the Irish literary field, it was a field held together by common assumptions about the expressive capacity of the subject to represent the object. In 'Recent Irish Poetry', Beckett suggests the possibility of a third position that goes well beyond either the nativism of Corkery or the cosmopolitanism of O'Faolain by calling into question such assumptions about representation.

2

Beckett's relocation to Paris, his personal connections to modernist circles that included art and sculpture as well as literature, and his eventual decision to write many of his works in French all identify him with a modernist notion of cosmopolitanism. It has become one of the commonplaces of Beckett criticism that he rejected the supposed insularity of post-colonial Ireland by opting instead for European cosmopolitanism. Consequently, the importance Irish culture had for Beckett has sometimes been a controversial matter. A standard approach that identifies him as an international modernist has often glossed over his relation to Irish cultural politics (other than assumptions about his supposed adversarial relation to the place in which he grew up).[32] Questions regarding his Irishness often go unasked; occasionally, some of this commentary is openly hostile to those who

32 For a selection of early critical explorations of Beckett's relation to the land of his birth, see Vivian Mercier, *Beckett/Beckett* (Oxford, 1977) and J. C. C. Mays, '"Mythologized Presences": *Murphy* in Its Time', in Joseph Ronsley, ed., *Myth and Reality in Irish Literature* (Waterloo, Ontario, 1977), 197–218; Eoin O'Brien, *The Beckett Country: Samuel Beckett's Ireland* (Dublin, 1986); and Seamus Deane, 'Joyce and Beckett', in *Celtic Revivals*, 123–34; for more recent analyses of Beckett's Irishness, see Kiberd, *Inventing Ireland*, 454–67, 530–50; Harrington, *The Irish Beckett*; Lloyd, *Anomalous States*, 41–58; and W. J. McCormack, *From Burke to Beckett: Ascendancy, Tradition and Betrayal in Literary History* (Cork, 1994), 375–433. Anthony Cronin's biography, *Samuel Beckett: The Last Modernist* (New York, 1997), also pays close attention to Beckett's Irish background.

do raise such questions.[33] Yet his brief essay about Irish writing in the 1930s shows that interpretative questions about cosmopolitanism or nativism were for Beckett rooted in his perception of other Irish writers. The position he takes emerged specifically out of an Irish modernist tendency that begins with Joyce. This is most evident in Beckett's representation of the literary intellectual. In fact, Beckett's formulation of intellectual labour in 'Recent Irish Poetry' and his representation of the lazy idle schemer who is the eponymous hero of the novel *Murphy* place him firmly within the conventions of a specifically Irish brand of modernism.

An account of Beckett's representation of would-be intellectuals like Murphy that addresses the context of decolonization might help to soften this dispute. This can be done without losing sight of such typical concerns as epistemology and philosophy.[34] *Murphy* alternates between chapters that focus on the title character and his attempt to cultivate a process of contemplation that will bring about some form of intellectual autonomy, and chapters that concern a group of people from Murphy's past life in Ireland. J. C. C. Mays, in a pioneering exploration of the book's Irish dimension, argues that the plot involving Murphy and his cognitive processes demonstrates Beckett's investment in an Irish version of experimental modernism, and that the plot involving the pursuit of Murphy by his former associates provides Beckett the opportunity to parody various aspects of the Revival.[35] In a more recent critical inquiry into the relationship between Beckett's early novels and philosophical formulations of modernity, Richard Begam also examines the two evident narrative modes in the novel, arguing that the chapters that concern Murphy comprise an experimental 'inner' novel dealing with 'Murphy's psychotic contraction into himself', and that the chapters concerning Murphy's associates constitute an 'outer' novel that enables Beckett to parody the conventions of nineteenth-century fiction.[36] Though the interpretations offered by Mays and Begam are different, it is possible to bring them closer together by approaching *Murphy* through looking at Beckett's representation of intellectual labour. If that form of imaginative work is taken to mean both the act as well as the result of intellectual work, then it is possible that the 'inner' novel of *Murphy* concerns an alternative form of creative labour, which, on the one hand, brings about literary innovation, as Mays would have it, and on the other hand,

---

33 C. J. Ackerley in *Demented Particulars: Annotations for* Murphy (*Journal of Beckett Studies* 7.1/2, 1988), plays down the Irish dimension to that work: 'Attempts to reclaim Beckett for the Irish, from Harrington to Cronin, have proved unconvincing' (xi). The lack of detail concerning an Irish context to *Murphy* — and even slight hostility towards a critical interest in that context — is symptomatic in mainstream Beckett criticism. For example, in *Chronicles of Disorder*, 176, Weisberg rejects Lloyd's examination of Beckett's relation to cultural nationalism by arguing that 'Lloyd implicitly assumes that because Beckett was born in Ireland, he is an Irish writer; Beckett himself (unlike Joyce) had no interest in being an Irish writer and throughout his works he parodies such a notion'.

34   But see Casanova, *Samuel Beckett: Anatomy of a Literary Revolution*, 38.

35 Mays, '"Mythologized Presences": Murphy in Its Time', 206–07.

36 Richard Begam, *Samuel Beckett and the End of Modernity* (Stanford, 1996), 57. Begam discusses the relation between the 'inner' and 'outer' novels of *Murphy* on 57–65.

delineates the practice of thinking itself, as Begam argues. If a discussion of the 'outer' novel focuses on the representation of Murphy's associates *as* types of intellectuals, then it is possible to discern Beckett's satirical critique of conventional, acceptable modes of intellectual work, whether they are rooted in Ireland, as Mays suggests, in the nineteenth century, as Begam suggests, or, as in the case of the Revival, in both.

Among other things, *Murphy* explores how the lazy idle schemer eventually comes to understand a position that goes beyond both cosmopolitanism and traditionalism, as described in 'Recent Irish Poetry'. Because it is a position regarding intellectual work that depends upon the failure of representation in the first place, Murphy ultimately fails to practise an alternative form of intellectual labour that demonstrates the third position described in Beckett's essay. Yet Murphy encounters something like it by eventually finding employment in an insane asylum. There, the inmates — or, as Beckett refers to them, 'the microcosmopolitans' — inhabit an idle utopia in their isolation from the world of work and responsibility outside the walls of the asylum: 'The great majority preferred simply to hang about doing nothing.'[37] I want to suggest that 'microcosmopolitanism' is a particularly useful term to describe the position Beckett articulates in 'Recent Irish Poetry' as the sort of aesthetic he argues for. A 'microcosmopolitan' form of intellectual labour would necessarily go beyond the limitations of both 'antiquarianism' and cosmopolitanism as those terms were understood in Ireland in the 1930s. Microcosmopolitanism implies a cultural politics rooted in a local version of disinterested worldliness; it can initially be explained by identifying what it is not.

To begin with, it is neither the cosmopolitanism of O'Faolain nor the nativism of Corkery. Beckett suggests that the literary intellectual cannot work to represent the *Gemeinschaft* of rural, Catholic, Gaelic Ireland, as Corkery's ideology of the aesthetic insists, or, as O'Faolain would have it, the *Gesellschaft* of modern Ireland as it actually was. Microcosmopolitan intellectual work also stands contrary to the antiquarianism of the Revival, to an idealized conception of Irish tradition, and to the creation of a nation-state devoted to the construction of a capitalist form of modernity.[38] Temporality is linked to capitalism from the very first page of *Murphy*: 'Somewhere a cuckoo-clock, having struck between twenty and thirty, became the echo of a street-cry, which now entering the mew gave *Quid pro Quo! Quid pro Quo!*' (M, 5). The outside world is bound by time and defined by exchange. It is a reality that would-be microcosmopolitans like Murphy seek to escape ('These were sights and sounds that he did not like. They detained him in the world to

37   M, 95; Beckett refers to the inmates as 'microcosmopolitans' on 134.
38   In this sense, my argument is consistent with Nicholas Allen's suggestion that the 'acute examples of temporal deconstruction' (113) evident in Beckett's early prose register the degree to which Beckett's modernist aesthetics strive to articulate a condition of temporality outside of the progressive time of the state. Beckett's attention to temporality not only has to do with Murphy's status as a lazy idle schemer, as I suggest, but as Allen argues, situates him in relation to broader debates concerning the relationship between republicanism and modernism in Ireland in the 1930s. See Allen, *Modernism, Ireland and Civil War*, 113–35.

which they belonged. But not he, as he fondly hoped.' M, 6). Finally, microcosmopolitanism is not Trinity sloth. As an extreme form of social Cartesianism, Trinity sloth convinces itself that through an absolute devotion to intellectual contemplation for its own sake, the collective 'mind' of the Anglo-Irish Protestant intelligentsia can detach itself from the 'body' of the rest of Ireland. This is, philosophically speaking, a risky position. Alfred Sohn-Rethel suggests,

> as it assumes representation as the *ego cogito* of Descartes or of the 'subject of cognition' of philosophical epistemology, the false consciousness of intellectual labour reaches its culmination: the formation of thinking which in every respect merits the term 'social' presents itself as the diametrical opposite to society, the EGO of which there cannot be another.[39]

A form of intellectual work premised upon some concept of philosophical autonomy is ultimately rooted in what Sohn-Rethel terms the fundamental 'division of head and hand' that brings about the social divisions, contradictions, and exploitation of capitalism — and in the case of Trinity sloth, was also complicit with colonial rule. Throughout most of the novel, Murphy seems to be a spectacular example of Trinity sloth, who finally becomes aware of a microcosmopolitan approach to life that overcomes the contradictions inherent in it, even if that microcosmopolitan ideal proves to be as elusive and impossible to attain as any coherent form of literary representation that Beckett had formulated in 'Recent Irish Poetry'.

Microcosmopolitanism grows out of Beckett's suggestion in that essay that any familiar form of literary work is impossible because of the 'rupture in the lines of communication', or breakdown in perceptual relationship, between the writer as subject and the object of representation. This does not mean that the object of perception does not exist — for Murphy, such objects as the sounds of time passing or cries in the street exist all too readily for him as things to be escaped from — but rather that no hitherto realized form of literary representation can realize it; instead, it can only register the absence of its own conditions of possibility. Both Peter Boxall and David Lloyd argue that the paradoxical nature of Beckett's position provides an opening for a more political understanding of Beckett. For Boxall, the ruptured aesthetic evident throughout Beckett's writing registers 'both a drive to negate the political world and a drive to find a way of belonging to it', ultimately leaving the reader of Beckett's writing, 'in all its indeterminacy, its partiality, its uncertainty, with two "unlessenable" cultural conditions — that of belonging to the world, and that of being estranged from it'.[40] Lloyd argues that the writing of Beckett and the work of his friend and mentor Jack B. Yeats offers: 'the enactment of a failure of

---

39 Alfred Sohn-Rethel, *Intellectual and Manual Labour: A Critique of Epistemology* (Atlantic Highlands, NJ, 1978), 77.
40 Peter Boxall, 'Samuel Beckett: Towards a Political Reading', *Irish Studies Review*, 10, 2 (2002), 159–70, 162, 169.

representation, a failure to either retrieve or to abandon the object. The formal means employed in this virtually obsessive work of representation are at once the analogue and the performance of this predicament.[41] Thus, Beckett's paradoxical position, that aesthetic representation is obliged to re-enact its own impossibility, does not in itself offer an explicit political position. But it does disengage aesthetic from political ends; that disengagement has deep affinities with the principle of non-domination of a republicanism that opposes the post-colonial state.[42]

The lives of the microcosmopolitans in *Murphy* (particularly the schizophrenic Mr. Endon) provide examples of the paradoxical nature of representation highlighted in the essays by Boxall and Lloyd. Despite Murphy's hope that it will, microcosmopolitanism does not afford an extreme degree of detachment from the outside world. It is not just the case that the microcosmopolitan version of the lazy idle schemer refuses to work as an intellectual in any conventional manner, but that no fulfilling, alternative form of work will ever be possible — at least for those who have any desire to find such work. For those inmates of the insane asylum specifically identified as microcosmopolitans in *Murphy* function at a level at which the distinction between work and idleness has ceased to have meaning.

Beckett's identification of microcosmopolitanism with insanity is not to be romanticized; it emphasizes the abject dimension of lazy idle scheming, which implies that the postulation of any alternative form of intellectual labour will ultimately be doomed to failure or extreme marginality. But Beckett's microcosmopolitanism shows how inherently problematic intellectual endeavour is. Adorno's later reading of Beckett's *Endgame*, in the context of the triumph of an administered society after World War II, reminds us that there was no theoretical resource in Ireland in the 1930s for making sense of Beckett's notion of intellectual work premised upon the ultimate impossibility of intellectual work. However, the apparently contradictory or aporetic nature of Beckett's position serves in some way as an implicit critique of the conditions that make it appear so.[43] In its ambiguity, microcosmopolitanism, as a version of lazy idle scheming, continued to resist the nationalist project of building the nation, even though the intensity of that demand began to wane in de Valera's Ireland.

41 Lloyd, 'Republics of Difference: Yeats, MacGreevy, Beckett', 64.
42 Lloyd, 'Republics of Difference', 66: 'In other words, where an aesthetic of representation that had become tied to a mode of political thinking becomes, along with the political state, a means to domination, only in the ruins of that aesthetic can an alternative be excavated.'
43 See Theodor Adorno, 'Trying to Understand *Endgame*', in *Notes to Literature: Volume One* (New York, 1991), 241–75.

3

During his time in London from 1934 through 1935 as a patient of Bion, Beckett specifically identified his habitual 'désoeuvrement' as both a symptom and a cause of his need for therapy.[44] Eventually, Bion's influence and Beckett's secular reinterpretation of the quietest elements of Thomas à Kempis' *The Imitation of Christ* enabled him to come to terms with his indolence through an understanding of both his personal habits and the depression he felt while at Trinity.[45] Such afflictions extended to Beckett's fraught composition of *Murphy* in the mid-1930s (most notably in the form of writer's block);[46] it is little wonder that his representation of idleness in the novel is profoundly ambiguous. Before his employment, as a nurse in the Magdalen Mental Mercyseat hospital, Murphy plays the role of lazy idle schemer very well. His lover, Celia, describes him to her grandfather, Mr. Willoughby Kelly:

> Taking the first point first, Celia replied that Murphy was Murphy. Continuing then in an orderly manner she revealed that he had no profession or trade; came from Dublin — 'My God!' said Mr. Kelly — knew of one uncle, a Mr. Quigley, a well-to-do ne'er-do-well, resident in Holland, with whom he strove to correspond; did nothing that she could discern; sometimes had the price of a concert; believed that the future held great things in store for him; and never ripped up old stories. He was Murphy. He had Celia. (M, 14)

Prior to 12 September 1935, Murphy had departed Ireland for London, 'the Mecca of every young aspirant to fiscal distinction' (M, 34), supposedly to make enough money to support an earlier, since-abandoned lover named Miss Counihan. But he quickly severs his communications with Miss Counihan and never bothers to find employment. Instead, Murphy lives by arranging to have his landlord overcharge the uncle who pays his rent and gives the landlord a portion of the profit, while he spends his days in idleness. Neither Murphy nor Celia is an average Irish emigrant.

In the 1930s emigration intensified; close to 6 percent of the population left Ireland in search of work. Because of the institution of quotas that severely restricted the number of Irish emigrants permitted to enter the United States during this period, Britain became the most common destination.[47] The persistence of Irish emigration was a source of embarrassment to the social architects of post-colonial Ireland: 'in an independent Ireland, emigration was an embarrassment best ignored. Perhaps it was difficult for the leaders of the Irish Free State to recognize or identify with thousands of young, able and

44 See *Letters I*, 254.
45 *Letters I*, 257–59.
46 See Pilling, *Beckett before Godot*, 127–29.
47 See John Archer Jackson, *The Irish in Britain* (London, 1963), 97–98.

energetic people who continued to leave home and settle in the land of the conqueror.[48] The Irish government, especially in its early years, did little to reduce the outflow. Lee sarcastically notes this development was particularly galling to de Valera:

> De Valera yearned for a self-sufficient, bucolic, Gaelic utopia. He detested contaminating economic contact with a certain neighbouring island race, who, through some unfortunate oversight in divine regional policy, had been located within smelling distance of the chosen people. But his aim of frugal self-sufficiency, bucolic bliss, and growing population were logically incompatible. The Irish people, for better or worse, were not prepared to accept the level of frugality that a primarily agricultural society imposed on them. The result was sustained emigration.[49]

One of the chief arguments made by nationalists before 1922 was that independence would enable emigrants to return and contribute their skills to the work of the nation. Murphy and Celia belong to a world beyond the horizons of Irish nationalist ideology. Celia is a prostitute; conservative nationalists refused to admit Irish women would enter such a profession.[50] Murphy, for the most part, refuses to work at all.

This is the key point of contention in his relationship with Celia. Celia longs to enter into a conventional domestic life with Murphy, but he repeatedly refuses to find a job. His justification for his laziness ranges from the practical to the mythological, and centres upon a sense of eternal punishment:

> He begged her to believe him when he said he could not earn. Had he not already sunk a small fortune in attempts to do so? He begged her to believe that he was a chronic emeritus. But it was not altogether a question of economy. There were metaphysical considerations, in whose gloom it appeared that the night had come in which no Murphy could work. Was Ixion under any contract to keep his wheel in running order? Had any provision been made for Tantalus to eat salt? Not that Murphy had ever heard of. (M, 16)

Eventually, the couple runs out of money and Celia demands that either he finds a job or she leaves him and returns to her work. Despite his protestation that 'work would be the

48 Graham Davis, 'The Irish in Britain, 1815–1939', in Andy Bielenberg, ed., The Irish Diaspora (Harlow, 2000), 19–36, 33.
49 Lee, Ireland 1912–1985: Politics and Society, 187.
50 On the problematic nature of Beckett's representation of Celia in Murphy, as well as the misogynistic qualities of More Pricks than Kicks and Watt, see Susan Brienza, 'Clods, Whores, and Bitches: Misogyny in Beckett's Early Fiction', in Linda Ben-Zvi, ed., Women in Beckett: Performance and Critical Perspectives (Urbana, 1990), 91–105. See also Wills, 'Joyce, Prostitution, and the Colonial City', 79–95, and Katherine Mullin, 'Don't Cry for Me, Argentina: "Eveline" and the Seductions of Emigration Propaganda', in Attridge and Howes, eds., Semicolonial Joyce, 172–200.

end of them both' (M, 16), Murphy finally agrees to look for a job. He and Celia move into a flat 'between Pentonville Prison and the Metropolitan Cattle Market' (M, 40), between a prison and a slaughterhouse.

In a letter to MacGreevy, written before the publication of *Murphy*, Beckett stressed that the title character should not be taken too seriously; Murphy's suffering in his search for employment is indeed comic.[51]

> Murphy on the jobpath was a striking figure. Word went round among the members of the Blake league that the Master's conception of Bildad the Shuhite had come to life and was stalking about London in a green suit, seeking whom he could comfort. But what is Bildad but a fragment of Job, as Zophar and the others are fragments of Job. The only thing that Murphy was seeking was what he had not ceased to seek from the moment of his being strangled into a state of respiration — the best of himself. (M, 44)

Unlike Bildad the Shuhite, a figure who tried to comfort Job by telling him that his punishments from God were deserved, Murphy does not attempt to rationalize his tortured experience of having to enter the workforce. Just as William Blake represented Bildad in his illustrations for the Book of Job as belonging to a collective humanity brought together by a shared suffering, symbolically endured by Job, so Beckett represents a comically self-important Murphy as a figure who endures the most notable latter-day version of acute suffering — modern humanity's need to work. Unfortunately, as Murphy reflects to himself, working in modern times means working for someone else: 'For what was all working for a living but a procuring and a pimping for the money-bags, one's lecherous tyrants the money-bags, so that they might breed' (M, 47). Murphy has trouble finding suitable work.

To Celia's surprise, Murphy's everyday departures and returns are regularly timed,[52] even though he spends the day aimlessly wandering the streets of London. If idleness is indeed of an 'unlimited duration', as Benjamin suggests, Murphy's punctuality only intensifies it; he symbolically acknowledges the existence of the regulated work time of modernity, while he actually devotes his energies to the alternative temporality of dwelling in 'embryonal repose' on what he calls (after the character in Dante that also provides the name of the lazy idle schemer in *More Pricks than Kicks*) his 'Belacqua fantasy' of committed inactivity

---

51 Beckett wrote in a letter to MacGreevy in 1936, while the manuscript was circulating among various publishers, of Murphy's grotesque death: 'I chose this because it seemed to me to consist better with the treatment of Murphy throughout, with the mixture of compassion, patience, mockery, and "tat twam asi" that I seem to have directed on him throughout, with the sympathy going so far and no further (then losing patience) as in the short fantasy of his mind's fantasy on itself. There seemed to me always the risk of taking him too seriously and separating him too sharply from the others.' (D, 102)

52 M, 43.

(M, 48).[53] Tyrus Miller writes that 'Murphy, bluntly put, is a portrait of the artist who no longer works, from whom works should not be expected. For Murphy's art is expressed not in works but in not working.'[54] Yet there is no evidence that Murphy is some sort of a literary intellectual; it is suggested that he was once a 'theological student' (M, 44) under the tutelage of the philosopher Professor Neary, who is now part of the group in search of Murphy on behalf of the abandoned Miss Counihan. Like Corkery and O'Faolain, Neary and another former student named Wylie are from Cork. Beyond that geographical reference and occasional jokes at the expense of the national tradition (at one point Beckett ridicules one of the key mythological figures by having Neary, in a depressed fit of irrationality, attempt to kill himself by hitting his head against the buttocks of Oliver Sheppard's statue of Cuchulainn in the General Post Office in Dublin), there is very little reference to the Irish literary world, let alone any evidence that Murphy inhabits it. Yet Murphy is clearly an intellectual of some kind; in addition to his educational background and apparently broad knowledge of the history of philosophy, meditation is his greatest pleasure.

To achieve this, he ties himself naked to a rocking chair, in which 'only the most local movements were possible' (M, 5), and slowly rocks himself into a state of self-hypnosis. Murphy hopes to achieve thereby the liberation of the mind:

> He sat in his chair this way because it gave him pleasure! First it gave his body pleasure, it appeased his body. Then it set him free in his mind. For it was not until his body was appeased that he could come alive in his mind, as described in section six. And life in his mind gave him pleasure, such pleasure that pleasure was not the word. (M, 6)

Murphy hopes to leave the limitations of the body behind in order to experience intellectual work and creation: 'As he lapsed in body he felt himself coming alive in mind, set free to move among its treasures. The body has its stock, the mind its treasures' (M, 65). However, Murphy is not much of a Cartesian; unlike René Descartes and his followers, who held that such experience allowed for the recognition of the immensity of divine love and will, Murphy's desire to gaze upon the terrain of his mind is directed entirely inwards towards a self-indulgent knowledge of himself alone.[55]

Chapter 6 of Murphy is devoted to what he understands to be this terrain ('Happily we need not concern itself with this apparatus as it really was — that would be an extravagance and an impertinence — but solely with what it felt and pictured itself to be', M, 63). The Latin epigraph to the chapter translates as 'the intellectual love with

---

53 As Benjamin suggests: 'The student "never stops learning"; the gambler "never has enough"; for the *flâneur*, "here is always something more to see". Idleness has in view an unlimited duration, which fundamentally distinguishes it from simple sensuous pleasure, of whatever variety.' AP, 806
54 Tyrus Miller, *Late Modernism: Politics, Fiction, and the Arts between the World Wars* (Berkeley, 1999), 186.
55 On Beckett's interest in the Cartesian thinker Arnold Geulincx, see Knowlson, *Damned to Fame*, 206–07.

which Murphy loves himself alone' and concerns the three zones of the mind Murphy passes through in his meditations.[56] The first zone has to do with direct experience, the place where he finds 'the elements of experience available for a new arrangement' (M, 65). Murphy's greatest pleasure in this zone involves the fantasy of reprisal, in which events and relationships that have not gone well throughout the day are re-arranged to his liking. Next, Murphy enters a zone devoted to thought and the act of cognition; here the act of contemplation itself is the greatest pleasure, and Murphy identifies it with the 'Belacqua bliss' (M, 65) of idleness. The passage through each of these zones and its attendant pleasures is only a prelude to entry into the third and final zone, 'a flux of forms, a perpetual coming together and falling asunder of forms' (M, 65). This zone is the location of pure abstraction, a place where identity dissolves. As Murphy's mind loses its will by becoming just one momentary form among others, Murphy attains a great degree of pleasure at the ultimate recognition of his own insignificance: 'Here he was not free, but a mote in the dark of absolute freedom. He did not move, he was a point in the ceaseless unconditioned generation and passing away of line' (M, 66). In this zone, Murphy transcends temporality, the body, and even matter in order to enter into a realm of universal marginality in which the ruptured relationship between the subject and object characterizes being. Through his contemplative method, Murphy believes that he arrives at a momentary sense of the breakdown of subject and object in the face of the infinite. In doing so, Murphy achieves a form of epistemological autonomy, in which the intellectual — as one who labours by thinking — no longer has to work as he surrenders his will. It is difficult to draw a connection between Murphy's contemplative 'work' as he rocks in his chair and more familiar forms of intellectual labour. The details of how he achieves the knowledge of his own mind seem designed to make him appear somewhat ridiculous, as is Murphy's desire to attain a sense of cosmic marginality through an intellectual love in which he loves himself alone. If the third zone of Murphy's mind is characterized by the complete lack of the will, he can only reach it by wilfully tricking himself that he is able to transcend the body and material reality in the first place; he must lie to himself as he wills himself into a condition premised upon the complete absence of will in the experience of pure abstraction. Taken as an intellectual process, Murphy's work of contemplation can only succeed by fetishizing its own abstraction.

In a metaphorical sense, Murphy's work of contemplation resembles Trinity sloth. This is not to suggest any literal connection between Murphy's meditative self-abasement and the actual practices of the faculty of Trinity College in the 1930s. But Murphy's focus on the Cartesian split between mind and body parallels Trinity's disconnection from the rest of Ireland. Both deny any connection to the material world in which they are grounded;

---

56 The quote reads 'Amor intellectualis quo Murphy se ipsum amat' (M, 63). Ackerley notes the phrase parodies Spinoza's dictum, 'Deus se ipsum amore intellectuali infinito amat', or, 'God loves himself with an infinite intellectual love.' Ackerley, 101.

both assume the feasibility of intellectual autonomy, despite the fact that epistemological concepts like abstraction are firmly rooted in material conditions. As Sohn-Rethel argues, abstraction itself has its origins in the abstract dimension of the exchange process:

> This abstract and purely social physicality of exchange has no existence other than in the human mind, but it does not spring from the mind. It springs from the activity of exchange and from the necessity for it which arises owing to the disruption of communal production into private production carried on by separate individuals independently of each other. This real abstraction is the arsenal from which intellectual labour throughout the eras of commodity exchange draws its conceptual resources.[57]

An internal logic characterizes the intellectual work of abstraction; abstraction appears to originate in the mind of the intellectual alone, detached from the material conditions in which the intellectual is situated.[58] Yet historically, abstraction has depended upon a fundamental split between 'head and hand'; the philosophical work of abstraction is the fetish by which the division between head and hand is naturalized and the elite status of dominant social groups reinforced. While the philosophers and other academics of Trinity College might work lazily at various forms of abstract intellectual labour that claim to be far removed from the material world they inhabit, the position that enables such apparently autonomous forms of work only exists in the first place as a consequence of the whole process of social division, exploitation, and — because this is Ireland — imperialist violence by which an Anglo-Irish elite became a dominant social group. The problem facing the practitioners of Trinity sloth in the 1930s was that the form of abstraction that characterized their intellectual labour no longer corresponded to the needs of the new dominant social group in post-colonial Ireland. If 'the socially necessary forms of thinking of an epoch are those in conformity with the socially synthetic functions of that epoch', the casual work of Trinity sloth ran the risk of becoming a useless, residual remainder of an older social order, since it was not in conformity with the socially synthetic function of the work of the nation.[59]

It is possible to read Beckett's *Murphy* as a satire of the way in which intellectuals devoted to traditional forms of intellectual work lie to themselves in order to create the illusion that they have somehow transcended the material conditions they inhabit. The representation of Murphy's relation to intellectual work can be read as a comic echo of Trinity sloth of the 1930s: though Murphy is devoted to a fetishized form of abstraction in

---

57 Sohn-Rethel, *Intellectual and Manual Labour*, 57.
58 Sohn-Rethel, *Intellectual and Manual Labour*, 68: 'It must further be understood that because it is cut off from its social origin, the abstract intellect emerges with a peculiar normative sense all its own, serving as its "logic".'
59 Sohn-Rethel, *Intellectual and Manual Labour*, 4–5.

his contemplative endeavours, he inhabits a moment in which the utilitarian dimension of such intellectual work is questionable. But it is difficult for Murphy to find a socially conventional form of employment in which he can perform his version of intellectual work, although, unlike other lazy idle schemers, he finally does find a job. While on the 'jobpath', Murphy coincidentally meets up with the irritating Austin Ticklepenny, an old acquaintance from Ireland and 'Pot Poet from the County of Dublin' (M, 51) known for his antiquarian 'gaelic prosodoturfy' (M, 53) and now working in the Magadalen Mental Mercyseat hospital as a male nurse.[60] He is desperate to leave his job, but first must find someone to replace him; Murphy readily agrees to take that position.

Murphy is immediately attracted to the marginality of the inhabitants of the institution, and, as noted earlier, their tendency to 'simply to hang about doing nothing' (M, 95). Unlike many of the other workers in the asylum who are troubled by or fearful of the patients, Murphy idealizes the microcosmopolitans (except for those whose symptoms are manifested in a high level of activity rather than a total commitment to idleness) and admires the fact that they seem permanently to exist in a state that he is only able to reach as a result of his contemplative efforts in the rocking chair:

> They caused Murphy no horror. The most easily identifiable of his immediate feelings were respect and unworthiness. Except for the manic, who was like an epitome of all the self-made plutolaters who ever triumphed over empty pockets and clean hands, the impression he received was of that self-immersed indifference to the contingencies of the contingent world which he had chosen for himself as the only felicity and achieved so seldom. (M, 96)

Murphy can only escape the 'contingencies of the contingent world' through an elaborate form of work in which the body must be suppressed in order to free the mind; the mind having been freed, Murphy must then continue the work of contemplation beyond the realm of rationality to enter into a condition in which there is no stable relation between subject and object and identity dissolves into nothingness along with the material conditions in which the body remains. In Murphy's view, the distinction between mind and body does not function in the same manner for the microcosmopolitans; due to their mental afflictions — which Murphy refuses to regard as affliction, or, for that matter, as a form of suffering — neither their minds nor their bodies are rationally grounded in the here and now of the contingent world. The microcosmopolitans do not need to invent an intricate form of contemplative labour to escape the material conditions imposed on

---

60 Ticklepenny is quite clearly a mean-spirited parody of Beckett's contemporary Austin Clarke, an 'antiquarian' poet criticized in 'Recent Irish Poetry'. On Austin Clarke's relation to the nascent Irish modernism of the 1930s, as well as Beckett's representation of him in Murphy, see W. J. McCormack, 'Austin Clarke: The Poet as Scapegoat of Modernism', in Patricia Coughlan and Alex Davis, eds., Modernism and Ireland: The Poetry of the 1930s (Cork, 1995), 75–102.

mind and body, for lacking any sense of their reality, they already exist in a condition
that Murphy identifies with the third zone of his mind. Murphy objects that this state is
classified by the rational world as insane:

> All this was duly revolting to Murphy, whose experience as a physical and rational
> being obliged him to call sanctuary what the psychiatrists called exile and to think
> of the patients not as banished from a system of benefits but as escaped from a
> colossal fiasco … The issue therefore, as lovingly simplified and perverted by
> Murphy, lay between nothing less fundamental than the big world and the little
> world, decided by the patients in favour of the latter, revived by the psychiatrists on
> behalf of the former … His vote was cast. 'I am not of the big world, I am of the little
> world' was an old refrain with Murphy … How should he tolerate, let alone cultivate
> the occasions of fiasco, having once beheld the beatific idols of his cave? In the
> beautiful Belgo-Latin of Arnold Geulincx: *Ubi nihil vales, ibi nihil velis.* (M, 101)

Geulincx's 'beautiful Belgo-Latin' translates as 'Where you are worth nothing, there
you should want nothing'. Murphy experiences that sense of cosmic insignificance
in the contemplation of the third zone of his mind; it produces an absence of will so
overwhelming that it can be identified as the most absolute commitment of all the various
formulations of idleness he considers throughout the novel. Murphy sees in the life of the
microcosmopolitans the realization of everything he has not worked in his life for, and
attempts to enter into the first-hand experience of that idle utopia by severing his ties to
Celia and moving into a garret in the hospital.

But in choosing to live to the greatest degree possible as a microcosmopolitan, Murphy
makes a fundamental mistake. To choose to do anything involves an act of will, and
microcosmopolitan life is defined by the absence of will. Just as Murphy celebrated the value
of seemingly detached abstract thought as the means for escaping the material conditions
that ultimately produce abstraction in the first place, he ignores the contradictory crux
that ultimately dooms to failure his desire to become a microcosmopolitan. That failure
emerges most explicitly in Murphy's relationship with the schizophrenic Mr. Endon,
the patient who, because of the completeness of his detachment from the world, can be
regarded as the most extreme microcosmopolitan.[61] Throughout the day, Murphy and
Mr. Endon habitually play slow-motion chess games, in which each player makes a move
in the absence of the other; the games are never resolved, but the practice gives Murphy

---

61 It is possible that Beckett's use of the word 'microcosmopolitan' to describe the condition of the mental
    patients in *Murphy* and my use of that word to describe the modernist form of literary work Beckett calls for
    in 'Recent Irish Poetry' come together in the character of Mr. Endon; according to Mays, '"Mythologized
    Presences": *Murphy* in Its Time', 209–10, a number of Mr. Endon's characteristics can be identified with
    the personality and literary work of MacGreevy, one of the poets Beckett singles out for praise for being
    aware of the breakdown of subject and object.

a feeling of kinship with Mr. Endon. On the night of Murphy's first night-shift duty, Mr. Endon initiates a game of chess; because Murphy does not have as many other duties as he does during the day, he devotes more of his attention to the game and it takes place at a quicker tempo than usual. In this chess game Mr. Endon makes a series of moves according to a symmetrical pattern that refuses to take into account the moves of his opponent. As hard as Murphy tries to force Mr. Endon to respond in some way to his own moves, Mr. Endon holds to his closed system, which completely shuts out any recognition of Murphy. As a result, Murphy eventually surrenders the game because no game is possible, and comes to the realization that Mr. Endon is a subject that has no relationship whatsoever to any perceived object, since he exists permanently in a condition in which the lines of communication are ruptured; to Mr. Endon, Murphy is not a perceived object, but rather a remote stimulus that triggers his habit of playing chess.

In coming to this realization, Murphy momentarily becomes conscious of what he presumes to be the condition in which Mr. Endon lives; not surprisingly, it bears a resemblance to the third zone of his mind, and even improves upon it:

> Mr. Endon's finery persisted for a little as an after-image scarcely inferior to the original. Then this also faded and Murphy began to see nothing, that colourlessness which is such a rare postnatal treat, being the absence (to abuse a nice distinction) not of *percipere* but of *percipi*. His other senses also found themselves at peace, an unexpected pleasure. Not the numb peace of their own suspension, but the positive peace that comes when something gives way, or perhaps simply add up, to the Nothing ... Time did not cease, that would be asking too much, but the wheel of rounds and pauses did, as Murphy with his head among the armies continued to suck in, through all the posterns of his withered soul, the accidentless One-and-Only, conveniently called Nothing. (M, 138)

As the object not perceived (*percipi*) by the subject Mr. Endon, Murphy becomes aware of the complete breakdown of the perceptual relationship between the subject and the object. But this is only an echo of Mr. Endon's sense of that breakdown, rather than a direct experience of it. As a rational subject, Murphy still perceives Mr. Endon as an object, even if Mr. Endon as subject cannot perceive Murphy; Murphy can only become aware of the breakdown of the relationship between subject and object indirectly. Murphy finally comes to realize the contradictory impossibility of the microcosmopolitan ideal as he stares closely into Mr. Endon's eyes:

> 'The last Mr. Murphy saw of Mr. Endon was Mr. Murphy unseen by Mr. Endon. This was also the last Murphy saw of Murphy.'
> A Rest.

'The relation between Mr. Murphy and Mr. Endon could not have been better summed up by the former's sorrow at seeing himself in the latter's immunity from seeing anything but himself.'
A long rest.
'Mr. Murphy is a speck in Mr. Endon's unseen.' (M, 140)

Unlike Murphy, Mr. Endon does not need to devise an elaborate form of contemplative intellectual labour to enter into a condition in which everything is a speck in his unseen, a mote in the dark of absolute freedom. Murphy idealizes Mr. Endon because his microcosmopolitan consciousness succeeds better than Murphy's contemplative labours in transcending the material world, for Murphy can only approach Mr. Endon's consciousness temporarily and through great effort. The revelation that Mr. Endon has permanently transcended the conditions of material reality exposes the faulty basis of Murphy's faith in the power of abstraction as a means to leave the situated body behind, for Murphy's wilful act of contemplation can only succeed temporarily and must always return him to the here and now. It is a revelation comparable to Sohn-Rethel's suggestion that the intellectual labour of philosophical abstraction — the form of work practised by the traditional intellectuals of Trinity College that Murphy's contemplative practices at a remote level resembles — serves as a fetish that disguises the material conditions that make abstraction possible in the first place. The microcosmopolitan non-work of Mr. Endon becomes more preferable to Murphy than his own form of contemplative intellectual labour. Murphy cannot wilfully become a microcosmopolitan like Mr. Endon, who had no choice in the matter of coming into his condition; he can only register from a distance a sense of the breakdown between subject and object as it characterizes microcosmopolitan life. Paradoxically, the possibility of an absolute form of intellectual autonomy through a process of pure abstraction — the primary value of Murphy's contemplative practice — is only available to those who have lost their connection to a tangible reality and are no longer able to perform acts of cognitive labour. Everyone else must eventually return to the sordid material conditions in which their bodies are situated.

Notably, one of the pervading characteristics of Murphy's sense of the nothingness he identifies with Mr. Endon's inability to perceive is the experience of a different relationship to the passage of time. Murphy's awareness of Mr. Endon's experience of the breakdown of subject and object enables him to contemplate an alternative temporality in which time does not entirely disappear, as 'that would be asking too much', but passes differently than it would in relation to Murphy's scheduled duties on the night-shift. Murphy's momentary contemplation of the breakdown of the subject and the object enables him to encounter a different form of temporality than the work-time which not only characterizes his daily life, but modernity in general. Thus, the aftermath of the chess game has an effect upon Murphy very similar to the effect produced by the modernist texts celebrated by Beckett in his critical essays concerning Joyce, Proust, and the Irish literary field. Murphy's consequent realization that he cannot wilfully become a microcosmopolitan can be read as an allegorical moment that dramatizes Beckett's formulation of an alternative form of modernist literary work in 'Recent Irish Poetry'. At the end of the novel, Murphy is in a similar position to the aspiring modernist writer who longs to devise a new form of literary work, different from conventional modes of writing that remain subordinate to sacred values like tradition. That innovative form of writing aspires to register the breakdown of the relationship between subject and object but is unable to do so because that very breakdown of subject and object has already brought about the failure of representation. Just as Murphy can only come to know of the microcosmopolitan Mr. Endon's sense of the breakdown of subject and object in an indirect way, the 'microcosmopolitan' literary aesthetic of writers like Devlin and Coffey cannot straightforwardly represent the 'rupture in the lines of communication' after the failure of representation, since they can only represent the echo of that breakdown in an indirect manner. The microcosmopolitan ideal, as implicitly formulated by Mr. Endon in *Murphy*, represents something like the realization of a philosophy of non-practice for lazy idle schemers seeking to invent a new form of alternative intellectual labour that challenges the socially acceptable values of conventional literature by emphasizing the breakdown of representation as a process. Yet it is an ideal that can never be realized; one can never successfully represent the breakdown of the relation between subject and object, just as Murphy cannot consciously choose to become a microcosmopolitan. Microcosmopolitan literary work can only ever represent its own impossibility as literary work-ethic; it is a lazy, idle scheme that can never become an alternative form of intellectual work because scheming has become impossible.

Murphy's recognition of this fundamental contradiction to his form of intellectual work — such as it is — is a monumental crisis for him. He finally resolves to return to his rocking chair one last time in order momentarily to encounter the pleasures of the contemplation of the third zone of his mind before he leaves the microcosmopolitan world of Magdalen Mental Mercyseat hospital behind and returns to Celia and some form of responsibility. Yet we never discover what would happen to Murphy and his commitment to laziness after his realization that the contemplative work of abstraction is doomed to failure because it can never be permanent. For reasons that Beckett takes great pains to demonstrate but never really fully explains, the gas that heats Murphy's garret leaks when one pulls the chain on the water closet. Someone pulls the chain as Murphy rocks one last time, and his garret explodes as Murphy's obliterated body literally becomes a mote in the dark of absolute freedom. Murphy ultimately finds his last resting place among the cigarette ashes and dirt of a seedy London pub as the package containing his remains is converted into a temporary football by the pub's patrons. But he had different wishes for the disposal of his body. Murphy's last will and testament, discovered as Celia, Neary and the others finally catch up with him too late, provides one more dig on Beckett's part at the values of the Irish literary world:

With regard to the disposal of my body, mind, and soul, I desire that they be burnt and placed in a paper bag and brought to the Abbey Theatre, Lr. Abbey Street, Dublin, and without pause into what the great and good Lord Chesterfield calls the necessary house, where their happiest hours have been spent, on the right as one goes down the pit, and I desire that the chain be there pulled upon them, if possible during the performance of a piece, the whole to be executed without ceremony or show of grief. (M, 151)

The Abbey Theatre, founded by Yeats and Lady Gregory, was the central institution of the 'antiquarians' criticized in 'Recent Irish Poetry'; it was the primary social space in which a sacred concept of Irish tradition was articulated. The ignoble nature of Murphy's final desire to be flushed down its toilet during a performance deflates the solemnity that characterized the conventional literary work that paraded tradition as a crucial social value.

Though the Revival is not as much a target for critique in Murphy as it is in 'Recent Irish Poetry', Beckett nevertheless provides one last co-ordinate for the novel's relation to the Irish literary field that makes the Revival seem somewhat ridiculous. To Beckett, the Revival entailed a form of respectable intellectual labour in which the antiquarians endlessly repeated themselves and produced the same idea of tradition through a stable understanding of the relationship between subject and object. Yet the alternative to this repetition, which he poses in Murphy, is maddening because it can never be completed, never succeed in its attempt at representation, never go beyond self-reflexively accounting for its own ruined aesthetic. In this sense, the form of idleness in Murphy that I have termed 'microcosmopolitanism' turns out to be an even starker version of Blanchot's désoeuvrement. It registers a realization of an even darker time, one in which the revolutionary potential of an independent Ireland committed to multiplicity and freedom from domination rather than sameness and the state, seemed to have receded even further. Whether it originated in the traditional form of intellectual work he encountered at Trinity College or as an important motif of the modernist writing he was invested in, laziness stands as an important component of Beckett's version of an alternative form of intellectual labour. Roughly a year after completing the first draft of Murphy, in a letter to his childhood friend, the actress and playwright Mary Manning, written in August 1937, Beckett concedes that idleness retains a sense of the utopian that continues to register the sort of willlessness Murphy aspired to, even if it is problematic and ambiguous:

I do nothing, with as little shame as satisfaction. It is the state that suits me best. I write the odd poem when it is there, that is the only thing worth doing. There is an ecstasy of accidia — willess in a grey tumult of idées obscures. There is an end to the temptation of light, its polite scorching and consolations ... The real consciousness is the chaos, a grey commotion of mind, with no premises or conclusions or problems or solutions or cases or judgment. I lie for days on the floor, or in the woods, accompanied and unaccompanied, in a coenaesthia of mind, a fullness of mental self-aesthesia that is entirely useless ... I used to pretend to work. I do so no longer.[62]

But for Beckett, who suffered anxiety attacks because of his own inability to work, laziness can never be a completely effective metaphor for a socially unrecognized form of work because, strictly speaking, it is the opposite of work. The 'microcosmopolitan' aesthetic one can derive from Beckett's writing of the 1930s presents the only possibility of a form of literary work that reproduces neither the conventional values of tradition nor abstraction. Because it is premised upon an absolute commitment to idleness, it can never really be a feasible form of work in its own right, as it can only register how literary work is no longer possible in any productive sense.

Such an extreme position would suggest that the radical possibilities of laziness as a metaphor for alternative forms of intellectual labour diminished as the work of decolonization came to an end in the early years of the de Valera era. Yet all was not lost, not even to Beckett. In the very same letter to Manning cited above, in which Beckett praised the 'ecstasy' of idleness, he also mentions that he had been to see Charlie Gilmore and his partner Lily Donaghy. Gilmore and Donaghy were bohemian lovers who moved between artistic and dissident republican circles. Charlie Gilmore was the brother of George Gilmore, organizer of the Republican Congress of 1934 and one of the most prominent Irish leftists of the time, and shared his brother's views. Beckett was impressed with the manner in which Gilmore seemed to live as 'a gipsy, on the dole'.[63] By the mid-1930s, Gilmore and Donaghy were living in a cottage they borrowed from the poet Joseph Campbell; they had no gainful employment. Their refusal to work somewhat anticipates the Italian autonomist Marxist principle of exodus, in which one refuses to participate in a social or political sphere one is opposed to through a strategy of withdrawal as a means of self-empowerment. Beckett considered that 'the Gilmores are on the right track. After a bit one wouldn't mind the filth and discomfort. One would want less and less. That is the right direction.'[64] In this observation, Beckett's earlier praise of the pleasures of idleness comes together with a politically inspired model of how to live one's life in opposition to the dominant values of the time. The Gilmore and Donaghy's living situation offers a brief glimpse of dissent by those who brought together affection for modernist literature with a republican refusal to recognize the legitimacy of the state. Because of this, their cottage in Co. Wicklow, admired by Beckett as one practical way to pursue the quietist goals of withdrawal and contemplation that he identified with idleness, provides one small part of Ireland reserved for the lazy idle schemer. Unfortunately, the days of the lazy idle schemer were numbered. There was still the chance that laziness could be converted

62 Letters I, 546.
63 Letters I, 351.
64 Letters I, 547.

into something useful and productive by the state. It was a possibility that Flann O'Brien would address a year after the publication of *Murphy* in his novel *At Swim-Two-Birds*.

7   Flann O'Brien and the Politics of Idleness

In the contradiction between derivation and difference that lies at the basis of anti-colonial nationalism, derivation proved to be more dominant in the early years of the Irish Free State. John P. Fitzgibbons's admission in the *Saorstát Eireann Official Handbook* that 'in its main features the framework of the local government service is the same as that taken over from the British regime' extends to many facets of post-colonial Ireland.[1] By the mid-twenties, no more than a few dissidents remained to claim that the issue of decolonization had not yet been effectively addressed by the new state. In an essay entitled 'Irish Time', published in the *Dublin Magazine* in 1927, J. F. MacCabe wrote that 'some differences of opinion exist as to whether the (Irish) Free State is, indeed, free'.[2] Questions about sovereignty, loyalty oaths to the British Crown, partition, and the existence of two different state apparatuses professing different degrees of fealty to the British Empire on the same island were all symptoms of a deeper condition: the time in Ireland was out of joint.

Although MacCabe's essay does not refer to Irish cultural production in any general sense, nor demonstrates any knowledge of the experimental works of literature of the 1920s, it raises several issues directly relevant to the Irish modernist novel. He begins by

---

1   Bulmer Hobson, ed., *Saorstát Eireann Official Handbook* (Dublin, 1932), 171. My understanding of anti-colonial nationalism is indebted to Partha Chatterjee's highly influential *Nationalist Thought and the Colonial World*.

2   Luke Gibbons identifies MacCabe's essay with other similarly obscure explorations regarding the specificity of Irish time written in the early decades of the twentieth century, though his reading of MacCabe is slightly different from mine; see Gibbons, 'Spaces of Time through Times of Space: Joyce, Ireland, and Colonial Modernity', *Field Day Review*, 1 (2005), 71–86 (81–82).

noting an important historical coincidence. In 1916 the Easter Rising began the war for national independence, which culminated in the creation of the Irish Free State in 1922; but it also marked the introduction into Ireland of Greenwich Mean Time. Irish time had hitherto been twenty-five to forty minutes behind British time. MacCabe argued:

> It cannot be disputed that the imposition of 'Summer Time' on Ireland was a definite invasion of our national habits of thought, work, and outlook. It was, and is, a product of English town and industrial life ... Let us keep a clear mind as to what we really want. Surely we should not borrow a foreign system that is visibly breaking down under its own weight, and that before our very eyes ... For centuries Ireland fought bitterly against English methods and ideas. Have we clearly in our mind our own objective? The answer is that we probably have, however dimly.[3]

For MacCabe, that dim objective was an assertion of Irish national difference. He felt that there should be a specifically Irish temporality that would have economic as well as cultural repercussions:

> And the beginning of all of these things is, necessarily, our own Time Standard. In itself it is an indication of our separate, Irish entity. It would even influence our English commercial visitors. The fact of having to alter one's watch is a potent reminder of both physical realities and eternal verities. It would also convenience our Irish cows and help our Irish harvesters. This is no light cause, lightly put forward ... So therefore let us blaspheme neither space nor time, but combine them for Irish purposes in the centre of Ireland.[4]

MacCabe's declaration can be dismissed as typical of the out-and-out nationalism that could be found in any moment of intensified decolonization, in any part of the post-colonial world. Yet it makes an important point — that the then current understanding of temporality in the Irish Free State assumed a colonial model as the norm, whereas his version of 'Irish time' does not; for him, 'Irish time' is the time of uneven development.

'Irish time' was never implemented in post-colonial Ireland (although the issue has been revived recently by Lloyd as part of his ongoing critique of dominant forms of modernization in Ireland). MacCabe's notion of 'Irish time' is in many respects consistent with the official ethos of the new nation-state.[5] But in other respects, the concept of 'Irish time' captures exactly what that new state hoped to leave behind, as it became a sovereign nation. The difference between 'Irish time' and the temporality of modernization recalls

---

3   MacCabe, 'Irish Time', *Dublin Magazine* 2.1 (1927), 35–36.
4   MacCabe, 37–38.
5   See Lloyd, *Irish Times*, esp. 1–9.

Seamus Deane's distinction between national character and the character of nations.[6] A distinct time zone set twenty-five to forty minutes after Greenwich Mean Time could be taken to represent backwardness in economic or cultural development. Yet it could also raise the question of how 'backwardness' is measured. The persistence of fragmentary traces of the past — like the time-zone difference — within the present may call into question the narrative of modernization that renders them 'archaic'.

MacCabe, perhaps unwittingly, raises some interesting questions about Irish modernist works of literature of the period. What are the interpretative ramifications of a differential notion of Irish time? If narratives — whether cultural, legal, or political — can be understood as particular structural arrangements of time, in what form do they exist within the period in which MacCabe is still able to discern the traces of a specifically Irish time? What impact would the assertion of a distinct Irish temporality or differential sense of modernity have for an understanding of Irish narrative? As Lloyd argues, such forgotten, displaced, fragmentary or suppressed remainders of a radical Irish past represent the location of the

> non-modern ... a name for such a set of spaces that emerge out of kilter with modernity but none the less in dynamic relation to it ... a space where the alternative survives, in the fullest sense of that word, not as a preserve, or as an outside, but as an incommensurable set of cultural formations historically occluded from, yet never actually disengaged with, modernity.[7]

In other words, the 'non-modern' might be regarded as precisely that conceptual site — both actual and symbolic — in which the possibility of a distinct form of 'Irish time' might persist, despite the fact that it disappeared in 1916. Just such a different understanding of temporality might provide grounds for an alternative to the supposed inevitability of the triumph of a progressive form of modernization characteristic of capitalism and colonialism.

The question of what the 'non-modern' has to do with Irish narratives — and more specifically, with the Irish modernist novel — remains. In *Ulysses* or O'Duffy's Cuanduine trilogy, the lazy idle schemer lives in a world in which traces of a pre-modern past collide or uneasily coexist with the contemporary. Eagleton has argued that such collisions and contradictions bring about an 'archaic avant-garde'; uniquely, Irish modernism is more a consequence of Ireland's political, social, economic, and cultural backwardness rather than of its progressive modernity.[8] This view underestimates the frequently progressive qualities of the Irish Free State (like the achievements recorded in the *Saorstát Éireann Official Handbook*), and also underestimates the possibility of a distinct form of Irish time.

6   See Deane, *Strange Country*, 49–99.
7   Lloyd, *Ireland after History*, 2.
8   See Eagleton, *Heathcliff and the Great Hunger*, 273–319.

To identify a polity as 'backward', 'archaic' or 'anachronistic',[9] in Marxist or liberal terms, is to accept a 'stagist' version of historical progress, in which the 'archaic' will inevitably diminish with the passage of time. Dipesh Chakrabarty argues that 'the modern sense of "anachronism" stops us from confronting the problem of the temporal heterogeneity of the "now" in thinking about history'. He suggests these vestiges of the past might in fact exemplify alternative constructions of self and community that gesture towards a different, parallel modernity—although 'modernity' itself deserves scare quotes in such an account.[10]

While the foreclosure of the radical possibilities offered by dissident variations of Irish nationalism began well before MacCabe wrote his article in 1927, within ten years the process was complete, as the period of decolonization in Ireland ended. The defining moment of the consolidation of both the state and Irish nationalism can be assigned the symbolic date of 1 July 1937 — the date on which the people of Ireland approved a new constitution initiated by de Valera, who was possibly the first hegemonic leader of the whole nation in Irish history. He enjoyed the consent of the masses, not because he effectively represented some general political consensus but because, in classic populist fashion, he was able to articulate a policy that appeared to resolve the society's contradictions.[11] He and Fianna Fáil argued that while the Irish Free State was no more than a compromise with Britain, the new Constitution of 1937 achieved a decisive separation from the British Empire. Bunreacht na hÉireann, which technically abolished the Irish Free State by officially renaming the country Éire, sought to define a conservative, exclusionary version of Irishness and to tie that identity closely to the state form. Legally speaking, it provided the means to resolve a number of contradictions (such as those between what Deane calls the national character and the character of nations, between Chatterjee's notion of the thematic and problematic within nationalist discourse, and Lloyd's distinction between modernity and the non-modern) in a manner that would stabilize the state. Most of all, it signalled the triumph of political modernization. It is a text in which the national character is invoked in order to establish the superiority of the character of the nation. In temporal terms, an ongoing nationalist narrative of

9   In addition to the hierarchical orientation of such concepts as the 'archaic', there is also the matter of precisely what relation the present has to the past; as Joe Cleary argues in a critique of Eagleton's argument: 'the embrace in modernist hands of the archaic premodern worlds of aristocracy, epic past, and rural countryside or that of the metropolis and technology can be equally reactionary. From a political standpoint, what is decisive is not whether a modernist writer embraces the archaic or the modern elements, the country or the city, on this spectrum, but rather how the dialectic between the two is actually elaborated.' See Cleary, Outrageous Fortune, 70.

10 See Dipesh Chakrabarty, Provincializing Europe: Postcolonial Thought and Historical Difference (Princeton, 2000), 243, 37.

11 See Ernesto Laclau, Politics and Ideology in Marxist Theory (London, 1977), 161: 'a class is hegemonic not so much to the extent that it is able to impose a uniform conception of the world on the rest of society, but to the extent that it can articulate different versions of the world in such a way that their potential antagonism is neutralized'.

anti-colonial struggle culminates in the production of Bunreacht na hÉireann itself, as Ireland takes its place among the sovereign nation-states of the world.

Yet the persistence of Irish time presents itself in displaced fashion in another contemporary narrative. As I have argued so far, those contradictions that the Constitution sought to resolve also serve as the formal and thematic conditions of possibility for Irish modernism. The novel At Swim-Two-Birds by Flann O'Brien (the pseudonym of Brian O'Nolan) offers a particularly acute example of a text that operates according to a temporality completely distinct from the teleology of linear progress identified with modernization; it stands as a final instance of the modernist trajectory that I have traced thus far. It draws liberally upon a wide range of sources, ranging from the archaic to the contemporary, yet the relation between past and present in At Swim-Two-Birds is neither hierarchical nor linear. When read in relation to Bunreacht na hÉireann — a narrative to which I will argue it is closely related — At Swim-Two-Birds formally undoes the logic of authority and temporality of development evident in the Constitution. In this sense, the temporality of the novel is akin to what MacCabe calls Irish time. In fact, O'Brien's novel goes even further. MacCabe's understanding of Irish time was grounded in pre-industrial agrarian forms of work, but the temporality of At Swim-Two-Birds emerges out of an ongoing commitment to avoid work as much as possible. The unnamed central character — an Irish university student in the 1930s who is attempting to write a novel — is the most thoroughgoing lazy idle schemer in all of Irish modernism. He frequently demonstrates the virtuosity of his idleness by emphasizing performativity over material production. O'Brien's representation of idleness goes further than any of the works I have yet discussed by making performativity the dominant, preferred form of cultural production in the novel, despite the fact that it is a written text.

In At Swim-Two-Birds, idleness registers the simultaneous, out-of-kilter relationship between several different temporalities at once. This dimension of O'Brien's novel proposes an alternative to progressive modernization, just as idleness is an alternative to work. The disavowal of conventional forms of labour, as well as the suggestion that a prolonged commitment to idleness could become a more satisfying and different form of work in its own right, was not at all what was demanded for the character of the nation. But this is not to say that the novel is a straightforwardly political text in any sense.[12] Nor does it unabashedly celebrate idleness. Ultimately, it parodies the way in which idleness became the conventional Irish modernist refusal of the imperative to do the work of the nation, even while it participates in such conventions. At Swim-Two-Birds is as much a self-reflexive, critical satire of the limitations of the lazy idle schemer and of Irish modernism as it is a celebration of either. Crucially, the narrator does not fall back upon his own impotentiality

12 Michael Cronin argues that At Swim-Two-Birds is a 'ludic' text, in which the narrative goal 'is not to communicate a coherent world-view but rather to challenge the very premises on which world-views, political, aesthetic or otherwise are presented in fiction'. See Cronin, 'Mental Ludo', in Anne Clune and Tess Hurson, eds., Conjuring Complexities: Essays on Flann O'Brien (Belfast, 1997), 47–52, 51.

at the end of the novel in order to dissent from the dictates of propriety and responsibility, but instead actualizes his potentiality in a rather conventional way. For all of these reasons, it presents the end of the era of the lazy idle schemer within Irish literary history.

Yet idleness is not only a characteristic of Irish modernism parodied by O'Brien. Nor, in the form of it practised by the narrator, does it lack the evident subversive potential it had in the literary works he attempts to emulate. Idleness retains a radical potential in *At Swim-Two-Birds* in at least two ways. The formal demands of the narrative transform it into a distinct mode of cultural production in its own right. Moreover, the representation of elements drawn from the Irish past invokes a form of heroic indolence that satirizes conventional proprieties and the policies of modernization pursued with both eagerness and hesitation by the increasingly conservative state.

2

Throughout my discussion of Irish modernism I have argued that one of its most prominent formal characteristics is the process that Jameson identifies as the autonomization of the text, that tendency for narratives to become increasingly compartmentalized; distinct sections have singular characteristics that define their formal autonomy. In an Irish context, I have suggested, those autonomous units often have generic or stylistic registers, both historical and contemporary. The juxtapositions of these produce the non-simultaneity of the synchronic condition of *Erlebnis* rather than the diachronic condition of *Ehrfahrung* typical of the Revivalist/nationalist text that subtends the belief in the inevitability of modernization. The formal qualities of the work make it a paradigmatic example of 'autonomization'. But O'Nolan took autonomization further by extending it to the persona of the literary intellectual. Under the name Flann O'Brien, he both performed and parodied the role of the literary intellectual as lazy idle schemer. When writing for newspapers and journals, he used a number of pseudonyms like 'Count Blather' and 'George Knowall', but became most famous for his daily column in the *Irish Times* as Myles na Gopaleen a 'legendary' inventor, playwright, politician and all-round public intellectual with a 'biography' that stretched back to the seventeenth century. In the personae of Myles na Gopaleen and Flann O'Brien, O'Nolan lampooned both the engaged public writer of the Revivalist school, as well as the Joycean self-referential modernist artist.

Of all the writers discussed in this book, O'Nolan was the least bohemian. He never left Ireland; moreover, he was the only one among them who had a conventional salaried position. He 'entered the civil service in 1935 and was assigned to the Department of Local Government', remembers John Garvin, his immediate superior. 'He quickly picked up a working knowledge of our administration but it took some time to channel his rich linguistic flow within the bounds of objectivity and exactitude and to make him realize that official letters were not an appropriate medium for expressing his personality.'[13] O'Nolan rose quickly through the ranks and had a largely successful career as a civil servant, although a slow decline into alcoholism and his involvement in a local scandal led to his early retirement in 1953.[14] Meanwhile, he channelled his 'rich linguistic flow' that exceeded bureaucratic constraints into the literary works he published under the names Flann O'Brien and Myles na Gopaleen.

As Walter Benjamin suggests, it is necessary to regard idleness within the historical context in which it appears, and idleness meant something different in the late 1930s than it had in 1922.[15] By the late 1930s, the post-colonial state was more stable than it ever had been, and the initial, founding work of the nation could be said—at least from the perspective of de Valera and Fianna Fáil—to have been accomplished. Chatterjee has argued that the expansion and consolidation of bureaucracy is key to the national and international legitimation of the post-colonial state.[16] Additionally, to many in 1930s Ireland, the civil service seemed a career that was safe, reliable and not overly strenuous. Anthony Cronin, O'Nolan's biographer, explained:

> The position the Civil Service occupied in the public mind and consciousness in Ireland in those days is now somewhat difficult to grasp. In a country where jobs had always been scarce, it offered not only jobs but absolute security as well; and it offered them to those without any qualification except a talent for passing examinations. It was widely believed that once 'established' in the Civil Service you were required to do little except wait for promotion and it was known that once there you were virtually unsackable.[17]

Thus, bureaucratic labour provided the means by which the lazy idle schemer could be remade as a competent, professional functionary of the state. Authorial ambitions are relegated to 'spare-time literary activities', where idleness, the pre-eminent vocation of the protagonists of Irish modernism, finds its apotheosis.

Most of this chapter will focus on 'Flann O'Brien' and *At Swim-Two-Birds*, the novel that most clearly interrogates the emancipatory possibilities of idleness. But it would be remiss to omit Myles na Gopaleen, that parody of the engaged intellectual. Between 1940 and 1965, in his column 'Cruiskeen Lawn' in the *Irish Times*, Myles na Gopaleen claimed to have been born, variously, in Montevideo in 1646, in London in 1863, in Paris in both 1691 and

---

13 John Garvin, 'Sweetscented Manuscripts', in Timothy O'Keefe, ed., *Myles: Portraits of Brian O'Nolan* (London, 1973), 54–61, 54.
14 See Anthony Cronin, *No Laughing Matter: The Life and Times of Flann O'Brien* (London, 1989), 198–204.
15 AP, 805.
16 Partha Chatterjee, *The Nation and Its Fragments* (Princeton, 1993), 203, 205.
17 Cronin, *No Laughing Matter*, 83.

1801, and at or in a number of other different times and places.[18] In his career as a public intellectual, he served as provost of Trinity College, Dublin, Minister for Justice in 1931, member of the Irish Senate from 1925 to 1927, District Justice of Ballybofey, president of Ireland — against his will — in 1945; further, he founded the Myles na Gopaleen Research Bureau as well as Cruiskeen Industries, and wrote several unproduced plays — 'nobody in Ireland knows more about bad plays than myself ... since 1932 I have written 156 of them'.[19] He was friend and mentor to Albert Einstein, James Joyce, John McCormack, Georges Clemenceau, William Wordsworth, and George Frederick Handel. In an appraisal of the column, Thomas Hogan noted in the *The Bell* (itself a frequent target of Myles's satire): 'Myles na Gopaleen's biographical note on himself is probably not entirely accurate, but it is a fairly illuminating introduction to his work.'[20]

Myles na Gopaleen is an embodiment of the absurd, and many of his recurring antics and stories — such as his frequent anecdotes about Keats and Chapman, or the Brother — follow the conventions of comic journalism. On the other hand, Myles's assaults on O'Faolain bring the role of the literary intellectual into dispute and even disrepute by questioning the values that defined the literary field of production in Ireland in the 1940s. O'Faolain flaunted a literary cosmopolitanism that favoured contemporary American and European writing, yet was opposed to the more experimental aspects of modernist writers like Joyce. O'Faolain argued strenuously that the ideals of his former mentor, Corkery, were provincial and subordinate to official political values, not at all compatible with the 'high purposes of art' one might find in European and American literature and, sporadically, within Irish writing.[21] O'Faolain also advocated realism as the most suitable genre for exposing the shortcomings and flaws of life in post-colonial Ireland. Yet, if literary intellectuals were to be politically engaged — and O'Faolain felt very strongly that they should — their primary duty was to the preservation of the freedom of artistic expression and their role was to stand as 'the sole bulwark between the national character and the disintegrating influences of the censorial mind'.[22] O'Faolain derived a great deal of his understanding of the role of intellectual labour from Yeats, even though their specific positions were often opposed. O'Faolain's valorization of the 'high purposes of art' and his liberal political values often overlapped with positions Yeats had famously espoused (such as the opposition to censorship and the restriction of civil liberties) while serving in the Irish Senate in the 1920s. Most of all, the engaged form of writing that

18　The title is an anglicization of the Irish phrase 'crúiscín lán', or 'the little overflowing jug'. The brief biography here is drawn from Cronin, *No Laughing Matter*, 128, and Thomas Hogan's article 'Myles na Gopaleen', *The Bell*, 13, 2 (1946), 129–30.

19　Quoted by Steve Curran in '"No, This is Not from *The Bell*": Brian O'Nolan's 1943 *Cruiskeen Lawn* Anthology', *Eire/Ireland*, 32, 2–3 (1997), 83.

20　Hogan, 'Myles na Gopaleen', 129.

21　Sean O'Faolain, 'Daniel Corkery,' *Dublin Magazine*, 11, 2 (1936), 49–61, 61.

22　Sean O'Faolain, 'The Dangers of Censorship', *Ireland To-day*, 1, 6 (1936), 57–63, 63.

O'Faolain called for coincided with a basically Yeatsian model of the literary intellectual in its focus on the articulation of social values through the representation of Irish life.

O'Nolan was initially offered the opportunity to become Myles na Gopaleen as a consequence of a controversy involving O'Faolain and Frank O'Connor, which he engineered in the letters section of the *Irish Times*.[23] The object of O'Nolan's satirical campaign was not the quality of O'Faolain's or O'Connor's writing, but rather their assumption of the role of public intellectuals with a privileged insight into the representation and interpretation of contemporary Ireland. Right from the beginning, O'Nolan challenged the position that the obligation of the literary intellectual was to work in a public and progressive manner on behalf of the liberal modernization of Irish society. The ratio of Irish in his *Irish Times* column gradually diminished until it was written entirely in English. It was in English that Myles na Gopaleen mounted a prolonged satirical attack on the public literary intellectual O'Faolain exemplified.[24]

His strategy was to present himself as a serious and legitimate rival to O'Faolain while parading his own more ridiculous qualities. Myles's parody of 'Waama' and his subsequent foundation of the 'Myles na Gopaleen Book Club' provide a typical example.[25] In 1941 O'Faolain founded an organization called the Irish Writers' Artists' Actors' and Musicians' Association (IWAAMA), designed to promote the public position of cultural intellectuals. Not long after, Myles na Gopaleen presented a description of the organization's first meeting, declaring that in the public interest he was offering to sacrifice his own needs to those of the group by presenting himself as a potential leader. After being rebuffed by the other members because of his scandalous reputation, Myles breaks with the group in disgust when it decides to elect O'Faolain ('One shrinks from gratuitous comparisons, but man for man, novels for novels, plays for plays, services to imperishable Irish nation for services to i.I.n., popularity as drawingroom raconteur for p. as d.r., which was the better choice?') and founds his splinter faction known as the 'Myles na Gopaleen Waama League'.[26] Over the next several columns, he supplies an ongoing description of the work of Waama, which eventually puts most of its energy into the Myles na Gopaleen Book Club. After determining that the most important social function of the highbrow literary efforts of O'Faolain and his group was to provide prestige for the contents of the bookcases of an expanding middle class comprised largely of government functionaries, Myles offers a service for a monthly fee to this newly ascendant class — a supply of renowned works of literature that have the worn appearance of having been read. For an additional fee, the book club will provide underlined passages and insightful marginalia ('Rubbish!'; 'How true, how true!'; 'Yes, but cf. Homer, Od., iii, 151'; 'But

23 See Cronin, *No Laughing Matter*, 118–19.
24 Curran provides a detailed account of the various parodies of and attacks on O'Faolain and his journal *The Bell* in "'No, This is Not from *The Bell*'".
25 See *The Best of Myles* (New York, 1968), 15–35.
26 *The Best of Myles*, 15–16.

why in heaven's name?'; 'I remember poor Joyce saying the very same thing'), as well as personal dedications from the author of the work in question ('From your devoted friend and follower, K. Marx'; 'Dear A.B.,— Your invaluable suggestions and assistance, not to mention your kindness, in entirely re-writing chapter 3, entitles you, surely, to the first copy of 'Tess'. From your old friend T. Hardy').[27] The book club is so successful that Myles na Gopaleen initiates the Waama League Escort Service, which, through the medium of a highly educated undercover escort ventriloquist, enables its customers to appear to have highly intelligent and pithy conversations at public events (such as dramatic productions at the Abbey Theatre) without actually saying anything. This story continues for several days until the ventriloquists, dissatisfied with their working conditions, force Myles na Gopaleen to surrender his control of Waama to them: at an organizational meeting, one of the ventriloquists vocalizes Myles's cession of control of the group for him before Myles is able actually to say anything on his own behalf.

While this sequence was written primarily as a form of comic relief in a generally stuffy and traditional newspaper, it was nevertheless a serious inquiry into the institutionalization of culture. Decades before Bourdieu coined the phrase 'cultural capital' to denote the manner in which the symbolic prestige of cultural expertise legitimated a given class position, Myles na Gopaleen provides in this column a comic representation of a similar process.[28] The columns suggest that the function of highbrow literature was not to create or transmit social or political values, but rather to provide a source of symbolic authority for a section of society that was growing into a position of social dominance— whatever the content or aesthetic qualities of the literature. Such a position was considerably at odds with O'Faolain's reassertion of a Yeatsian version of the role of the literary intellectual in Irish society. Myles na Gopaleen does not refuse this position, as other lazy idle schemers had before him; instead, he takes on that role eagerly, exaggerating it to the point where it is revealed as a thinly disguised and ultimately ineffective form of elitism.

O'Faolain was not the only target of Myles na Gopaleen. Many conservative nationalists glorified the rural peasant as the embodiment of the frugal, hard-working, morally pure, religious Ireland espoused by de Valera. Literary works that idealized rural life acquired a canonical status in this period; Tomás Ó Criomhthain's *An tOileánach* was an outstanding example. O'Nolan, a native Irish speaker who genuinely admired *An tOileánach*, objected to the way in which a stereotypical image of the Irish peasant was constructed as a national symbol that repressed the more ribald qualities of writing in the Irish language.[29] His response was to have Myles na Gopaleen write a short comic novel in Irish entitled *An Béal*

---

27 *The Best of Myles*, 20–21.
28 See Pierre Bourdieu, *Distinction: A Social Critique of the Judgement of Taste* (Cambridge, MA, 1984), 6–7.
29 See Tomás Ó Criomhthain, *An tOileánach* (Baile Átha Cliath, 1980). O'Nolan's enthusiasm for *An tOileánach* and other Irish language works is remarked upon by his brother Ciarán, who was an Irish language writer and activist of some note, in his memoir of his brother, *Óige an Dearthár*; see the translation of that book *The Early Years of Brian O'Nolan/Flann O'Brien/Myles na Gopaleen* (Dublin, 1998), 106–07.

Bocht (Drochscéal ar an Drochshaol) that parodied the conventions of peasant autobiography by a process of exaggeration similar to that used in the 'Waama' parodies.[30] An Béal Bocht offers a critique of the nationalist literary intelligentsia that O'Faolain opposed, just as Myles's satirical attacks in 'Cruiskeen Lawn' on IWAAMA and The Bell provided a critique of O'Faolain.

Yet O'Nolan satirized alternatives to the engaged literary intellectual as well. Before the first appearance of Myles na Gopaleen in 1940, O'Nolan had already written two novels under the name Flann O'Brien (though The Third Policeman, the second novel, was rejected for publication and did not appear until after O'Nolan's death). If Myles na Gopaleen produced a parody of the writer as public intellectual, Flann O'Brien in At Swim-Two Birds presents the most sustained interrogation into the role of the lazy idle schemer, the counterpart to figures like O'Faolain. More specifically, the persona of Flann O'Brien allowed O'Nolan at once to enact and parody the model of the Joycean modernist intellectual. Much of At Swim-Two-Birds in particular mocks the final chapter of A Portrait of the Artist as a Young Man in its representation of an artistic student milieu. Yet O'Brien's writing demonstrated both a remarkable reproduction of the values and characteristics of Irish modernism, while also suggesting that it had reached a sort of endpoint at which it could no longer sustain its emphasis on innovation, iconoclasm, and the celebration of idleness. The formal virtuosity of At Swim-Two-Birds presents another aspect of the critique of figures like O'Faolain by demonstrating that modernist technique still had much to contribute to Irish culture.

Later in life (and primarily through the Myles na Gopaleen persona) O'Nolan was more openly critical of Joyce and his writing.[31] In 1951, writing as Brian Nolan in a special issue of the Irish literary journal Envoy devoted to Joyce, he identified isolation, resentment, self-indulgent intoxication, and a complete inability to effect forces greater than oneself as the primary characteristics of the Joycean modernist writer.[32] At Swim-Two-Birds is nowhere near as critical as that in its engagement with the version of Irish modernism typified by Ulysses. But just as the state seemingly managed to make idleness productive by converting it into bureaucratic labour, At Swim-Two-Birds demonstrates the manner in which the more iconoclastic critique of the Revival evident in the emergence of Irish modernism had become simply another literary movement safe for the consumption of an emerging upper middle class. Idleness nevertheless continues to retain a truly radical potential in At Swim-Two-Birds — particularly when it is conceived of in terms that recall the heroic indolence

30 See Myles na Gopaleen, An Béal Bocht (Drochscéal ar an Drochshaol) (Baile Átha Cliath, 1941). The novel was translated into English by Patrick Power as The Poor Mouth (A Bad Story about the Hard Life) (London, 1973).
31 Carol Taaffe suggests that at least some of the criticism of Joyce authored by Myles na Gopaleen was actually written by O'Nolan's friend, Niall Montgomery; see Ireland Through the Looking Glass: Flann O'Brien, Myles na gCopaleen, and Irish Cultural Debate (Cork, 2008), 15.
32 See Flann O'Brien, 'A Bash in the Tunnel', in John Ryan, ed., A Bash in the Tunnel: James Joyce by the Irish (Brighton, 1970), 18.

valorized in O'Duffy's Cuanduine trilogy. While that heroic indolence does not ultimately lead to utopia in Flann O'Brien's novel — despite its considerable humour, At Swim-Two-Birds in many ways is a much darker book than anything to be found in O'Duffy's trilogy — it nevertheless retains the capacity to unsettle the official positions of the state. Even if the representation of idleness in At Swim-Two-Birds suggests that its function within Irish modernism has come to an end, it still proves useful for the implicit critique of de Valera's consolidation of the post-colonial state through the enactment of Bunreacht na hÉireann.

3

At Swim-Two-Birds, written between 1935 and 1938, was O'Nolan's first novel and the first publication by Flann O'Brien.[33] Although it received several positive reviews and was praised by Joyce upon its publication in 1939, it failed to gain a wide readership.[34] It has been regularly republished since its rediscovery in the 1960s and its reputation continues to grow; but it has not yet been completely assimilated into the canon of high modernist writing that so clearly inspires it. The narrative operates on several different levels. It is about an astonishingly inactive undergraduate in his final year at University College Dublin and his relationships with his uncle (whom he lives with) and his classmates. At this level, the narrative seems to be clearly patterned after the final chapter of Joyce's Portrait of the Artist as a Young Man, a book that the undergraduate narrator appears to own. Much of the narrative has its origins in O'Nolan's work as a writer for the student newspaper Comhthrom Féinne. Like Joyce before him, O'Nolan presented fictionalized versions of his friends as characters.[35] The narrator's primary interest is his 'spare-time literary activities', which are devoted to the writing of a novel that is about another writer called Dermot Trellis, a fierce moralist, who is also writing a novel. This realist (and to a certain degree naturalist) novel is devised as a cautionary tale against the dangers of immorality. But, in order to win a wide readership, Trellis intends to include as much smut and obscenity as possible. Through a mysterious process called 'aestho-autogamy', Trellis's characters come to physical life as he creates them. This is O'Brien's solution to a puritanical Catholic nationalism's problem — a mode of physical reproduction untainted by the immoral dangers of sexual pleasure. To save time and effort — he is accustomed to spending most of the day in bed — Trellis borrows characters already in existence from a wide range of sources, from popular American western novels to ancient Irish mythology. He houses both his own and his

33 Since 'Flann O'Brien' will be the focus of this chapter, all subsequent references to the author of At Swim-Two-Birds will be to O'Brien and not to Brian O'Nolan.
34 The novel's obscurity can at least in part be attributed to the destruction of the publisher's warehouse containing most of the existent copies of the book during the Battle of Britain in 1940. See Cronin, No Laughing Matter, 85–94, 99.
35 Taaffe argues that O'Nolan's experiences as an editor of the student literary journal Comhthrom Féinne are are central to Flann O'Brien's representation of the unnamed narrator and his friends; see Taaffe, Ireland Through the Looking Glass, 41–49.

borrowed characters with him in a low-rent hotel in suburban Dublin, 'so that he can keep an eye on them and see that there is no boozing' (ASTB, 47).

While Trellis is at work on his novel, the characters are compelled to obey him, but discover that they have absolute freedom when he is asleep. Disturbed by what Trellis demands of them in his vice-ridden novel and generally dissatisfied with their working conditions, the characters conspire to drug him so that he sleeps for twenty hours a day. While he is asleep, they commit themselves to prolonged sessions of story-telling. These stories provide another level of narrative. The characters realize that this arrangement cannot last forever, so they recruit an additional writer to write a novel in which Trellis is forced to act as a character. They find a willing author in Orlick Trellis, the half-fictional, illegitimate offspring of Dermot Trellis and one of his characters (Dermot Trellis is a hypocrite who does not live by the puritanical principles he preaches). Orlick Trellis's novel — yet another level of narrative — recruits an Irish 'member of the devil class' named the Pooka MacPhellimey to torture Dermot Trellis mercilessly and brutally (ASTB, 9). Dermot Trellis is finally put on trial and condemned to death 'by a jury of his own manufacture' in a surreal courthouse that resembles a particularly dissolute pub and takes place in the Antient Concert Rooms, first home of the Irish Literary Theatre. Before Dermot Trellis can be executed, however, his servant Teresa by mistake burns the manuscript that contains the vengeful characters, thus ending their existence and ensuring Dermot Trellis's survival. The narrator's manuscript ends with Dermot Trellis's reflection 'I have done too much thinking and writing, too much work', as he contemplates the failure of art that self-consciously reveals its own fictional nature (ASTB, 313–14). Meanwhile — if such a temporal identification is still possible for such a text — the narrator is reconciled with his uncle by successfully passing his final exams with high honours, despite his own devout commitment to idleness.

None of the narrative levels persists for more than a few pages before another narrative intervenes. Advertisements for betting shops, fragmentary extracts from the eighteenth-century encyclopedia *A Conspectus of the Arts and Sciences* and bad translations of ancient Irish legends are incorporated into the text. Taken in isolation, many of these fragmentary mini-narratives provide brief, unique archaeologies into the over-determined culture of post-colonial Ireland. The collisions between these different sections of the text register a number of different forms of antagonism evident within the Irish literary field. The juxtaposition of mass-market culture with the literary tastes and beliefs of the narrator exemplifies the tension between high and low culture. The distinction between the Revival and the realist and naturalist writing that succeeded it and the juxtaposition of the archaic and the contemporary are among O'Brien's many variations on that 'divide'. Legal rhetoric and bureaucratic terminology invoke an important dimension of the warped humour visible among the various styles, motifs, allusions and wholesale appropriations from both traditional and contemporary Irish culture. This is not surprising considering that O'Nolan was a civil servant. The narrator frequently draws upon the form of the questionnaire as if he were collecting data for a metafictional reflection on the meaning of his novel. Several conversations (such as a long discussion between the Pooka and the Good Fairy, which ranges from the nature of good and evil to whether the Pooka's wife is actually a kangaroo) have the intricate, crazed logic, or illogic, of bureaucratic regulations. But the influence of O'Nolan's job as a bureaucrat goes further. The drafting of de Valera's new Constitution between 1935 and 1937 coincided with the writing of At Swim-Two-Birds. O'Nolan had direct access to the conversations and debates that informed the writing of the Constitution. The connection between At Swim-Two-Birds and Bunreacht na hÉireann lies in the distinction, visible in both, between, on the one hand, the temporality of modernization and the state, and on the other, 'Irish time'.[36] The political meaning of At Swim-Two-Birds and its relationship to Irish history can be found within that distinction.

The enactment of Bunreacht na hÉireann was the final moment of the long period of Ireland's anti-colonial struggle and post-colonial state formation.[37] The new Constitution was meant to provide an explicitly nationalist articulation of Ireland's arrival into the political modernity of the parliamentary state. The preamble of the document begins by invoking 'the Most Holy Trinity', and concludes with the restoration of national unity and 'concord established with other nations'.[38] The document then summarizes the historical emergence of independent Ireland. If the past was uniquely marked by the centrality of struggle and the heroic spirit that sustained it, the present was governed by the prevalence of those attributes and values that made Ireland like other modern states. Ireland's emergence as a distinct nation-state was the state-form itself, as codified by the Constitution. But that characteristic political structure of Western modernity had already arrived in Ireland as a result of Britain's long colonial presence in the country, prior to national independence. Any articulation of the national singularity of the Irish state Bunreacht na hÉireann might achieve would require the translation of a colonial political structure into more identifiably local terms. Though the new Constitution did introduce the presidency and the Senate, it left intact a political and legal structure that dated back to the British colonial period (though it did translate the words for the more significant

36 See Kiberd, Irish Classics, 519, and Deane, Strange Country, 158.
37 On the background of Bunreacht na hÉireann, see Ronan Fanning, 'Mr. De Valera Drafts a Constitution', in Brian Farrell, ed., De Valera's Constitution and Ours (Dublin, 1988), 31–39, and Lee, Ireland 1912–1985, 201–11. Lee also provides a detailed (and generally more favourable) close reading of the respective sections of the Constitution in his article 'The Irish Constitution of 1937', in Seán Hutton and Paul Stewart, eds., Ireland's Histories: Aspects of State, Society and Ideology (London, 1991), 80–93.
38 The preamble states: 'In the name of the Most Holy Trinity, from Whom is all authority and to Whom, as our final end, all actions both of men and States must be referred, We, the people of Éire, Humbly acknowledging all our obligations to our Divine Lord, Jesus Christ, Who sustained our fathers through centuries of trial, Gratefully remembering their heroic and unremitting struggle to regain the rightful independence of our Nation, And seeking to promote the common good, with due observance of Prudence, Justice, and Charity, so that the dignity and freedom of the individual may be assured, true social order attained, the unity of our country restored, and concord established with other nations, Do hereby adopt, enact, and give to ourselves this constitution.'

offices and institutions into their nearest equivalents in the Irish language).[39] The most significant changes Bunreacht na hÉireann introduced concerned the clarification and legal codification of Irish identity.

Articles 40 to 45 guarantee the liberal rights common to most Western democracies, including the right to private property, freedom of expression, freedom of the press and of religion. However, a conditional clause is included with each right that seems to limit its fullest extension. In each case that limit is linked with a conservative version of national identity. Women, for example, are represented only in their roles as mothers, within the domestic sphere. The state also recognized the 'special position' of the Catholic Church. While the importance of the freedom of the press and of expression is duly admitted, this right is rescinded if it disturbs conventional notions of 'public order and morality'. This gave a legal basis for the most powerful state censorship. Many of these provisions proved controversial in subsequent decades, and many of them have been deleted or revised. These articles have been said to reflect the essentially authoritarian nature of the de Valera period.[40] They do formalize a preferred form of Irish national identity: Catholic, nationalist, intolerant of 'immorality', and characterized by a strictly gendered split between the public and private spheres. Bunreacht na hÉireann fixes the nature of Irish identity according to the terms of a dominant form of conservative Catholic nationalism. One of its most unusual features, the position that the Irish language was the primary language of the state, paradoxically posed a threat to its own authority. Article 8 affirms 'the Irish language as the national language is the first official language', though it also recognizes English as the 'second official language'. In a point of clarification, Article 25.6 states, 'in case of conflict between the texts of a law enrolled under this section in both the official languages, the text in the national language shall prevail'. However, no political terminology for liberal democracy existed in Irish. Key sections of the Constitution were drafted in English, translated into a form of Irish, and then retranslated into an English version that was deemed to be subordinate to the Irish. This led at least one critic to see in the Constitution a post-structuralist crisis of the authority of the text that is comically worthy of a writer as fanciful as Flann O'Brien.[41] Certainly O'Nolan, a native Irish speaker, hostile to the official policy towards the language, was amused by the paradoxical foundation of the Constitution's linguistic authority.

---

39 Article 50, the final section, asserted that all the laws not addressed in the new Constitution — and very few laws were addressed — would be the same as those that were codified in the older Constitution. Article 50 meant that the legal and political forms of British colonialism continued to mould de Valera's Ireland.

40 Lee argues, for example, that the legal recognition and protection of Judaism articulated in Article 44.1.3 presented a considerably notable act within the greater context of Europe in the late 1930s, especially in a country that had had anti-Semitic episodes in its own history. See Lee, 'The Irish Constitution of 1937', 83.

41 See Eagleton, *Heathcliff and the Great Hunger*, 126.

One of the goals of the Constitution is to harness the erratic specificity of the past for the purposes of the contemporary state by seeking permanently to establish an authorized conception of Irish identity appropriate for citizenship. One could not find a clearer example of the manner in which elements identified with the pre-colonial national character — in this case the Irish language — have the power to subvert or interrupt the authority of a discourse of modernization that seeks to assimilate the ostensibly 'archaic' as a means of containing it. In temporal terms, the 'Irish time' of national character emerges here as an implicit threat to the standard modern time of the state. *At Swim-Two-Birds* also echoes the manner in which the past threatens the order of the present. O'Brien's novel represents this threat by putting into question the notion of fixed identity by linking its dissolution with oral story-telling, associated with ancient Irish literature and therefore respectably archaic but, as an oral tradition, less secure than a written one. The conditions of possibility for story-telling, in turn, rest upon the utopian pleasures of idleness.

In what seems to be a parody of Stephen Dedalus in Joyce's *Portrait*, the narrator of *At Swim-Two-Birds* formulates an elaborate aesthetic theory that implicitly refers to the form of the novel that contains it. Unlike Stephen Dedalus, who earnestly draws on Aquinas and Aristotle for his theory, the narrator of *At Swim-Two-Birds* ironically appropriates constitutional rhetoric for his purposes. His theory of cultural production registers the illusion of permanence that characterizes certain genres more than others. He records an early conversation in the novel:

> It was stated that while the novel and the play were both pleasing intellectual exercises, the novel was inferior to the play inasmuch as it lacked the outward accidents of illusion, frequently inducing the reader to be outwitted in a shabby fashion and caused to experience a real concern for the fortunes of illusory characters. The play was consumed in wholesome fashion by large masses in places of public resort; the novel was self-administered in private. The novel, in the hands of an unscrupulous writer, could be despotic. In reply to an inquiry, it was explained that a satisfactory novel should be a self-evident sham to which the reader could regulate at will the degree of his credulity. It was undemocratic to compel characters to be uniformly good or bad or poor or rich. Each should be allowed a private life, self-determination and a decent standard of living. This would make for self-respect, contentment, and better service. It would be incorrect to say that it would lead to chaos. Characters should be interchangeable as between one book and another. The entire corpus of existing literature should be regarded as a limbo from which discerning authors could draw their characters as required, creating only when they failed to find a suitable existing puppet. The modern novel should be largely a work of reference. (ASTB, 32–33)

By stressing that authors should borrow existing characters wholesale from other works, the narrator demonstrates an awareness of and commitment to the modernist practice of a 'mythic method' that transposes older literary characters into modern contexts in a manner similar to Yeats's plays and poems about Cuchulainn or in Joyce's use of Homeric analogues. Various analogies between the narrator's aesthetic theory and the Constitution offer themselves: the characters of the novel are its citizens, the author is like the state, and the written text of the novel provides the legal rhetorical structure through which the author/state organizes a productive and stable life for its citizens/characters. Unlike de Valera's Constitution of 1937, however, the narrator is wary of the threat posed by the writer's capacity to fix identity permanently. As his aesthetic theory demonstrates, the narrator realizes that the author is in a position to produce a narrative that imparts a 'moral of the story' or message. Dermot Trellis's novel, written for the express purpose of exposing and condemning vice in modern Ireland, presents a prime example of just such a pedagogical work. Trellis's realist novel is the antithesis of the 'self-evident sham' — or, in more constitutional language, legal fiction. The novel as self-evident sham emphasizes the mobility rather than the permanence of identity.[42] At least, when they are not officially working as Trellis's characters within his novel, the characters of the narrator's manuscript hilariously affirm this flexibility.

At Swim-Two-Birds exemplifies Homi Bhabha's theorization of the 'nation as narration', which describes anti-colonial nationalist discourse as split between the axes of pedagogy and performativity.[43] On the one hand, nationalism draws upon a historicist, 'continuist' narrative of modernization that brings the colonized subject into the modern temporality of national sovereignty; this is the same concept Deane terms the character of nations. Nationalism serves a pedagogic function in this sense, since it transforms the colonized people into modern national citizens through the rhetoric of progress. On the other hand, the people must first act to transform a colonial province into a nation. Because this occurs before they have yet become fully modern through the pedagogic project of nationalism, the masses inevitably utilize older forms and practices — in other words, Deane's concept of national character — for the modern purposes of achieving independence. Thus, the progressive temporality of nationalism depends on its subsumption of older, different temporalities. At the same time, the 'occult instability' of such older temporalities continually threatens to undercut the pedagogical, modernizing project of nationalism. MacCabe's notion of 'Irish time' is a case in point.

Although they obviously have very different functions, the distinction between the performative and the pedagogical in At Swim-Two-Birds is analogous to the tension between national character (as suggested by the memorialization of struggle and implied by the

42 Taaffe argues that the narrator's aesthetic theory responds to the increasing politicization of literary aspirations in the 1930s exemplified by agitprop literature; see Taaffe, Ireland Through the Looking Glass, 39.
43 See Homi Bhabha, 'DissemiNation: Time, Narrative, and the Margins of the Modern Nation', in The Location of Culture, 145–46.

particularities of the Irish language) and the character of nations (as represented by the institutions of the state and the grounds for proper citizenship) in Bunreacht na hÉireann. In both texts is a persistent form of 'Irish time', subordinate to, but nevertheless implicitly threatening, the progressive temporality favoured by the state and authority. Therein lies the relationship At Swim-Two-Birds has to the Constitution — the novel dramatizes the manner in which the recalcitrant past might effectively overwhelm the establishment of authority. The 'occult instability' of Irish time in At Swim-Two-Birds is not exactly the same thing MacCabe wrote about in 1927. MacCabe linked his sense of Ireland's distinct temporality to pre-modern agricultural work. The temporality of At Swim-Two-Birds also emerges out of an older mode of production — oral story-telling. Oral story-telling depends upon the refusal of conventional forms of work. That enabling idleness, as it is construed in the multiple narrative layers of At Swim-Two-Birds, is a mode of performativity in itself that involves a lot of hard work.

4

At Swim-Two-Birds presents a late variation of the modernist celebration of inactivity, as the paradoxically rigorous commitment to idleness demonstrated by the narrator suggests the degree to which laziness had become a fashionable pose by the 1930s, no longer as scandalous as it had been for earlier writers. The narrator of the novel thinks of himself as a modernist; Joyce, Pound, and Eliot are the key literary influences on him and his friends (also aspiring writers); in their conversations about literature they assert 'the primacy of America and Ireland in contemporary letters and ... the inferior work produced by writers of the English nationality' (ASTB, 62) so often that it becomes a cliché. Central to the group's shared notion of how to be a modernist is 'the importance of being at all times occupied with literary activities of a spare-time or recreative character' (ASTB, 32). But the repeated claim that writing must be a spare-time activity is too strong for the narrator, for he never engages in any activity, literary or otherwise, that is not of a spare-time literary character. For the narrator and his friends, the alternative intellectual labour of the lazy idler seems to be an attractive vocation while they seek 'those competitive plums which make the Civil Service and the Banks so attractive to the younger bread-winners of to-day' (ASTB, 56).

Nevertheless, the narrator's uncle, the most obvious authority figure in the book, is scandalized. 'Idleness, you might say, is the father and the mother of the other vices', is his mantra As a respectable member of the lower middle class — he is a clerk at the Guinness brewery — he has very little time for the laziness of those who have been offered more opportunities than he had:

> As you know yourself, I have strong views on the subject of idling. Lord save us, there is no cross in the world as heavy as the cross of sloth, for it comes to this, that the lazy man is a burden to his friends, to himself and to every man woman or child

he'll meet or mix with. Idleness darkens the understanding; idleness weakens the will; idleness leaves you a very good mark for the sinful schemes of the gentlemen down below. (ASTB, 308–09)

Disinclination towards work was not only an economic matter that prevented the growth of a self-sufficient middle class and a political problem that arrested the energy necessary for the creation of a new nation; idleness raised moral difficulties as well. As a form of unproductive, self-involved enjoyment, idleness overlaps with such sins as masturbation, something duly noted by the uncle:

Aren't you very fond of your bedroom now ... Why don't you study in the dining-room here where the ink is and where there is a good book-case for your books? Boys but you make a great secret about your studies ... I know the studying you do in your bedroom, said my uncle. Damn the studying you do in your bedroom.
I denied this. (ASTB, 12)

Idleness thus avoids the work required for the nation's survival, and indicates a deeply flawed and unproductive moral character. The state's policing of public morality enforced a Jansenist form of Catholicism. In Bunreacht na hÉireann freedom of expression was restricted if it violated the state's very strict notions of immorality. O'Brien was at pains to point out that ideas, practices, and modes of speech quite common in pre-Christian Ireland were frowned upon in modern Ireland. At Swim-Two-Birds never makes specific reference to the Constitution, though the rhetoric of the narrator's aesthetic theory implicitly invokes it in order to provide the basis for a novel that will symbolically challenge its authority. In a more general sense, O'Brien's frequent juxtaposition of the pagan bacchanalian qualities of traditional Irish culture against the more puritanical values of post-colonial Ireland presents yet another example of something out of the 'Irish time' of the past that does not consort with the progressive goals of the modern state.

The uncle certainly has reason to complain of his nephew, who is perhaps the laziest character in all of Irish literature. 'A contemplative life has always been suitable to my disposition. I was accustomed to stretch myself for many hours upon my bed, thinking and smoking there', he states early in the narrative, articulating the form of inactivity that will remain predominant throughout the rest of the novel (ASTB, 11). Though he occasionally feels some guilt about his inactivity and vows to reform ('I resolved at the time to make an end of my dissolute habits and composed mentally a regime of physical regeneration which included bending exercises'), his efforts usually fail ('One consequence of my resolve, at any rate, was that I attended at the College every day and walked through the Green and up and down the streets, conducting conversations with my acquaintances and occasionally talking with strangers on general topics') (ASTB, 61). At one point, he decides to catalogue his own idleness:

Biographical reminiscence, part the eighth: While I was engaged in the spare-time literary activities of which the preceding and following pages may be cited as more or less typical examples, I was leading a life of a dull but not uncomfortable character. The following approximate schedule of my quotidian activities may be of some interest to the lay reader. (ASTB, 212)

The description that follows provides an estimate of the average number of hours (6.63) the narrator devotes to 'spare-time or recreative pursuits'.[44] It is followed by two further accounts of other quotidian experiences.

The first, extracted directly from *A Conspectus of the Arts and Natural Sciences*, is a letter written in 1766 by the English poet William Cowper, best known for his lengthy poem *The Task*. Though *The Task*, written nearly two centuries later, demonstrates a certain investment in the representation of idleness, the letter cited by O'Brien clearly does not. Instead, it is a succinct articulation of that approach to work that Weber would later identify with the Protestant work-ethic. It describes Cowper's daily life in an evangelical community led by the preacher John Newton: 'As to amusements, I mean what the world call such, we have none ... We refuse to take part in them, or to be accessories to this way of murthering (sic) our time, and by so doing have acquired the name of Methodists' (ASTB, 213). Cowper's daily life consists entirely of work and prayer, and idleness has no place in such a devout and disciplined regime. But *At Swim-Two-Birds* does not mention that Cowper turned to Methodism in an attempt to counter severe periods of mental illness characterized by melancholic indolence. Cowper's letter belongs to a world outlandishly foreign to that of Finn Mac Cool, a legendary hero of Irish mythology who appears as a minor character as one of Dermot Trellis's characters. Finn traditionally spent 'a third of the day watching the boys — three fifties of boys has he at play in the ball-yard; a third of the day drinking sack; and a third of the day in the calm sorcery of chess' (ASTB, 214). Finn's idleness belongs to the distant, mythological time of the 'archaic' and pre-colonial. The juxtaposition of Finn's heroic indolence and Cowper's faith in work as a means of avoiding damnation highlight the narrator's predicament. His idleness, once an admired avocation, is now anathematized as immoral. Arduous laziness is not a virtue in the modern, post-colonial world.

---

44 '*Nature of daily regime or curriculum:* Nine-thirty a.m. rise, wash, shave, and proceed to breakfast; this on the insistence of my uncle, who was accustomed to regard himself as the sun of his household, recalling all things to wakefulness on his own rising. 10.30. Return to bedroom. 12.00. Go, weather permitting, to College, there conducting light conversation on diverse topics with friends, or with acquaintances of a casual character. 2.00 p.m. Go home for lunch. 3.00 Return to bedroom. Engage in spare-time literary activity, or read. 6.00. Have tea in company of my uncle, attending in a perfunctory manner to the replies required by his talk. 7.00. Return to bedroom and rest in darkness. 8.00. Continue resting or meet acquaintances in open thoroughfares or places of public resort. 11.00. Return to bedroom ... *Minutiae:* No. of cigarettes smoked, average 8.3; glasses of stout or other comparable intoxicant, av. 1.2; times to stool, av. 2.65; hours of study, av. 1.4; spare-time or recreative pursuits, 6.63 circulating.' (ASTB, 212–13)

But if such a critique is predicated upon such a commitment to idleness and a consequent mistrust of the written word, how does one construct a narrative form committed to the possibility of a flexible conception of identity that is nevertheless arduous in its laziness? One of the narrator's solutions is to draw upon the model of oral story-telling, the foremost mode of cultural production in the world Finn originates in. The subordinate status of the task of this performative form of narrative is something that ancient characters are aware of. Finn, who now 'works' as a minor character in Trellis's novel on account of his elderly venerable appearance, resents the passage of time that has made his art of story-telling subordinate:

> Small wonder, said Finn, that Finn is without honour in the breast of a sea-blue book, Finn that is twisted and trampled and tortured for the weaving of a story-teller's book-web. Who but a book-poet would dishonour the God-big Finn for the sake of a gap-worded story? ... Indeed, it is true that there has been ill-usage to the men of Erin from the book-poets of the world and dishonour to Finn ... (ASTB, 24–25)

Finn's complaint betrays a suspicion of the fixity of the written text that has affinities with the narrator's theory of the novel. Moreover, he knows his characteristic mode of narrative is now outmoded, replaced by the novel, the genre Benjamin identifies as 'a concomitant symptom of the secular productive forces of history'.[45] The frequent interruptions by those listening to Finn's tale ('You can't beat it, of course, said Shanahan with a reddening of the features, the real old stuff of the native land ... But the man in the street, where does he come in? By God he doesn't come in at all as far as I can see' (ASTB, 105–06), the wonderful digressions, in one of which Mad King Sweeny of Dal Araidhe, the primary character of Finn's tale, appears as a character in the narrator's manuscript in order to play poker with other characters and to recite lyrical narratives of his own, certainly make a nonsense of the linear narrative's assumptions, such as the secure identity of its characters. These comic instabilities threaten the pedagogical project of the author/authoritarian, Dermot Trellis. Story-telling within At Swim-Two-Birds demonstrates its capacity to challenge the novel as a genre, while of course remaining an element of it.[46]

Writing itself becomes a disciplinary form of coercion. The section written by Orlick Trellis is more coercive and brutal in its violence than Dermot Trellis's 'novel' had ever been. Orlick's representation of the trial of Dermot Trellis offers a brief allegory of the dangers of revolutionary justice, in which the oppressed become oppressors. Writing is complicit with power in At Swim-Two-Birds, and the darkly comic and gratuitous manner in which Orlick's monological manuscript shuts down any alternatives demonstrates the difficulty of bringing about the utopian, egalitarian promise of the narrator's constitutional aesthetic theory. Despite such authoritarian dangers, the narrator works

---

45 I, 87.
46 See Walter Benjamin, *Reflections* (New York, 1968), 181.

very hard — even if he does present such labours routinely and consistently as 'idle and perfunctory' — to retain the characteristics of story-telling in his manuscript. This produces a narrative that consistently looks like an interrupted or digressive conversation. More important, in the form of both the manuscript and *At Swim-Two-Birds* as a whole, is O'Brien's transformation of idleness, associated with both the telling of stories and the writing of a novel, as a necessary condition for either or both. The narrator incorporates his own laziness into his aesthetic project by refusing to revise or even reread his writing:

> My literary or spare-time compositions, written not infrequently with animation and enjoyment, I always found tedious of subsequent perusal. This sense of tedium is so deeply seated in the texture of my mind that I can rarely suffer myself to endure the pain of it. One result is that many of my shorter works, even those made the subject of extremely flattering *encomia* on the part of friends and acquaintances, I have never myself read, nor does my indolent memory enable me to recall their contents with a satisfactory degree of accuracy. (ASTB, 84)

The narrator's reluctance fully to work out his novel in a complete or satisfying fashion provides one of the central narrative energies of *At Swim-Two-Birds*. O'Brien reproduces for the reader the fragmentary and incomplete sense the narrator has of his own work by consistently bringing seemingly unrelated sections of the manuscript together throughout. Aside from a prolonged section on the battle for the soul of Orlick Trellis between the forces of good and evil (as represented by the comic characters of the Good Fairy and the Pooka MacPhellimey) and the concluding section in which Dermot Trellis is tortured and put on trial, none of the narrative segments of the manuscript advances the plot in any significant manner. Instead, those parts of the narrator's manuscript that do make their way into the text of *At Swim-Two-Birds* generally concern digressive conversations and stories told by the characters as they refuse to do the narrative work Trellis demands of them in his role as author of his book. Rather than having to endure the tedium of rereading and revising the manuscript so that a coherent plot emerges — that would simply involve too much work — he instead opts for a variety of narrative shortcuts:

> Without seeking independent advice on the matter, I decided — foolishly perhaps — to delete the entire narrative and present in its place a brief resumé (or summary) of the events which it contained, a device frequently employed by newspapers to avoid the trouble and expense of reprinting past portions of their serial stories. (ASTB, 84–85)

The two-page synopsis he produces provides the first clear sense of the manuscript's plot. Synopses of this kind become a narrative technique.[47] The narrator has managed to make idleness into a formal technique, airily dismissing difficulties with the claim, 'all this [is] being provided for in the plot' (ASTB, 86).

The narrator's autobiographical reflections are also narrative shortcuts. The reproduction of various texts the narrator has read saves O'Brien from the labour of having to represent the formative experiences of the narrator's past. When the narrator drinks alcohol for the first time, for example, O'Brien merely includes an extract from a Christian Brothers textbook on the dangers of intemperance, in order to suggest his memory of how such forms of idle and immoral intoxication were presented while he was at school.[48] Elsewhere, O'Brien reverts to the minimalist classificatory schemas of bureaucratic description ('*Description of my uncle:* Red-faced, bead-eyed, ball-bellied. Fleshy about the shoulders with long swinging arms giving ape-like effect to gait. Large moustache. Holder of Guinness clerkship the third class', ASTB, 2); ('I denied this. *Nature of denial:* Inarticulate, of gesture', ASTB, 13). At every level of the narrative, both the narrator and O'Brien represent writing as a form of work, even if it is the chosen labour of the idler. Idleness makes the work of writing appealing; it does not, on that account, lose its charm for the writer, does not become alienated from him. In addition, the state unwittingly managed to make idleness productive through the expansion of its own bureaucracy.

The various, loosely assembled segments that make up the text of *At Swim-Two-Birds* — all of the interruptions and digressions that take place in the stories it contains, all of the random interpolations drawn wholesale from other texts, all of the shortcuts, summaries, and substitutions that take the place of a coherent narrative due to the narrator's laziness — produce a narrative that is in some fundamental way about a cultural and historical moment in which, due to the spiralling contradictions between the modern and the archaic in the context of post-colonial state formation, a normative conception of temporality is always in question. But *At Swim-Two-Birds* is not just a novel *about* how 'Irish time' is out of joint. Instead, it is a novel that *is*, in a narratological sense, Irish time out of joint. It is noteworthy that the pocket-watch that the narrator receives as a gift from his uncle at the end is six minutes slow. Texts like Bunreacht na hÉireann, which marked Ireland's arrival into a form of sovereign statehood characteristic of Western modernity, were proof of the apparent triumph of the process of modernization. But the legitimation of such narratives of modernization depended upon an appeal to certain aspects of the Irish past that often had unruly qualities that could potentially undermine the apparent stability and finality of that authority. *At Swim-Two-Birds* heightens such contradictions between non-modern forms of recalcitrance and a more familiar, dominant form of modernity and shows how such elements of the apparently archaic undermine the teleologies of progress, which both

47 Further synopses occur on pages 145, 214 and 235.
48 See ASTB, 27–28.

enable the existence of, and legitimate, the state. The form of modernity identified with the state more or less triumphs in At Swim-Two-Birds also, for even though it emphasizes the centrality of such unproductive practices as idleness and story-telling in its form and narrative, it nevertheless remains a written novel. It may progress more haphazardly than other novels but it progresses nevertheless — thus presenting a final contradiction that the egalitarian aspirations of its narrator's advocacy of the novel as a self-evident sham ultimately cannot resolve. The novel does not end on an optimistic note; the third and final ending concerns the relationship between madness and intellectual labour and concludes with a final rumination on suicide. The three endings — Trellis's decision to stop writing rather than to risk insanity, the student's reconciliation with his uncle and entry into a sort of respectability, and finally suicide — provide the three possibilities for the future that Stephen Dedalus specifically rejects at the triumphant close of A Portrait of the Artist as a Young Man. The distance between its conclusion and that of At Swim-Two-Birds shows how completely the initial optimism of the modernist response to the Revival had dissipated by the end of the 1930s.

However, by dramatically representing the disruption of the linear progress of the modern novel by the lazy, performative pleasures of story-telling, At Swim-Two-Birds nevertheless demonstrates the so-called non-modern's interruption of the apparent logical inevitability of modernity and calls into question the totalizing drive of modernization — even if it also indicates that the high modernist period in Ireland had come to an end. Both in the narrator's relation to his friends and in the discussions and stories of his characters, the central value of At Swim-Two-Birds is the desire to avoid work by seeking, as the Good Fairy puts it to the Pooka MacPhellimey, to 'spend an hour in fine talk, and to enter into a colloquy with you' (ASTB, 146). Idleness retains a utopian quality in At Swim-Two-Birds. This is especially so when the novel is considered in the light of Adorno's assertion that one of the fundamental characteristics of modernity was the way in which even the imagination is colonized by a form of rationalism that itself arises out of work discipline.[49] If one of the more oppressive characteristics of modernity is the process by which even relaxation and free time take on structural forms derived from alienated labour, as Adorno suggests, then At Swim-Two-Birds offers a dialectical reversal of this condition, in which work — identified there as writing — takes on the structural forms of idleness by assimilating the digressive, dialogical, and immediate characteristics of story-telling to as great a degree as possible. 'Irish time' may have already passed into a more familiar version of the time of modernity by 1940, but the utopian pleasures of doing nothing, so central to its narrative, nevertheless provide the resources for a critique of that very process that ended 'Irish time' in the first place.

Unfortunately, Flann O'Brien himself provided a depressing postscript to the place of idleness in Irish modernism twenty-five years later, long after the active period of the

49   See Theodor Adorno, 'Free Time', in Critical Models, 167–75.

high modernist moment had ended and writers like Yeats and Joyce had won unassailable positions within the canon of international modernism. Brian O'Nolan had great success via Myles na Gopaleen with 'Cruiskeen Lawn'. By the 1950s, however, a combination of alcoholism, bitterness, and frustration led him to a desultory and reactionary position. O'Nolan's late writing, whether under the guise of Myles na Gopaleen or Flann O'Brien, betrays a reactionary blend of dissatisfaction, reflecting spiritual confusion about his own relation to the Catholic Church, his disillusion with the international success of a conception of modernism that failed to include him but canonized Joyce, and the provincialism of Irish society. In the words of Carol Taaffe, his last and worst novel, The Dalkey Archive, 'ends O'Nolan's career on a downward note, a rushed job in which his ambition was not matched by his powers of execution'.[50] The Dalkey Archive, written under the name Flann O'Brien and at a moment in which At Swim-Two-Birds had recently been rediscovered by the public, attempts to rewrite significant sections of his unpublished novel The Third Policeman. Rather than presenting a lazy idle schemer as a central figure of late Irish modernism, The Dalkey Archive presents a central character named Mick, who prides himself on his industry: 'Perhaps sheer laziness was the explanation, and Mick was pleased to reflect that sloth was not a sin that could be laid at his own door.'[51]

Beyond this disavowal of the lazy idle schemer as a central character type of Irish modernist literature, O'Brien goes much further. The character of De Selby, an eccentric philosopher-scientist with whom the lazy idle schemer of The Third Policeman is obsessed, is committed to the annihilation of the universe. O'Brien makes use of familiar literary figures: St. Augustine and James Joyce himself. In Augustine, O'Brien humorously attempts to reflect on the relationship between blasphemy and Catholic doctrine. Despite his attempts to walk the line between humorous blasphemy and malevolent orthodoxy, his efforts amount to nothing more than a racist joke about Augustine that fails to be funny. His representation of Joyce is more developed and deeply resentful. In The Dalkey Archive, James Joyce is alive and well in the 1960s, living anonymously as a bartender in Skerries. Part of Mick's quest is to employ Joyce's literary talents to persuade De Selby against going through with his apocalyptic plans. When Mick finally meets Joyce, however, he learns that Dubliners was the only literary work Joyce was responsible for (and even then, half of it was written by Oliver St. John Gogarty, who was afraid to sign his name to it), that Joyce is unaware of the novels A Portrait of the Artist as a Young Man and Finnegans Wake, and that Ulysses was written by a wide variety of criminals, pornographers, and vagabonds, under the direction of Sylvia Beach, who, upset by her supposed unrequited love for Joyce, published the novel under Joyce's name. Ultimately, the Joyce of The Dalkey Archive dreams of becoming a Jesuit priest late in life, but must unfortunately settle for a position as the launderer and mender of undergarments for Jesuit priests in Dublin.

50   Taaffe, Ireland Through the Looking Glass, 194.
51   Flann O'Brien, The Dalkey Archive (London, 1986), 139.

Harold Bloom's notion of 'the anxiety of influence' has rarely appeared as obvious as it does in *The Dalkey Archive*. The reactionary resentment of O'Nolan's earlier essay about Joyce, 'A Bash in the Tunnel', culminates in this novel. Taaffe argues that O'Nolan's representation of Joyce has as much to do with his own frustrated literary ambitions as it does with any kind of critical assessment of Joyce.[52] By the time *The Dalkey Archive* was published in 1964, of those who made the lazy idle schemer a central figure in their fiction, only Beckett and O'Nolan were still alive. The difference between the two writers could not have been greater. While it is not difficult to see a line of continuity between *More Pricks than Kicks*, *Murphy*, and *At Swim-Two-Birds*, it is much harder to determine how O'Nolan's later works relate to such later prose texts by Beckett as *All Strange Away*, *Imagination Dead Imagine*, *Enough*, or *Ping*. Beckett's later writing presents an even more radical presentation of the aesthetic positions he elaborated earlier — that identity itself no longer seems possible, as the central personae of those texts inhabit a condition of complete immobility. Between the two extremes — the absolute stillness found in Beckett, and the absolute ineffectivity evident in O'Brien's *The Dalkey Archive* — lies the fate of the Irish lazy idle schemer. The trope of impotentiality indicated the need for a new form of intellectual labour in that moment in which the publication of *Ulysses* and the realization of Irish independence coincided. Forty years later it either served as an indication of the inevitability of a failure, in the case of Beckett, or the opportunity for a Catholic moralistic conception of Irish futility, in the case of O'Brien. In either case, the subversive possibilities of 'Irish time', visible in *At Swim-Two-Birds*, had been lost.

52   Taaffe, *Ireland Through the Looking Glass*, 203, 204.

Afterword

Falling into Old Ways

Flann O'Brien wrote *The Third Policeman* in 1940. Its bleak humour was not considered appropriate for wartime; it was not published until 1967, a year after his death.[1] Like O'Brien's previous novel, it focuses on an unnamed, would-be intellectual narrator who is not interested in doing any kind of practical work. He has inherited a family farm and pub from his parents, but has no desire to run it. His abiding obsession is with the mysterious De Selby, a condition that is comically manifested in footnotes that slant the narrative towards one of De Selby's many eccentric positions on various issues.[2] This parody of the conventions of academic intellectual work echoes O'Brien's earlier parody of a modernist literary work in *At Swim-Two-Birds*.

The narrator hires a man named Divney to run both the farm and the pub while he works on his ambitious 'De Selby Index', a compilation of all recorded criticism of De Selby. The bizarre plot then unfolds with the murder by our narrator — talked into it by Divney — of an elderly farmer, Mathers, for his money. The narrator is thereafter dispatched on a surreal, quest through a strange version of rural Ireland. But events start to recur; the end of the narrator's quest repeats the beginning. It is revealed that not long after killing Mathers, Divney also killed the narrator, whose quest has been a hell of endless repetition. O'Nolan commented in a letter appended to the end of the novel:

1   Flann O'Brien, *The Third Policeman* (London, 1974).
2   O'Brien, *The Third Policeman*, 9.

It is made clear that this sort of thing goes on forever — and there you are. It is supposed to be very funny but I don't know about that either ... Hell goes round and round. In shape it is circular and by nature it is interminable, repetitive and very nearly unbearable.[3]

Hell, in this case, is the ultimate form of *Erlebnis*: time is frozen, things are always the same. *The Third Policeman* is indeed very funny, just as O'Nolan hoped it would be. But it also risks being very boring, partly because it mimics the repetitiveness of boredom. The pleasures of laziness experienced by the narrator of *At Swim-Two-Birds* optimistically suggested that some satisfying, non-alienated form of intellectual work might still be possible, despite the state's productive transformation of idleness into a form of bureaucratic labour. The situation is very different for the lazy idle schemer in the hell of *The Third Policeman*. Nothing of consequence ever happens; hell is remarkably similar to the version of de Valera's rural, mediocre Ireland.

In Beckett's *Watt*, the novel he wrote after *Murphy*, the defining formal principle is grammatical repetition, as the same sentences are repeated with only the slightest permutations over and over again. Beckett does not identify Watt's world as hell — Watt attempts to work as a servant in a Big House — but it certainly is bleak. A stunned and frozen condition, implacably and painstakingly presented as an experience of inexhaustible repetitiveness and of lethal boredom, presides in many Irish novels of this period of the late thirties and early forties. Máirtín Ó Cadhain's *Cré na Cille*, perhaps the last, high modernist novel by an Irish writer,[4] is not known outside Ireland; it has never been officially published in an English translation. Its formal experimentation and the comic-grotesque exploration of post-colonial Ireland, align it with the worlds of Beckett and O'Brien. *Cré na Cille* takes place in a graveyard in Connemara that opened in 1916, and concerns the ongoing, endless — and for the most part, petty, cynical, and cruel — conversations among the dead who are buried there. Its representation of an eternal afterlife, devoid of hope and characterized by banality, recalls *The Third Policeman*. Stylistically, with its frequent repetitions with minor variations, it echoes *Watt*. Most of all, like the other two novels, *Cré na Cille* brings the innovative energies of modernist experimentation to bear on a thorough examination of Irish boredom.

Finally, there is the matter of Joyce's *Finnegans Wake*, the most significant liminal text of Irish modernist literature. It too marks the transition from the preoccupation with idleness to a cultural fixation on post-colonial boredom. It is the most elaborate product of lazy idle scheming of the period. Beckett's suggestion in 'Dante ... Bruno ... Vico ... Joyce', that *Finnegans Wake* is not only an instance of alternative intellectual labour but that its experimental form demands new types of intellectual work on the

---

3   O'Brien, *The Third Policeman*, 173.
4   Máirtín Ó Cadhain, *Cré na Cille* (Baile Átha Cliath, 1996).

part of the reader as well, is accurate. It cannot be read like any other text; it demands that its readers commit to a productive form of idleness as they grapple with its difficulties. Whatever pleasures may be involved, the act of reading such a formally radical text involves some experience of boredom. In suggesting this, I am by no means casting aspersion on its merits, one of which is to provide deeply interesting insights into the nature, even the function, of boredom. The Viconian cyclical theory of history, which provides its narrative structure, is premised upon perpetual repetition. Joyce's compositional technique of combining more than sixty-five different languages into one universal language, which, when read aloud, sounds very much like English spoken with an Irish accent, demonstrates how an extreme form of linguistic particularity undergoes a dialectical reversal into a form of homogeneity. Deane argues that this principle is at the essence of Joyce's relationship to boredom:

> for all of the diversity of its representations, the Joycean text is constantly referring difference, local or personal eccentricities, national or imperial formulations, back to sameness. The same, the elision of difference, the iterative reproduction of the same story or style within a diversity of other stories or styles, is the ultimate site of boredom.[5]

According to Deane, an increasing emphasis on the representation of boredom in Irish modernism is not surprising for at least two reasons. Boredom, writes Deane,

> is a feature of the advanced industrial world, where the monotony of work, the vacuousness of leisure, the atomization of traditional communities and practices are all routine experiences that make the representation of boredom inescapable, whether in poetry or fiction. Further, boredom is both a symptom and a technique of repression, both in its psychic and political forms.[6]

The stultifying, insular version of Ireland is clearly one of the main targets of satire in *The Third Policeman*, *Watt*, and *Cré na Cille*. Yet, as Deane notes, collective Irish boredom during this period was also a symptom of the transition from colonial to sovereign status. If the right to sovereignty was in part grounded in the suggestion that Ireland has as much right to independence as any other nation, the emphasis upon sameness integrates the 'strange country' into a more recognizably typical global condition:

> Ireland's colonial history was both a history of emancipation from the monotonies of tyranny and, after the emancipatory movement, a restoration of the same

5   Deane, *Strange Country*, 167.
6   Deanc, *Strange Country*, 168.

monotonies under the name of freedom. It was economically, politically, culturally, half-baked … But in this condition it also had (or bore?) a striking resemblance to all those advanced countries in which the relation between tradition and modernity had become, or had been understood to have become, inert.[7]

The boredom is paradoxical in nature. It signals the historical memory of a particular past that makes Ireland different from other countries in the world, especially from its immediate neighbours; but it also indicates that Ireland has moved beyond that past into a general condition of typicality that had long been the goal of progressive modernization. Irish boredom, in other words, neatly encapsulates Gibbons's influential assessment that 'Ireland is a First World country, but with a Third World memory'.[8]

Deane argues that Irish boredom — whether as an imagined ideal designating a form of economic normality or as an appropriate description of the post-colonial condition — has long been an integral part of what he identifies as the national paradigm. Since at least the eighteenth century, a thematic and formal negotiation with the trope of boredom in Irish writing has worked in a dialectical relationship with a similar interrogation with the trope of apocalypse in order to register the temporality of the national paradigm.[9] Idleness in Irish modernism presented a brief but important interruption of that dialectic in order to signal the lost possibilities of Irish independence before the attendant processes of modernization reinstituted boredom as the prevailing cultural condition. Those writers most invested in the literary uses of idleness were also those who registered a shift in their later works towards an overwhelming sense of boredom. Throughout this book I have argued that idleness is a crucially important dimension in Irish modernism. Joyce and O'Duffy, Beckett, and O'Brien used idleness as a trope that could contribute to a critique of colonial modernity and of the post-colonial state. Within the texts of Irish modernism, the lazy idle schemer attempts to live outside of the process of modernization driven by work. Lazy idle scheming refashioned what had been a colonial stereotype of Irishness and then reconfigured it again in the light of the nationalist ambition to modernize Ireland.

By the 1940s, the prevailing sense of collective boredom Deane identifies as a recurring trait in Irish discourse had clearly arrived with a vengeance. Whatever radical possibilities idleness may have offered only seemed to be available while the work of decolonization was an ongoing national project. After the stabilization of the state with the implementation of the Constitution of 1937 and the pronounced sense of isolation Ireland experienced as a result of a policy of neutrality during World War II, the work of the nation gradually came

7   Deane, *Strange Country*, 168.
8   Gibbons, *Transformations in Irish Culture*, 3.
9   See Deane, *Strange Country*, 145–97.

to an end.[10] This does not mean that de Valera's Ireland in the late 1940s was no longer interested in constructive social policies or in the economic process of modernization. But precisely because that nation-state had finally become stable, the intensity of the national work-ethic diminished and laziness seemed a less radical alternative possibility than it once had been. Once nation-building had become a more or less complete project in Ireland, then dissenting literature, which had questioned the imperative of the work-ethic, switched its preoccupations to the absolute sense of boredom it had created. The lazy idle schemer no longer had a standard, conventional form of work to scheme against. Instead, he had to account for the boring form of modernity that had triumphed over any alternative form of intellectual labour.

This shift towards an emphasis on boredom was not unprecedented; boredom appears as a major thematic concern in many other modernist traditions as well.[11] Yet this last phase of Irish modernism did not survive the end of de Valera's rule. It was certainly never the cultural dominant that it may appear in hindsight to have been. Within the Irish literary field, the dominant mode of writing after the Revival — especially in fiction — was realism (especially in its naturalist form) rather than modernism. One might argue (as Cleary does) that this would remain the case up to the present day.[12] With its emphasis upon the way in which the conditions of Irish life — banal, repetitive, psychically repressed, impoverished — limit human possibility, naturalism too proved to be effective in its delineation of Irish boredom. Modernism had a continuing impact on Irish writing, particularly in the case of writers such as Thomas Kinsella or John Banville, but it never, as a movement, attained the position or the prestige of cultural authority enjoyed by the Revival. Particularly, its prestige was confined to cultural, 'creative' work; it did not extend to any comparable degree beyond that until Joyce and Beckett acquired a significant position within the international canon of modernism in general. Deane notes that the contradiction between the historical persistence of recalcitrance towards modernization along with a globalized conception of normality is resolved in one of two ways:

> One of the most enduring characteristics of a postcolonial state is the presence within it of remaindered communities, formations that cannot be incorporated politically and must be sustained by the life-support machine of the aesthetic or the touristic, two intimately related practices.[13]

---

10 On the period that went by the official term 'the Emergency', see Clair Wills, *That Neutral Island: A Cultural History of Ireland during the Second World War* (Cambridge, MA, 2007).
11 See Deane, *Strange Country*, 164.
12 See Cleary, *Outrageous Fortune*, 85–137.
13 Deane, *Strange Country*, 163.

Deane's suggestion here concerns the final relationship of what Chatterjee terms the thematic and the problematic within anti-imperialist nationalism after independence. The progressive drive of the thematic, the claim of nationalism to the rights to sovereignty enjoyed by any other modern nation-state, requires the presence of the problematic, that insistence on an authenticity that demonstrates the difference of the colonized from the colonizer and becomes the basis for the mobilization of the masses. After independence, when the modernizing efforts of the thematic become a priority of the state, the presence of the problematic is still required as a register of authenticity, but must be made safe for consumption through the aestheticization or commodification of the local. The transformation of Irish difference by aesthetic means began during the Revival, and continued in altered form after the Revival; the packaging of that difference for the purposes of tourism came slightly later, when Ireland became a privileged site for international visitors in the global economy that emerged after World War II. By the end of the twentieth century, aestheticization and tourism increasingly began to overlap. In international terms, Irish modernism gradually became a marker of Irish genius, wit, and authenticity. Eventually, it came to be regarded as a primary feature of Irish difference in its own right — and consequently, the tourism industry assimilated writers like Yeats, Joyce and Beckett into its own practices.[14] Irish modernism never did contribute to the social transformation of post-colonial Ireland in any realm beyond the aesthetic; but it did create the conditions of possibility for the Dublin Literary Pub Crawl.

The appropriation of the Irish modernist tradition by the tourism industry was only the latest moment in the long process of canonization in which Joyce and Beckett became dominant figures in the global literary field of production. It should come as no surprise that local entrepreneurs managed to take advantage of the fact that Irish modernism had long been made safe for consumption by the academy and the arbiters of high culture in metropolitan places like Paris and New York.[15] What is more surprising is the status that Irish modernism acquired — at least in the case of its more famous writers like Yeats and Joyce — within the recent historical context of the last decade and a half, the period identified with the so-called Celtic Tiger economy. At the time of writing, that economy has collapsed, and the culture of consumption that marked the transition from the twentieth century into the twenty-first has passed as unemployment statistics once again begin to resemble those of the 1980s. Immigration, one of the indices of Irish economic success during the period of the Celtic Tiger, has considerably reduced. Although that moment of neo-liberal triumphalism has ended, the Celtic Tiger nevertheless changed

14 On the relationship between Irish modernism and tourism, see Spurgeon Thompson, 'The Romance of Simulation: W. B. Yeats and the Theme-Parking of Ireland', *Éire-Ireland: A Journal of Irish Studies*, 30, 1 (1995), 17–34, and 'James Joyce and Tourism in Dublin: Quotation and the Mass Commodification of Irish Culture', *New Hibernia Review* (1997), 136–55.

15 On the assimilation of Irish writers into a canon of global modernism, see Pascale Casanova, *The World Republic of Letters* (Cambridge, MA, 2004), 303–23.

Ireland irrevocably. The global form of sameness that Deane identifies with a general sense of collective boredom reasserts itself in increasingly newer forms with great alacrity in contemporary Ireland. Alacrity itself seems to be one of the most significant values that emerged during the period of the Celtic Tiger. Michael Cronin argues that one of the most prominent consequences of the period involved the 'chrono-politicization' of Ireland, an event that brought about the standardization of Irish time — beginning crucially with labour-time — so that it is in sync with the international time of globalization.[16] The category of 'Irish time', whether in respect of the condition of uneven development, as in MacCabe's notion, or in relation to the more utopian temporality of idleness that recurs throughout Irish modernism, seems, as a defining cultural characteristic, more remote than ever. Instead, speed became the idol; it was important that as much work as humanly possible gets done in one day. Yet such an intensification of temporality has the contradictory result of blurring a sense of history. Jameson argues that contemporary finance capital eradicates a sense of the passage of time, because technology and global communication enable the work-day to go on without end. Any conventional notion of labour-time that once characterized modernity is distorted beyond recognition. What prevails is the illusion of a perpetual present that bears a distant relation to the past and tends toward the liquidation of futurity.[17] The chrono-politicization of Ireland recalls Benjamin's distinction between the unending *Erlebnis* of the ongoing moment and the lost sense of *Ehrfahrung*, which would include all of the records of experience necessary for us to make sense of our historical situation — with the crucial difference that the contemporary moment differs from *Erlebnis*, 'the phantasmagoria of the idler', in that idleness seems to be missing from it altogether.

Given the emphasis placed upon idleness in Irish modernism, it is reasonable to wonder if it has an even more fraught relationship to the values of contemporary Ireland than it did to the values of its own time. Yet the global recognition of the achievements of Irish writers and the conversion of their identities and writing by the tourism industry into a condition in which they are often cited but less often read have both contributed to a new understanding of them appropriate to the present — that they were the first premonitions of the rhetoric of international success that made up the cultural logic of the Celtic Tiger. This has occasionally been presented as a fully elaborated critical position.[18] The achievements of the Irish modernists are certainly important enough to be celebrated as some of the most significant moments in the cultural history of the nation, but they nevertheless make a poor fit with the cultural logic of the Celtic Tiger. As I have argued, one of the primary characteristics of Irish modernism was the

16   See Michael Cronin, 'Speed Limits: Ireland, Globalization and the War against Time', in Peadar Kirby, Luke Gibbons and Michael Cronin, eds., *Reinventing Ireland: Culture, Society and the Global Economy* (London, 2002), 54–66.
17   Fredric Jameson, 'The "End" of Temporality', *Critical Inquiry*, 29, 4 (2003), 695–718.
18   See Declan Kiberd's essay 'The Celtic Tiger: A Cultural History' in *The Irish Writer and the World*, 269–88.

antagonistic relationship it had towards the imperative to do the work of the nation. It makes little sense that the same texts would contribute to a contemporary work-ethic that is now intensified and constructed in the interests of global capital rather than the nation. The recovery of such recalcitrant practices as idleness, whether in the case of the modernist writers I have discussed here or in other dimensions of Irish cultural history such as film or contemporary poetry (both venues in which the persistence of idleness is evident), is important, for it demonstrates that those aspects of cultural history are just as difficult to assimilate to the contemporary values of global capitalism as they were to the social conventions that prevailed in their moment of origin. In turn, such instances of recalcitrance provide the basis for opposition to a triumphant rhetoric of success that suggests radical social change is less and less possible.

Irish modernism still has the capacity to jar conventional positions about work and propriety. If one of the singular qualities about Irish modernism was that it contributed to the rapprochement of popular and highbrow forms of culture, perhaps Irish popular culture itself has managed to retain the recalcitrant tendencies of the sorts of idleness found in the writing of Joyce, Beckett, and O'Brien. The Dublin-born musician Barry McCormack's song 'I Fell into Old Ways' from the album *Last Night, as I was Wandering* (2006) offers an example. The song, which McCormack sings with no musical accompaniment, concerns a latter-day lazy idle schemer who takes some money from his lover and falls into the old ways of dissolute life. The behaviour of the song's protagonist is not exemplary by any means, but it demonstrates resistance towards the intensified commitment to a neo-liberal work-ethic and the consequent propriety complicit with a triumphant form of modernity. This does not mean that 'I Fell into Old Ways' is a manifesto that insists that everyone should live in as irresponsible a fashion as possible in order to register some point of opposition to the common sense of the Celtic Tiger, but rather that despite all of the efforts of a process of modernization that dates back as far as the inception of cultural nationalism, its ideological twin, certain qualities of Irish life remain inassimilable to the conventions of proper citizenship attendant to contemporary capitalist notions of propriety. Through its title, MacCormack's song indicates the degree to which history continues to haunt the present in Ireland. Alongside such persistence is the suggestion that the subversive qualities of Irish modernism may not be entirely extinct, and that a life not circumscribed by the work-ethic of either the Revival or the Celtic Tiger might continue to be possible.

Bibliography

Ackerley, C. J., *Demented Particulars: Annotations for Murphy* (Tallahassee, 1998)

Adorno, Theodor W., *Minima Moralia: Reflections from Damaged Life* (London, 1974)

——, *Notes to Literature: Volume One* (New York, 1991)

——, *Prisms* (Cambridge, MA, 1994)

——, *Critical Models* (New York, 1998)

Æ (George Russell), *The National Being: Some Thoughts on an Irish Polity* (Dublin, 1916)

——, *The Interpreters* (London, 1922)

——, 'The Memories of a Poet', *Irish Statesman*, 4 December 1926, 301–03

Agamben, Giorgio, *Infancy and History: Essays on the Destruction of Experience* (London, 1993)

——, *Potentialities: Collected Essays in Philosophy* (Stanford, 1999)

Alatas, Syed Hussein, *The Myth of the Lazy Native* (London, 1977)

Allen, Nicholas, *Modernism, Ireland and Civil War* (Cambridge, 2009)

Althusser, Louis, *Lenin and Philosophy* (New York, 1971)

——, and Étienne Balibar, *Reading Capital* (London, 1970)

Ardis, Ann L., *Modernism and Cultural Conflict 1880–1922* (Cambridge, 2002)

Attridge, Derek, and Marjorie Howes, eds., *Semicolonial Joyce* (Cambridge, 2000)

Beckett, Samuel, *Murphy* (London, 1963)

——, *Watt* (London, 1963)

——, *Proust and Three Dialogues with Georges Duthuit* (London, 1965)

——, *More Pricks than Kicks* (New York, 1972)

——, *Collected Poems in English and French* (New York, 1977)

——, *Disjecta: Miscellaneous Writings and a Dramatic Fragment* (New York, 1984)

Begam, Richard, *Samuel Beckett and the End of Modernity* (Stanford, 1996)

Ben-Zvi, Linda, ed., *Women in Beckett: Performance and Critical Perspectives* (Urbana, 1990)

Benda, Julien, *The Treason of the Intellectuals* (New York, 1969)

Benjamin, Walter, *Illuminations: Essays and Aphorisms* (New York, 1968)
——, *Reflections* (New York, 1968)
——, *The Origin of German Tragic Drama* (London, 1977)
——, *The Arcades Project* (Cambridge, MA, 1999)
——, *Selected Writings: Volume 4, 1938–1940* (Cambridge, MA, 2003)
Benstock, Shari, and Bernard Benstock, *Who's He When He's at Home: A James Joyce Directory* (Urbana, 1980)
Bhabha, Homi, *The Location of Culture* (London, 1994)
Bielenberg, Andy, ed., *The Irish Diaspora* (Harlow, 2000)
Bourdieu, Pierre, *Distinction: A Social Critique of the Judgement of Taste* (Cambridge, MA, 1984)
——, *The Field of Cultural Production: Essays on Art and Literature* (New York, 1993)
Boxall, Peter, 'Samuel Beckett: Towards a Political Reading', *Irish Studies Review*, 10, 2 (2002), 159–70
Brady, Ciaran, ed., *Interpreting Irish History: The Debate on Historical Revisionism* (Dublin, 1994)
Breckinridge, Carol A., et al., eds., *Cosmopolitanism* (Durham, NC, 2002)
Brennan, Timothy, *At Home in the World: Cosmopolitanism Now* (Cambridge, MA, 1997)
Brienza, Susan, 'Clods, Whores, and Bitches: Misogyny in Beckett's Early Fiction', in Ben-Zvi, ed., *Women in Beckett*, 91–105
Bristow, Joseph, ed., *Wilde Writings: Contextual Conditions* (Toronto, 2003)
Brown, Nicholas, *Utopian Generations: The Political Horizon of Twentieth-Century Literature* (Princeton, 2005)
Brown, Julia Prewitt, *Cosmopolitan Criticism: Oscar Wilde's Philosophy of Art* (Charlottesville, 1997)
Brown, Terence, *Ireland: A Social and Cultural History, 1922 to the Present* (Ithaca, 1985)
——, 'Ireland, Modernism, and the 1930s', in Coughlan and Davis, eds., *Modernism and Ireland*, 24–41
——, *The Life of W. B. Yeats* (Oxford, 1999)
Buck-Morss, Susan, 'The Flaneur, the Sandwichman, and the Whore: The Politics of Loitering', *New German Critique*, 39 (1986), 99–140
——, *The Dialectics of Seeing* (Cambridge, MA, 1989)
Bunreacht na hÉireann/Constitution of Ireland (Dublin, 1951)
Casanova, Pascale, *The World Republic of Letters* (Cambridge, MA, 2004)
——, *Samuel Beckett: Anatomy of a Literary Revolution* (London, 2006)
Castle, Gregory, *Modernism and the Celtic Revival* (Cambridge, 2001)
Chakrabarty, Dipesh, 'The Time of History and the Time of the Gods', in Lowe and Lloyd, eds., *The Politics of Culture in the Shadow of Capital*, 35–60
——, *Provincializing Europe: Postcolonial Thought and Historical Difference* (Princeton, 2000)
Chatterjee, Partha, *Nationalist Thought and the Colonial World: A Derivative Discourse* (Minneapolis, 1993)

——, *The Nation and Its Fragments* (Princeton, 1993)

Cheng, Vincent, *Joyce, Race, and Empire* (Cambridge, 1995)

Cleary, Joe (Joseph), 'Toward a Materialist-Formalist History of Twentieth-Century Irish Literature', *boundary 2*, 31, 1 (2004), 207–42

——, *Outrageous Fortune: Capital and Culture in Modern Ireland* (Dublin, 2006)

——, and Claire Connolly, eds., *The Cambridge Companion to Modern Irish Culture* (Cambridge, 2005)

Clery, Arthur, *The Idea of a Nation* (Dublin, 2002)

Clune, Anne, and Tess Hurson, eds., *Conjuring Complexities: Essays on Flann O'Brien* (Belfast, 1997)

Coetzee, J. M., *White Writing: On the Culture of Letters in South Africa* (New Haven, 1988)

Connolly, Claire, 'Theorising Ireland', *Irish Studies Review*, 9, 3 (2001), 301–315

Connolly, James, *Collected Works*, 2 vols. (Dublin, 1987)

Connolly, Ruth, and Ann Coughlan, eds., *New Voices in Irish Criticism 5* (Dublin, 2005)

Coogan, Tim Pat, *The I.R.A.: A History* (New York, 1994)

Corkery, Daniel, *Synge and Anglo-Irish Literature* (Cork [1931], 1966)

Coughlan, Patricia, and Alex Davis, eds., *Modernism and Ireland: The Poetry of the 1930s* (Cork, 1995)

Cronin, Anthony, *No Laughing Matter: The Life and Times of Flann O'Brien* (London, 1989)

——, *Samuel Beckett: The Last Modernist* (New York, 1997)

Cronin, John, *The Anglo-Irish Novel: Volume Two: 1900–1940* (Belfast, 1990)

Cronin, Michael, 'Mental Ludo', in Clune and Hurson, eds., *Conjuring Complexities*, 47–52

Cronin, Mike, and John M. Regan, eds., *Ireland: The Politics of Independence 1922–49* (London, 2000)

Cullingford, Elizabeth Butler, *Yeats, Ireland, and Fascism* (London, 1981)

Curran, Steve, '"No, This is Not from *The Bell*": Brian O'Nolan's 1943 *Cruiskeen Lawn* Anthology', *Eire/Ireland*, 32, 2–3 (1997), 79–92

Davis, Alex, *A Broken Line: Denis Devlin and Irish Poetic Modernism* (Dublin, 2000)

Davis, Graham, 'The Irish in Britain, 1815–1939', in Bielenberg, ed., *The Irish Diaspora*, 19–36

De Grazia, Sebastien, *Of Time, Work, and Leisure* (New York, 1994)

Deane, Seamus, *Celtic Revivals* (Winston-Salem, 1987)

——, *A Short History of Irish Literature* (Notre Dame, 1986)

——, *Strange Country: Modernity and Nationhood in Irish Writing since 1790* (Oxford, 1997)

——, ed., *The Field Day Anthology of Irish Writing*, 3 vols. (Derry, 1991)

Dempsey, Pauric, 'Trinity College Dublin and the New Political Order', in Cronin and Regan, eds., *Ireland: The Politics of Independence 1922–49*, 217–31

Denning, Michael, *The Cultural Front: The Labouring of American Culture in the Twentieth Century* (London, 1996)

Devlin, Kimberly, 'Visible Shades and Shades of Visibility', in Devlin and Reizbaum, eds., *Ulysses: En-Gendered Perspectives*, 67–85

Devlin, Kimberly, and Marilyn Reizbaum, eds., *Ulysses: En-Gendered Perspectives: Eighteen New Essays on the Episodes* (Columbia, SC, 1999)

Donoghue, Denis, *William Butler Yeats* (New York, 1971)

Duffy, Enda, *The Subaltern Ulysses* (Minneapolis, 1994)

Dunphy, Richard, *The Making of Fianna Fáil Power in Ireland 1923–1948* (Oxford, 1995)

Eagleton, Terry, *The Ideology of the Aesthetic* (Oxford, 1990)

——, *Heathcliff and the Great Hunger* (London, 1995)

——, *Crazy John and the Bishop* (Cork, 1998)

——, *Scholars and Rebels in Nineteenth-Century Ireland* (Oxford, 1999)

Eglinton, John, *Literary Ideals in Ireland* (London, 1899)

Eglinton, John, and Frederick Ryan, 'Editorial', in Deane, ed., *The Field Day Anthology of Irish Writing*, vol 2, 975–76

Eliot, T. S., 'Ulysses, Order, and Myth', in *The Dial* (Nov. 1923), 480–83

——, 'Tradition and the Individual Talent', in *Selected Prose of* T. S. Eliot (New York, 1975), 37–44

Ellmann, Richard, *Ulysses on the Liffey* (Oxford, 1972)

——, *The Consciousness of Joyce* (London, 1977)

——, *James Joyce*, new and rev. edn. (Oxford, 1982)

——, *Oscar Wilde* (New York, 1987)

——, ed., *Letters of James Joyce: Volume II* (New York, 1966)

Emery, Lawrence K., 'Confessional', *The Klaxon* (Winter 1923–24), 1–2

Esty, Jed, *A Shrinking Island: Modernism and National Culture in England* (Princeton, 2004)

Fallon, Brian, *An Age of Innocence: Irish Culture 1930–1960* (Dublin, 1999)

Fanning, Ronan, 'Mr. De Valera Drafts a Constitution', in Farrell, ed., *De Valera's Constitution and Ours*, 31–39

Fanon, Frantz, *The Wretched of the Earth* (New York, 1963)

Farrell, Brian, ed., *De Valera's Constitution and Ours* (Dublin, 1988)

Feeney, W. J., 'Eimar O'Duffy's "A Military Causerie"', *Journal of Irish Literature*, 10, 3 (1981), 91–108

Fehsenfeld, Martha Dow, and Lois More Overbeck, eds., *The Letters of Samuel Beckett: Volume 1, 1929–1940* (Cambridge, 2009)

Finlay, John L., *Social Credit: The English Origins* (Montreal, 1972)

Forgacs, David, 'National-Popular: Genealogy of a Concept', in S. During, ed., *The Cultural Studies Reader* (London, 1993), 177–90

Fortunati, Leopoldina, *The Arcane of Reproduction: Housework, Prostitution, Labor, and Capital* (New York, 1995)

Foster, John Wilson, *Fictions of the Irish Literary Revival* (Syracuse, 1987)

Foster, R. F., *Paddy and Mr. Punch: Connections in Irish and English History* (London, 1993)

——, *W. B. Yeats: A Life: 1: The Apprentice Mage* (Oxford, 1997)

Frow, John, *Cultural Studies and Cultural Value* (Oxford, 1995)

Gagnier, Regenia, *Idylls of the Marketplace: Oscar Wilde and the Victorian Public* (Stanford, 1986)

Gaonkar, Dilip Parameshwar, ed., *Alternative Modernities* (Durham, NC, 2001)

Garvin, John, 'Sweetscented Manuscripts', in O'Keefe, ed., *Myles: Portraits of Brian O'Nolan*, 54–61

——, *James Joyce's Disunited Kingdom* (Dublin, 1976)

Gibbons, Luke, *Transformations in Irish Culture* (Cork, 1996)

——, 'Spaces of Time through Times of Space: Joyce, Ireland, and Colonial Modernity', *Field Day Review*, 1 (2005), 71–86

——, ed., 'Constructing the Canon: Versions of National Identity', in Deane, ed., *The Field Day Anthology of Irish Writing*, vol. 2, 950–1020

——, ed., 'Challenging the Canon', in Deane, ed., *The Field Day Anthology of Irish Writing*, vol. 3, 561–680

Gibson, Andrew, *Joyce's Revenge: History, Politics and Aesthetics in Ulysses* (Oxford, 2002)

Glynn, Sir Joseph, *Matt Talbot — A Dublin Labourer: 1856–1925* (Dublin, 1926)

Gramsci, Antonio, *Selections from the Prison Notebooks* (New York, 1971)

Gregory, Lady, ed., *Ideals in Ireland* (London, 1901)

Guy, Josephine M., 'The Soul of Man under Socialism: A (Con) Textual History', in Bristow ed., *Wilde Writings*, 59–85

Hardt, Michael, and Antonio Negri, *Labor of Dionysius: A Critique of the State-Form* (Minneapolis, 1994)

——, and Paolo Virno, eds., *Radical Thought in Italy: A Potential Politics* (Minneapolis, 1996)

Harrington, John P., *The Irish Beckett* (Syracuse, 1991)

Hobson, Bulmer, ed., *Saorstát Eireann Official Handbook* (Dublin, 1932)

Hodgkinson, Tom, *How to Be Idle* (New York, 2005)

Hogan, Robert, *Eimar O'Duffy* (Lewisburg, PA, 1972)

Hogan, Thomas, 'Myles na Gopaleen', *The Bell*, 13, 2 (1946), 129–40.

Holub, Renate, *Antonio Gramsci: Beyond Marxism and Postmodernism* (London, 1992)

Hopper, Keith, *The Portrait of the Artist as a Young Post-Modernist* (Cork, 1995)

Howes, Marjorie, *Yeats's Nations: Gender, Class, and Irishness* (Cambridge, 1996)

Hughes, Eamonn, '"You Need not Fear that I am not Amiable": Reading Yeats (Reading) Autobiographies', *Yeats Annual*, 12 (1996), 84–116

Hutchinson, Francis, and Brian Burkitt, *The Political Economy of Social Credit and Guild Socialism* (London, 1997)

Hutton, Claire, 'Joyce and the Institutions of Revivalism', *Irish University Review: A Journal of Irish Studies*, 33, 1 (2003), 117–32

Hutton, Seán, and Paul Stewart, eds., *Ireland's Histories: Aspects of State, Society and Ideology* (London, 1991)

Huyssen, Andreas, *After the Great Divide: Modernism, Mass Culture, Postmodernism* (Bloomington, 1986)

Ireland To-Day, 2, 5 (1937), 'Editorial', 2–3

Jackson, John Archer, *The Irish in Britain* (London, 1963)

Jacobsen, John Kurt, *Chasing Progress in the Irish Republic: Ideology, Democracy and Dependent Development* (Cambridge, 1994)

Jameson, Fredric, *The Political Unconscious* (Ithaca, 1981)

——, 'Third-World Literature in the Era of Multinational Capitalism', *Social Text*, 15 (1986), 65–88

——, *The Ideologies of Theory: Essays 1971–1986: Volume 2: The Syntax of History* (Minneapolis, 1988)

——, 'Ulysses in History', in Mary T. Reynolds, ed., *James Joyce: A Collection of Critical Essays* (Englewood Cliffs, NJ, 1993), 145–58

——, *Postmodernism, or, The Cultural Logic of Late Capitalism* (Durham, NC, 1991)

——, *Brecht and Method* (London, 1998)

——, *A Singular Modernity: Essay on the Ontology of the Present* (London, 2002)

——, 'The "End" of Temporality', *Critical Inquiry*, 29, 4 (2003), 695–718

——, *The Modernist Papers* (London, 2007)

Johnson, Samuel, *The Works of Samuel Johnson: Volume 2: 'Idler' and 'Adventurer'*, eds. W. Jackson Bate, et al. (New Haven, 1963)

Johnston, Dillon, *Irish Poetry after Joyce* (Notre Dame, 1985)

Joyce, James, *Dubliners* (New York, 1992)

——, *A Portrait of the Artist as a Young Man* (London, 1992)

——, *Ulysses* (New York, 1961)

——, *Finnegans Wake* (New York, 1974)

——, *Poems and Shorter Writings* (London, 1991)

——, *Occasional, Critical, and Political Writing* (Oxford, 2000)

Joyce, Stanislaus, *My Brother's Keeper* (London, 1958)

Kant, Immanuel, *Critique of Judgment* (Indianapolis, 1987)

Kearney, Richard, 'Beckett: The Demythologizing Intellect', in Richard Kearney, ed., *The Irish Mind: Exploring Intellectual Traditions* (Dublin, 1985), 267–93

Kennedy, Seán, '"Yellow": Beckett and the Performance of Ascendancy', in Connolly and Coughlan, eds., *New Voices in Irish Criticism 5*, 177–86

Kenner, Hugh, *Dublin's Joyce* (Bloomington, 1956)

Keogh, Dermot, *Twentieth-Century Ireland: Nation and State* (Dublin, 1994)

Kettle, Thomas, *The Day's Burden* (London, 1918)

Kiberd, Declan, *Inventing Ireland* (London, 1995)

——, *Irish Classics* (London, 2000)

——, *The Irish Writer and the World* (Cambridge, 2005)

Kinsella, Thomas, *The Táin* (Oxford, 1969)

Kirby, Peadar, Luke Gibbons, and Michael Cronin, eds., *Reinventing Ireland: Culture, Society, and the Global Economy* (London, 2002)

Knowlson, James, *Damned to Fame: The Life of Samuel Beckett* (New York, 1996)

Labriola, Antonio, *Essays on the Materialistic Conception of History* (Chicago, 1908)

——, *Socialism and Philosophy* (St. Louis, 1980)

Laclau, Ernesto, *Politics and Ideology in Marxist Theory* (London, 1977)

Lafargue, Paul, *The Right to be Lazy and Other Studies* (Chicago, 1907)

Lanters, José, *Unauthorized Versions: Irish Menippean Satire, 1919–1952* (Washington, DC, 2000)

Lazzarato, Maurizio, 'Immaterial Labor', in Hardt and Virno, eds., *Radical Thought in Italy*, 133–47

Lee, J. J., *Ireland 1912–1985: Politics and Society* (Cambridge, 1989)

——, 'The Irish Constitution of 1937', in Hutton and Stewart, eds., *Ireland's Histories*, 80–93

Lin, Lidan, 'Labor, Alienation, and the Status of Being: The Rhetoric of Indolence in Beckett's Murphy', *Philological Quarterly*, 79, 2 (2000), 249–71

Lloyd, David, *Anomalous States: Irish Writing and the Post-Colonial Moment* (Durham, NC, 1993)

——, *Ireland after History* (Cork, 1999)

——, 'Counterparts: Dubliners, Masculinity, and Temperance Nationalism', in Attridge and Howes, eds., *Semicolonial Joyce*, 128–49

——, 'Republics of Difference: Yeats, MacGreevy, Beckett', *Field Day Review*, 1 (2005), 43–67.

——, *Irish Times: Temporalities of Modernity* (Dublin, 2008)

——, and Paul Thomas, *Culture and the State* (London, 1998)

Lowe, Lisa, and David Lloyd, eds., *The Politics of Culture in the Shadow of Capital* (Durham, NC, 1997)

Lukács, Georg, *History and Class Consciousness* (Cambridge, MA, 1971)

Lutz, Tom, *Doing Nothing: A History of Loafers, Loungers, Slackers, and Bums in America* (New York, 2006)

Lyons, F. S. L., 'The Minority Problem in the 26 Counties', in MacManus, ed., *The Years of the Great Test*, 92–103

MacCabe, Colin, ed., *James Joyce: New Perspectives* (Sussex, 1982)

——, 'The Voice of Esau: Stephen in the Library', in MacCabe, ed., *James Joyce: New Perspectives*, 111–28

——, *James Joyce and the Revolution of the Word* (London, 2002)

McCarthy, Conor, *Modernisation: Crisis and Culture in Ireland 1969–1992* (Dublin, 2000)

McCormack, Jerusha, ed., *Wilde the Irishman* (New Haven, 1998)

McCormack, W. J., *From Burke to Beckett: Ascendancy, Tradition and Betrayal in Literary History* (Cork, 1994)

——, 'Austin Clarke: The Poet as Scapegoat of Modernism', in Coughlan and Davis, eds., *Modernism and Ireland*, 75–102

McCourt, John, *The Years of Bloom: James Joyce in Trieste 1904–1920* (Madison, 2000)

McDowell, R. B., and D. A. Webb, *Trinity College Dublin 1592–1952: An Academic History* (Cambridge, 1982)

MacManus, Francis, ed., *The Years of the Great Test* (Cork, 1967)

McMullen, Kim, 'Culture as Colloquy: Flann O'Brien's Postmodern Dialogue with Irish Tradition', *Novel*, 27, 1 (1993), 62–84

Maier, Corrine, *Bonjour Laziness: Why Hard Work Doesn't Pay* (London, 2005)

Manganiello, Dominic, *Joyce's Politics* (London, 1980)

Mao, Douglas, and Rebecca Walkowitz, 'The New Modernist Studies', *PMLA*, 123 (2007), 737–48

Martin, Augustine, 'Prose Fiction 1880–1945', in Deane, ed., *The Field Day Anthology of Irish Writing*, vol. 2, 1131–40

Martin, Wallace, *'The New Age' under Orage: Chapters in English Cultural History* (Manchester, 1967)

Marx, John, *The Modernist Novel and the Decline of Empire* (Cambridge, 2005)

Marx, Karl, *The Revolutions of 1848: Political Writings: Volume I* (London, 1973)

——, *Early Writings* (New York, 1975)

——, *Capital: Volume One* (London, 1976)

Mathews, P. J., *Revival: The Abbey Theatre, Sinn Féin, the Gaelic League and the Co-Operative Movement* (Cork, 2003)

Mays, J. C. C., '"Mythologized Presences": Murphy in Its Time', in Ronsley, ed., *Myth and Reality in Irish Literature*, 197–218

Mercier, Vivian, 'The Satires of Eimar O'Duffy', *The Bell*, 12, 4 (1946), 325–36

——, *The Irish Comic Tradition* (Oxford, 1962)

——, *Beckett/Beckett* (Oxford, 1977)

Miller, Elizabeth Carolyn, *Framed: The New Woman Criminal in British Culture at the Fin de Siècle* (Ann Arbor, 2008)

Miller, Tyrus, *Late Modernism: Politics, Fiction, and the Arts between the World Wars* (Berkeley, 1999)

Mohanty, Chandra Talpade, 'Cartographies of Struggle: Third World Women and the Politics of Feminism', in Chandra Talpade Mohanty, Ann Russo, and Lourdes Torres, eds., *Third World Women and the Politics of Feminism* (Bloomington, 1991), 1–47

Montaigne, Michel De, *The Complete Essays* (London, 1991)

Moretti, Franco, *The Way of the World: The Bildungsroman in European Culture* (London, 1987)

——, *Signs Taken for Wonders*, rev. edn. (London, 1988)

Moriarty, Dónal, *The Art of Brian Coffey* (Dublin, 2000)

Morris, William, *News from Nowhere and Other Writings*, ed. Clive Wilmer (London, 1993)

Mulhern, Francis, *The Present Lasts a Long Time* (Cork, 1998)

Mullin, Katherine, '"Don't Cry for Me, Argentina": "Eveline" and the Seductions of Emigration Propaganda', in Attridge and Howes, eds., *Semicolonial Joyce*, 172–200

Na Gopaleen, Myles, *An Béal Bocht (Drochscéal ar an Drochshoal)* (Baile Átha Cliath, 1941)

——, *The Best of Myles* (New York, 1968)

——, *The Poor Mouth (A Bad Story About the Hard Life)* (London, 1973)

Nancy, Jean-Luc, *The Inoperative Community* (Minneapolis, 1991)

Nelson, Cary, and Lawrence Grossberg, eds., *Marxism and the Interpretation of Culture* (Urbana, 1988)

Nolan, Emer, *James Joyce and Nationalism* (London, 1995)

——, 'Modernism and the Irish Revival', in Cleary and Connolly, eds., *The Cambridge Companion to Modern Irish Culture*, 157–72

Norris, Margot, *Joyce's Web: The Social Unraveling of Modernism* (Austin, 1992)

Nunokawa, Jeff, *Tame Passions of Wilde: The Styles of Manageable Desire* (Princeton, 2003)

Ó Cadhain, Máirtín, *Cré na Cille* (Baile Átha Cliath, 1996)

Ó Criomhthain, Tomás, *An tOileánach* (Baile Átha Cliath, 1980)

Ó Nualláin, Ciarán, *The Early Years of Brian O'Nolan/Flann O'Brien/Myles na Gopaleen* (Dublin, 1998)

O'Brien, Eoin, *The Beckett Country: Samuel Beckett's Ireland* (Dublin, 1986)

Flann O'Brien, 'A Bash in the Tunnel', in Ryan, ed., *A Bash in the Tunnel: James Joyce by the Irish*, 15–20

——, *At Swim-Two-Birds* (New York, 1976)

——, *The Third Policeman* (London, 1974)

——, *The Dalkey Archive* (London, 1986)

O'Brien, Kate, *Mary Lavelle* (London, 1984)

——, *The Land of Spices* (London, 1988)

O'Duffy, Eimar, *The Wasted Island* (Dublin, 1919)

——, *King Goshawk and the Birds* (London, 1926)

——, *The Spacious Adventures of the Man in the Street* (London, 1928)

——, *Asses in Clover* (London, 1933)

——, *Life and Money*, 3rd edn. (London, 1935)

——, 'Reviews', *Journal of Irish Literature*, 7, 1 (1978), 8–15

O'Faolain, Sean, 'Daniel Corkery', *Dublin Magazine*, 11, 2 (1936), 49–61

——, 'The Dangers of Censorship', *Ireland To-Day*, 1, 6 (1936), 57–63

O'Flaherty, Liam, *A Tourist's Guide to Ireland* (Dublin, 1998)

O'Grada, Cormac, *Ireland: A New Economic History 1780–1939* (Oxford, 1994)

O'Hegarty, P. S., *The Victory of Sinn Féin* (Dublin, 1998)

O'Keefe, Timothy, ed., *Myles: Portraits of Brian O'Nolan* (London, 1973)

Paseta, Senia, *Before the Revolution: Nationalism, Social Change, and Ireland's Catholic Elite, 1879–1922* (Cork, 1999)

Pettit, Philip, *Republicanism: A Theory of Freedom and Government* (Oxford, 1997)

Piccone, Paul, *Italian Marxism* (Berkeley, 1983)

Pilling, John, ed., *The Cambridge Companion to Beckett* (Cambridge, 1994)

——, *Beckett before Godot* (Cambridge, 1997)

Pilkington, Lionel, *Theatre and the State in Twentieth-Century Ireland: Cultivating the People* (London, 2001)

Pine, Richard, *The Thief of Reason: Oscar Wilde and Modern Ireland* (New York, 1995)

Plunkett, Sir Horace, *Ireland in the New Century* (London, 1905)

Pound, Ezra, 'James Joyce et Pécuchet', *Mercure de France*, 1 (June 1922), 307–20

Quintelli-Neary, Marguerite, *Folklore and the Fantastic in Twelve Modern Irish Novels* (Westport, CT, 1997)

Rainey, Lawrence, *Institutions of Modernism: Literary Elites and Public Culture* (New Haven, 1999)

Ramazani, Jahan, *The Hybrid Muse: Postcolonial Poetry in English* (Chicago, 2001)

Reynolds, Paige, *Modernism, Drama, and the Audience for Irish Spectacle* (Cambridge, 2007)

Robins, Stephen, *The Importance of Being Idle: A Little Lazy Book of Inspiration* (London, 2000)

Ronsley, Joseph, ed., *Myth and Reality in Irish Literature* (Waterloo, Ontario, 1977)

Ross, Kristin, *The Emergence of Social Space: Rimbaud and the Paris Commune* (Minneapolis, 1988)

Roughly, Alan, *James Joyce and Critical Theory* (Ann Arbor, 1991)

Rudmose-Brown, T. B., 'Review', *Dublin Magazine*, 10, 3 (1935), 73–77

Russell, Bertrand, *In Praise of Idleness* (London, 1996)

Ryan, John, ed., *A Bash in the Tunnel: James Joyce by the Irish* (Brighton, 1970)

Scott, Bonnie Kime, 'Diversions from Mastery in "Wandering Rocks"', in Devlin and Reizbaum, eds., *Ulysses: En-Gendered Perspectives*, 136–49

Share, Bernard, *Slanguage: A Dictionary of Irish Slang* (Dublin, 1997)

Shershow, Scott Cutler, *The Work and the Gift* (Chicago, 2005)

Sinfield, Alan, *The Wilde Century: Effeminacy, Oscar Wilde and the Queer Moment* (New York, 1994)

Smith, Adam, *The Wealth of Nations* (New York, 2000)

Smith, Barbara Herrnstein, *Contingencies of Value: Alternative Perspectives for Critical Theory* (Cambridge, MA, 1988)

Sohn-Rethel, Alfred, *Intellectual and Manual Labour: A Critique of Epistemology* (Atlantic Highlands, NJ, 1978)

Spiegelman, Willard, *Majestic Indolence: English Romantic Poetry and the Work of Art* (Oxford, 1995)

Spivak, Gayatri Chakravorty, 'Can the Subaltern Speak?', in Nelson and Grossberg, eds., *Marxism and the Interpretation of Culture*, 271–313

Spoo, Robert, *James Joyce and the Language of History: Dedalus' Nightmare* (Oxford, 1994)

Surette, Leon, *Pound in Purgatory: From Economic Radicalism to Anti-Semitism* (Urbana, 1999)

Synge, J. M., *Collected Works II: Prose* (Gerrards Cross, 1982)

——, *Collected Works III: Plays: Book 1* (Gerrards Cross, 1982)

Taaffe, Carol, *Ireland Through the Looking Glass: Flann O'Brien, Myles na gCopaleen and Irish Cultural Debate* (Cork, 2008)

Thompson, E. P., 'Time, Work-Discipline, and Industrial Capitalism', in his *Customs in Common: Studies in Traditional Popular Culture* (New York, 1993), 352–403

Thompson, Spurgeon, 'The Romance of Simulation: W. B. Yeats and the Theme-Parking of Ireland', *Éire-Ireland*, 30, 1 (1995), 17–34

——, 'James Joyce and Tourism in Dublin: Quotation and the Mass Commodification of Irish Culture', *New Hibernia Review* 1.1 (1997), 136–55

Valente, Joseph, 'The Perils of Masculinity in "Scylla and Charybdis"', in Devlin and Reizbaum, eds., *Ulysses: En-Gendered Perspectives*, 111–35

Virno, Paolo, 'Virtuosity and Revolution: The Political Theory of Exodus', in Hardt and
    Virno, eds., *Radical Thought in Italy*, 189–212

Walkowitz, Rebecca, *Cosmopolitan Style: Modernism beyond the Nation* (New York, 2006)

Ward, Margaret, *Unmanageable Revolutionaries: Women and Irish Nationalism* (London, 1983)

Wasserstein,Wendy, *Sloth* (Oxford, 2005)

Weber, Max, *The Protestant Ethic and the Spirit of Capitalism* (New York, 1930)

Weisberg, Phillip, *Chronicles of Disorder: Samuel Beckett and the Cultural Politics of the Modern
    Novel* (Albany, 2000)

Wenzel, Siegfried, *The Sin of Sloth: Acedia in Medieval Thought and Literature* (Chapel Hill, 1967)

West, Alick, *Crisis and Criticism, and Selected Literary Essays* (Norwood, PA, 1975)

Wicke, Jennifer, *Advertising Fictions: Literature, Advertisement, and Social Reading* (New York, 1988)

——, and Garry Leonard, eds., *Joyce and Advertising, James Joyce Quarterly*, 30, 4 & 31, 1 (1993)

Wilde, Oscar, *The Collected Works of Oscar Wilde: Stories, Plays, Poems and Essays* (London, 1966)

Williams, Raymond, *Culture and Society: 1780–1950* (New York, 1958)

——, *Problems in Materialism and Culture* (London, 1980)

——, *Keywords* (Oxford, 1983)

Wills, Clair, 'Joyce, Prostitution, and the Colonial City', *South Atlantic Quarterly*, 95, 1 (1996),
    79–95

——, *That Neutral Island: A Cultural History of Ireland during the Second World War* (Cambridge,
    MA, 2007)

Wood, Rupert, 'An Endgame of Aesthetics: Beckett as Essayist', in Pilling, ed., *The
    Cambridge Companion to Beckett*, 1–16

Woolf, Virginia, 'George Eliot', *Times Literary Supplement*, 10 (April 1919)

Yeats, W. B., 'A Postscript', in Lady Gregory, ed., *Ideals in Ireland*, 105–07

——, *Autobiographies* (New York, 1999)

——, *Essays and Introductions* (Dublin, 1961)

——, *Explorations* (New York, 1962)

——, *Uncollected Prose by W. B. Yeats, Volume 1: First Reviews and Articles 1886–1896*, ed. John P.
    Frayne (New York, 1970)

——, *The Collected Poems of W. B. Yeats: A New Edition*, ed. Richard J. Finneran (New York,
    1989)

Index